TRIBE AND CLASS IN MONROVIA

Centennial Memorial: the first and present Presidents
flanked by figures representing tribal and civilized women

TRIBE AND CLASS
IN MONROVIA

BY

MERRAN FRAENKEL

Published for the
INTERNATIONAL AFRICAN INSTITUTE
by the
OXFORD UNIVERSITY PRESS
LONDON   IBADAN   ACCRA
1964

Oxford University Press, Amen House, London E.C.4

GLASGOW   NEW YORK   TORONTO   MELBOURNE   WELLINGTON
BOMBAY   CALCUTTA   MADRAS   KARACHI   LAHORE   DACCA
CAPE TOWN   SALISBURY   NAIROBI   IBADAN   ACCRA
KUALA LUMPUR   HONG KONG

309.1666
F

Printed in Great Britain by
The Alden Press Ltd., Oxford

PREFACE

THE Republic of Liberia is, apart from Ethiopia, the oldest independent state in Africa, having had its own constitution since 1847. It is a small country—in area 43,000 square miles, in population less than two millions—but the peculiarities of its history and social structure make it an area of unique sociological interest. For it has no history of rule by a colonial power. Its government has, at least until recently, been in the hands of a small minority composed of Negro immigrants from America and their descendants, who are commonly known as Americo-Liberians, while the bulk of its population is made up of the members of about twenty indigenous tribes. During the first century of the republic's existence, interaction between Americo-Liberians and tribespeople produced a caste-like social system. However, since the Second World War, Liberia like other African territories has been through a period of unprecedented economic growth and social change. This study seeks to analyse how, during the present period of transition, a new and more open system of social stratification, more akin to a social class system, is appearing in Monrovia, the republic's capital and only sizeable city.

Such analysis can be meaningful only if viewed from the perspective of Liberia's peculiar history. Since the Liberian Republic is one of the most inadequately documented of all African countries, I start with an outline of the circumstances of its founding and of the main factors which determined its development during the first century of its existence. Chapter II describes present-day Monrovia: its sprawling physical lay-out; the main features of its population, today totalling over 53,000; its economic structure; and the manner in which it is administered. It has no large scale employers, a high proportion of self-employed persons, and a great deal of casual labour. There is no formal, overall administrative system, and government policy towards such matters as immigration and housing may be characterized as laissez-faire. In this situation, tribal and kinship bonds are particularly significant. Chapter III deals with the urban tribal communities, their history and organization, and the operation of urban tribal courts. I have here as in later chapters focused attention on the Kru tribe. The composition and role of households, and in particular of large extended family households in New Krutown, are discussed in Chapter IV. Chapter V analyses the role of the Christian churches, and of certain other types of voluntary association, and also shows why their membership tends to correspond with, rather than cut across, the general divisions of the population according to both class and tribe. Finally Chapter VI returns to discuss in more detail the process by which a new system of social stratification is emerging, the nature and extent of social mobility, and the present relationship of ethnic grouping to the social hierarchy.

The fieldwork on which this study is based was carried out in Monrovia between April 1958 and April 1959, while holding a fellowship from the International African Institute. I have, for the sake of simplicity, used the present tense, which should be understood as referring to the years 1958–9. For the first two months of my stay I lodged in a Liberian household in the area to which I have referred as the 'Town Centre'. Subsequently, I spent three months 'caretaking' two houses in succession on fashionable Mamba Point, then I moved to the community of stevedores and dockworkers in New Krutown. This nomadic existence had the advantage of providing me with first-hand experience of life in three quite different types of residential area. To my landlady, my neighbours, and my other good friends in each community, and especially to the Kru Governor and his councillors, I owe sincere thanks for their helpfulness and their hospitality. Between September and December 1958 I taught social anthropology to the senior class at the University of Liberia, and during the following semester I gave a course in English composition at one of the night schools in the town. Conversations and discussions with both groups of students were of great help in giving me insight into their lives and problems. The members of the university class were also of practical assistance in carrying out the questionnaire study of members of voluntary associations, to which reference is made in Chapter V.

I spent a great deal of time, especially during the first months of my stay in Monrovia, searching for documentary material— detailed departmental reports, reports of commissions of inquiry, recommendations of committees, and so on—of the type with which I was familiar from British territories. In fact, very little

documentation of this kind exists. In British territories, much of
the impetus for the recording of such material was provided by the
obligation to report to the colonial government. In Liberia such
impetus has been lacking, and, moreover, Liberians do not share
the Britisher's reverence for carbon paper and filing cabinets.
Indeed, a great deal of the administration of the town, as is apparent from Chapters II and III, is carried out on an *ad hoc* basis.
Written records are often lacking, not only on historical developments, but also on regulations at present in force. For the research
worker, this necessitates the devotion of an unusual amount of
time to interviewing officials of government departments and other
organizations, and to sifting basic information thus orally obtained.

The major part of my fieldwork was however undertaken by
means of informal conversations and participant observation,
especially, but not only, within the three communities where I
lived. I visited people and they me; I attended weddings, funerals,
church services, club meetings, court sessions, and so on. Where
these were held in the vernacular languages, I had to use an inter-
preter. In New Krutown, most of the men and perhaps half the
women spoke English, but my study would probably have gained
a great deal in depth if I could have followed directly not only
what was said to me, but also what was said around me. To learn
the language sufficiently well for this would, however, have occupied far too great a part of my time in the field. Neither could it
be learned in advance, because, for one thing, my advance information was insufficient to indicate which language would be the most
profitable one, and for another, even if I had planned to learn Kru
in advance I could not have done so because it has no written gram-
mar or literature.

During the last three months of my stay in Monrovia, in order
to test impressions gained by less formal methods and also to show
to what extent the communities I knew best were typical of the
town as a whole, I organized a social survey of eight residential
areas. The methods of sampling are described in Appendix A. The
bulk of the interviewing was done by a team of nine assistants, to
whom I owe a great deal for their enthusiasm and conscientious-
ness. I should also like to thank the members of the four hundred
households who bore with our curiosity and, in particular, the five
New Krutown households which co-operated in the budget study
described in Chapter IV.

A great many officers of the Liberian Government, and especially of the Departments of the Interior, Public Instruction, and Agriculture and Commerce, and the Bureaux of Information and Labour, gave most generously of their time and knowledge. I should also like to thank the staff of the UNESCO mission, of the Christian missions, of the university, and of the Monrovia schools, for their help. My gratitude is offered, above all, to President Tubman, whose permission and personal interest made it possible for this study to be carried out, and to the late ex-President King for his most valuable advice and encouragement.

For reading this book in manuscript and for their many helpful comments I am grateful to Professor Daryll Forde, Director of the International African Institute, to Dr. A. L. Epstein of the University of Manchester, to Mr. T. B. Bottomore of the London School of Economics, and to Dr. Kenneth Little of the University of Edinburgh. My husband, who spent three months with me in Monrovia, also read the manuscript and drew the maps, and has provided unfailing encouragement and moral support. For any errors of fact or interpretation, I of course take full responsibility.

MERRAN FRAENKEL

CONTENTS

TABLES

PLATES

Centennial Memorial: the first and present Presidents
flanked by figures representing tribal and civilized
women   *Frontispiece*

CHAPTER I

THE PAST

ACCOUNTS of the history of Liberia naturally centre on the fortunes and characteristics of the nineteenth-century immigrants from America and their descendants—today's Americo-Liberians. This tends to obscure the fact that, although they founded the republic and, at least until recently, have ruled it, the Americo-Liberians are a very small minority in its total population—possibly 25,000 out of an estimated two millions. The great majority of the population is composed of members of about twenty tribes, all of whom were established in their present habitat by the seventeenth century, and some considerably before that period.[1] On linguistic and cultural grounds they fall roughly into four groups, whose main representatives are the Kru and Grebo; the Bassa; the Vai and Gola; and the Kpelle and Loma. Their traditional social systems, in so far as they have been described,[2] were characterized by patrilineal descent and settlement in 'towns' whose populations frequently ran to several thousands. Political organizations varied from the markedly decentralized system of the Kru, who had a large number of autonomous towns, to the apparently more hierarchical system of the Vai, but there is no evidence that any of the tribes established unified states.[3] The tribal economies are based on farming, rice and cassava being staple crops. The coastal people are also fishermen. There are few cattle in the republic, apart from the herds brought down for slaughter by Mandingo and Fulani traders from Guinea. The Vai, who are today mostly Moslems, are famed for the syllabic form of writing which they developed during the nineteenth century. The

[1] Johnston, 1961, vol. ii, pp. 921 f.
[2] Apart from Westermann's work on the Kpelle and Schwab's survey of the tribes of the interior, especially the Gio-Mano, little has been published. Mr. James Gibbs has recently carried out research among the Kpelle, Mr. Warren d'Azevedo among the Gola.
[3] Azikwe quotes Delafosse as describing a Kru confederacy, but does not give the source. I found no evidence that such a confederacy has ever existed, even as a short-term phenomenon.

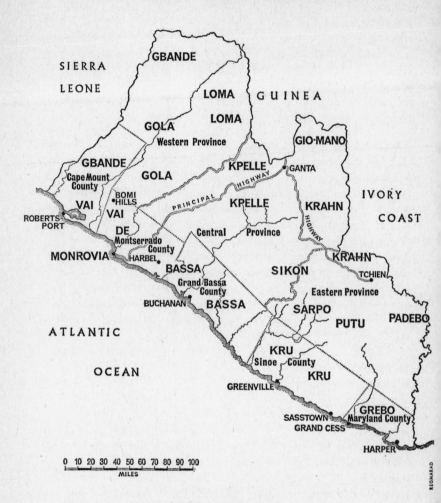

THE REPUBLIC
Administrative Divisions and Tribal Areas

Kru have for several centuries been travelling up and down the coast of West Africa as dock-workers and deck-hands, and they have established settlements in most of the ports from Dakar to Douala. A more recent movement into Liberia has consisted of immigrants from Guinea and territories farther inland who are collectively known in Liberia as 'Mandingoes'. These people have been coming to trade on the Liberian coast since the early nineteenth century,[4] and they now have several established chiefdoms within the republic. Finally, within recent decades, Fanti and other tribesmen have come from what is now Ghana to work especially as fishermen and clerks, and among them, as among the Mandingoes, are some who have adopted Liberian nationality.

The history of Liberia as a state, however, begins with the arrival in 1821 of the first boatload of American Negro settlers, and the establishment in the following year, on Cape Mesurado, of their first permanent settlement, which they named Monrovia after the American President James Monroe.

THE FOUNDERS

The Cape Mesurado region was originally within the territory of the De—a small tribe related to the Bassa. But the area was already ethnically mixed at the time when the American settlers arrived: the earliest accounts mention local villages of both Kru and Bassa as well as De, and indeed the 'King Peter' who made the original sale of land to the immigrants is said to have been of mixed Bassa-De descent. As can be seen from the accompanying map (opposite), the home territories of the Vai, Gola, Kpelle and Bassa are at no great distance from the Cape. For European trading ships it had long been a place of call. The Portuguese, who had a monopoly of trade on the coast from the fourteenth to the sixteenth centuries, named Cape Mesurado (as well as several other features of what is now the Liberian coast), but built no forts or permanent settlement there. From the seventeenth century, English and Dutch, as well as German and French, trading ships called. The English, particularly, are remembered on the Liberian stretch of coast as slave-traders. One such trader was John Hawkins, who in 1562 took three cargoes of slaves from the area to the West Indies, accompanied on his last trip by Francis Drake. Most of the coastal

[4] Johnston, op. cit., pp. 921-8.

tribes were engaged in the slave traffic. Cape Mount, in Vai territory about fifty miles north-west of Monrovia, was an important
shipping place for slaves brought from as far inland as Timbuctoo.
Trade Town, one of the most notorious slave 'factories', was also
on the Liberian coast, in Bassa territory about sixty miles south-
east of Monrovia. The rocky promontory of Cape Mesurado had
several times been suggested as a possible site for a European
settlement. During the eighteenth century, plans for colonizing
it were considered in turn by the (French) Senegal Company, by
the Swedish Government, and by a British philanthropic association. In 1787, the settlement of Freetown as a colony for freed
Negroes from England and other British territories commenced.
Accounts of this experiment reached the United States and stim-
ulated discussion of African colonization as a solution to the problems of the free Negro.[5]

At this period, there were in the United States just over 700,000
slaves, and by further import as well as by natural increase the
figure had risen to one and a half millions by 1820.[6] In addition,
by 1790 there were already 82,000 free Negroes, and twice as many
by 1830.[7] Several plans for freeing slaves and settling them abroad
had already been put forward when, in 1816, the voluntary association later known as the American Colonization Society was founded
Its aim[8] was

. . . to colonize, with their own consent, on the coast of Africa or in such
other place as Congress shall deem expedient, the people of colour in
our country, already free and those others who may hereafter be liberated by the humanity of individuals or the laws of the southern states.

A large part of the funds of the society came from Protestant
churches, who were interested in the possibilities of evangelizing
Africa. Individual supporters were, however, activated by a variety
of motives, including the desirability of ridding the country of a
class of free Negroes, many of whom were educated and able, dis-
satisfied with their own under-privileged status, and potential
trouble-makers for the slave-owners.[9] The society's project was
opposed both by slave-owners, who feared that the ultimate aim
was the total abolition of slavery, and by abolitionists, who held
that the presence in America of the free Negroes as an able and

[5] Johnston, op. cit., vol. i, p. 121, and Huberich, 1947, vol. i, pp. 1–17.
[6] Huberich, op. cit., pp. 7 and 19.   [7] Ibid., p. 45.
[8] As quoted by Brown, 1941, pp. 9–10.   [9] Huberich, op. cit., p. 47.

industrious group of people was a most crushing argument against the continuation of slavery.[10] Nor did it receive any direct support from the United States Government. Indeed, Huberich—the main authority on Liberian history—writes: 'The American Government at all times refused to take any responsibility with regard to the settlement'.[11] The colonists, once they left American shores, were regarded as expatriates to whom the Government owed no duty of protection; they had, of course, never been American citizens. Such military aid as the settlement did receive was provided by individual American and other coastal vessels which happened to be in the vicinity. Only towards the end of the century was a military aid agreement signed. The project did, however, receive a small amount of financial aid, indirectly, from the United States Government. Import of slaves into the United States had been declared illegal in 1807, and in 1819 the Federal Government passed a bill instructing the American Navy to seize any American vessels engaged in the slave traffic and to return all Negroes thus recaptured to Africa.[12] The American Colonization Society was made custodian for these recaptured Africans who, it was intended, should be under its protection until they found their way back to their own countries. To provide for these persons, the society received grants from the American Government.

Between 1822 and 1892, the American Colonization Society succeeded in sending just over 16,000 free Negroes to Monrovia and other places along what is now the Liberian coast, and to the population of these settlements were added some 6,000 Africans recaptured from slave ships and entrusted to the society by the United States Government.[13] Huberich gives the following figures indicating the status of those immigrants who arrived between 1822 and 1867, after which period immigration rapidly declined (Table 1).[14] Of the free Negroes, nearly half were emancipated specifically in order that they might be sent to Liberia: most, but not all, were illiterate and unfamiliar with any form of employment other than plantation labour. The remainder had at least some experience of life as free men—over 4,000 had in fact been born free—and they included individuals of some education and a number of artisans

[10] Brown, op. cit., p. 23.   [11] Huberich, op. cit., pp. 213, 257.
[12] Buell, 1947, p. 20; Brown, op. cit., p. 15.
[13] Huberich, op. cit., pp. 41–42.   [14] Ibid.

B

(carpenters, masons, bricklayers, etc.), although as an unfranchised section of the population they had no experience at all of participation in government. The recaptured Africans had of course not lived in America at all, although some cargoes were first taken to American ports for trans-shipment.

TABLE I. *Status of American immigrants 1822–1867*

Born free	4,541
Purchased their freedom	344
Emancipated to go to Liberia	5,957
Emancipated for other reasons	753
Sent in 1865 from Barbados, West Indies	346
Unknown	68
Settled in 'Maryland in Liberia' (Cap Palmas) by the Maryland Colonization Society, 1831 to 1862	1,227
Recaptured Africans sent by the United States Government	5,722
Total immigrants to 1867	19,858

The records[15] give a little more detail about the 4,000-odd immigrants of the first twenty-five years, who were the pioneers of the new state and who gave it its character. They were by no means a homogeneous group of people. They were fairly evenly divided among men and women, and included many children. Of those over ten years of age, about one in four was literate[16]—a very high proportion compared with the estimated 5 per cent among the slaves in the United States at the same period,[17] but a low proportion in view of the role of educating and civilizing Africa which was assigned to them. A few had a little property, but the majority were entirely dependent on the society during the initial months of their stay. Most were English-speaking, although one group from New Orleans spoke French. It is generally assumed that they were all Christians, and by 1841 all the recaptured Africans had adopted Christianity. Of the latter, ten were in fact from the vicinity of Monrovia, and they returned to their homes;[18] the remainder proved impossible to repatriate, joined the colonists, and became part of the population of present-day Liberia. It is generally thought

[15] As quoted by Huberich.
[16] These figures are compiled from statistical tables interspersed in Huberich, op. cit., vol. i.
[17] Myrdal, 1944, chap. 41.   [18] Huberich, op. cit., p. 625.

that tribespeople from the Congo region were numerous among
those who had been recaptured from the slave-ships; at all events,
the descendants of these people are today known in Liberia as
'Congoes'. We may note in passing that the proportion of free
Negro settlers to recaptured Africans was quite different from that
in the neighbouring colony of Sierra Leone, whose history closely
parallels that of Liberia in many other ways. In Freetown, black
settlers from England, Nova Scotia and Jamaica totalled less than
3,000, Africans recaptured from slave-ships 74,000. [19] In Liberia,
the overall number of immigrants was much smaller, and Negroes
who had lived in America outnumbered recaptured Africans by
four to one. For the former, no attempt seems to have been made
to record their African countries of origin, although these may have
been known in a few cases. It is generally supposed that they or
their forefathers had mostly come from the western coast of Africa,
and *today* some descendants of colonist families claim origins from
specific tribes, notably in Nigeria and Dahomey. But tribal origins
had no particular significance among the pioneers who, in fact,
did not consider themselves Africans at all.

Colour of skin did, however, have some social significance in
the early years. The colonists were not all of purely African descent,
but included a large number who were partly white or American
Indian. 'Ethnically they were truly American', writes Brown.[20]
According to Abayomi Karnga, who was himself a Congo,

Society . . . became divided into four distinct orders: the official
class (including the big traders), the common people, the Congoes, and
the natives. Social intercourse and marriage between these groups was
by custom forbidden.[21]

In the early years, the 'official class' tended to coincide with the
class of people of light skin—the first four presidents were all
partly white. Skin colour was, however, only one of several interrelated factors determining status. Those with light skins probably
tended also to be the better educated and more experienced, since
in the plantation days in America many white fathers freed their
illegitimate offspring and assisted their education.[22] Further, among
those who remained slaves the light-skinned were often chosen as
domestic servants, and they must therefore have become more

[19] Banton, 1957, pp. 3–4.   [20] Brown, op. cit., p. 341, fn. 2.
[21] Karnga, 1962, p. 24.   [22] See Myrdal, 1944, chap. 41.

familiar with the 'civilized way of life' which became the ideal in their new country. But the correlation between skin colour and social status did not persist beyond the first few decades.

The majority of the settlers then were illiterate, unskilled, penniless and without any experience at all of the art of administration. What did they—or for that matter the literate minority—expect, what did they hope for, when they embarked for Africa? Some indication is given by the wording of the 1847 Declaration of Independence, especially in a section listing the causes

... which induced them to expatriate themselves from the land of their nativity, and to form settlements on this barbarous coast.

The causes were almost entirely negative ones—that is, the emigrants were refugees rather than colonists. Further, they identified themselves closely with the way of life of the New World, despite their repudiation of the role in which they had been cast in it:

We the people of Liberia were originally the inhabitants of the United States of North America (my italics).

In some parts of the country, we were debarred from all the rights and privileges of men—in other parts, public sentiment, more powerful than law, frowned us down.

We were everywhere shut out from all civil office.

We were excluded from participation in Government.

We were taxed without our consent.

We were compelled to contribute to the resources of a country which gave us no protection.

We were made into a separate and distinct class, and against us every avenue to improvement was effectually closed ...

All hope of a favorable change in our country was thus wholly extinguished in our bosoms, and we looked with anxiety abroad for some asylum from this deep degradation.

They were expatriates rather than repatriated: they were not buoyed up—as were the Jews in Israel, for example—by the idea that they were returning to their ancestral continent. Indeed, the entire Declaration contains no mention whatsoever of Africa as the land of their forefathers, despite the fact that, for some of them, Africa may have been only one or two generations back. This was probably because conditions on the plantations had not permitted the existence of stable family units, let alone the persistence of family tradition.[23] Africa was a strange and barbarous continent; their

[23] See, for example, Frazier, 1939, chap. 1.

'native land' was America, and the 'God of their Fathers' the Christian God of whom they had learned in America.

The Western Coast of Africa was the place selected by American benevolence and philanthropy, for our future home. . . .

In coming to the shores of Africa, we indulged in the pleasing hope that we would be permitted to exercise and improve those faculties, which impart to man his dignity—to nourish in our hearts the flame of honorable ambition, to cherish and indulge those aspirations, which a beneficent Creator has implanted in every human heart, and to evince to all who despise, ridicule and oppress our race, that we possess with them a common nature, are with them susceptible of equal refinement and capable of equal advancement in all that adorns and dignifies man. . . .

Among the strongest motives to leave our native land—to abandon forever the scenes of our childhood and to sever the most endeared connexions, was the desire for a retreat where, free from agitations of fear and molestation, we could, in comfort and security, approach in worship the God of our Fathers. . . .

Their self-identification as 'inhabitants of North America', and their apparent lack of any feelings of sentiment towards Africa, were of vital importance in determining the manner in which the new settlement developed.

How in practical terms, was the new community to be organized, how was it to make a living? The American Colonization Society's white leaders envisaged it as

. . . an independent community of peasant farmers owning in fee simple a tract of land sufficient to enable them to support themselves and their families by their own labours, allotted out of the public domain without payment, but subject to their improving the land within a specified time.[24]

The actual social and economic organization of the new settlement took a quite different form. This might, perhaps, have been predicted from the characteristics of the settlers and the nature of the country to which they came.

COLONY AND COMMONWEALTH, 1821–47

The society's first emissaries attempted to found a settlement on Sherbro Island in what is now Sierra Leone. In 1821, after this experiment had ended in disaster, the fifty-four survivors of the

[24] Huberich, op. cit., p. 415.

first boatload of American emigrants moved to Cape Mesurado, where land had been purchased by the Colonization Society's agent from the local De chief, King Peter, and established their colony on the site of the present Monrovia. The doubtful legality of the land purchase[25]—as of many other such purchases from tribal chiefs—gave rise to later conflict, and the hostility of the tribes was further aroused by the colonists' attempt to stop the slave traffic, still very active in the area. In some accounts,[26] the European slave-traders incited the tribespeople against the colonists, in the hope of ridding themselves of interference. Whatever the case, several of the local chiefs certainly joined forces in attacking the colony, and bitter fighting ensued. This became the heroic period in Liberian history. During the fighting a British gunboat came offshore, and its commander offered help to the sorely pressed colonists, on condition that he could have a small piece of land on which to hoist the British flag. The refusal of Elijah Johnson, a colonist then in charge of the settlement during the agent's absence, is today known by every Liberian schoolchild:

We want no flag-staff put up here, that will cost us more to get it down than it will to whip the natives.

Another almost legendary figure from this period was Matilda Newport, who at the decisive moment in the final battle for Crown Hill lit a cannon with a coal from her pipe and wreaked havoc among the attacking tribesmen, an action today commemorated in the Republic by a public holiday. After this battle, peace seems to have been maintained within the immediate vicinity of Monrovia, although the colonists were involved from time to time in inter-tribal conflicts, and particularly in the Gola-De war of the 1830's when the Gola were reported to be practically exterminating the De.[27] At the death of King Peter of Bushrod Island his successor put the local De people under the protection of the colony, and several other local chiefs followed suit. 'The natives in our vicinity', wrote the society's agent in 1830, 'deem it no small privilege to be permitted to call themselves Americans.'[28] The settlers were joined by more boatloads of immigrants from America, further land was purchased, and by 1830 three other settlements

[25] See Staudenraus, 1961, pp. 64 f. for details.
[26] e.g. Yancy, 1954, p. 35.
[27] Huberich, op. cit., p. 539.
[28] Ibid., p. 408.

had been founded near by—Caldwell, Millsburg and New Georgia.
New Georgia was specifically founded as a settlement for Congoes
(i.e. recaptured slaves from ships on the high seas), although many
of the Congoes also joined the Monrovia population.

In the meantime, Monrovia's internal organization was taking
shape. Initially, each settler was allotted a tract of land in what was
to become the town centre, and a five-acre plot of farmland outside,
on the understanding that the plots should become his freehold
property if within two years he had cleared, fenced and built a
substantial house on the town lot, and cultivated at least two acres
of the farmland. Those wanting more land could purchase it from
the society. In the first months of their stay, the settlers received
food rations from the society, together with materials for house-
building. Each able-bodied man was expected to do public labour
for two days a week.[29] However, the projected 'community of peasant farmers, supporting themselves by their own labours' never
became a reality. The Monrovia settlers in particular were berated
in the early reports of the society for their lack of interest in farming. Several factors combined to produce this situation: the association of manual labour with the condition of slavery, the initial lack
of interest in local foodstuffs and preference for those accustomed
foods which were being imported from America, and the relatively
quick profits to be obtained from trading. Already in 1823 four
small Liberian schooners had gone down the coast while several
more were being built and fitted out in Monrovia. Exports at the
time were mostly products obtained by barter from the tribespeople—dye-wood, palm oil, ivory, gold, rice, tortoiseshell, wax,
hides and coffee.[30] By 1830, one settler had annual sales worth
$70,000, another sales worth $25,000 and property worth $20,000,
all accumulated within his seven years' residence in the colony.[31]
During the same period, a similar process was taking place in
neighbouring Freetown—that is, a thriving commercial community
was emerging at the expense of the projected community of
peasant farmers. In Freetown the settlers were being groomed for
government by the white administration, while the liberated
Africans took up commerce and trade and became wealthy.[32] In
Monrovia, on the other hand, the leaders and officials themselves

[29] Brown, op. cit., p. 111.
[30] Huberich, op. cit., pp. 436–7. Liberia has indigenous coffee.
[31] Huberich, op. cit., p. 437.
[32] Porter, 1963, pp. 42 f.

were the richest traders. J. J. Roberts, for example, an octoroon who arrived in 1829 and later became first President of Liberia, had one of the most prosperous trading firms in the country. But, of course, not all could succeed in trade, and the general population remained poor. The inhabitants of Caldwell, Millsburg and New Georgia, and of other settlements formed later in the vicinity of Monrovia, adopted agriculture with more enthusiasm than did the Monrovians, and by 1828 were planting cash crops in addition to their own food supplies, using native Africans or Congoes as labourers. The Upper Settlements, as they were called, became identified with the agricultural, conservative element; Monrovia with the commercial and liberal one.[33]

The local tribespeople were being drawn into the colony both politically—since their chiefs were putting them under its protection—and economically, since they were trading with the colonists and being employed as labourers by them. Further, from the earliest days, the colonists took tribal children into their households, sometimes adopting them, but more frequently using them as domestic help. In 1838 the practice was regulated by law as a system of apprenticeship, whereby clothing and some schooling were to be provided.[34] This custom was, over the ensuing century, to prove of the greatest importance in the process of assimilation of the tribal people into the community of Americo-Liberians. Finally, although according to Karnga 'social intercourse and marriage were by custom forbidden', unions of colonists and tribespeople were taking place, and their offspring seem to have been regarded as members of the colonist community. When the first census was made in 1843, the combined population of Monrovia and the Upper Settlements was 2,390, of whom twelve were recorded as of mixed Americo-Liberian and native parentage, forty-six of native parents and adopted into Americo-Liberian families.[35] This figure specifically excluded the Congoes and the 'loyal natives', estimated at about this time at 30,000.[36] The latter were not confined to their tribal areas: attracted by the economic opportunities, they seem to have been flocking into Monrovia. In 1835, the Monrovia Town Council passed an ordinance controlling the Kru fishermen and subjecting all native Africans not employed by

[33] Huberich, op. cit., pp. 431 and 487.
[34] Ibid., p. 523.   [35] Ibid., pp. 767–70.
[36] Ibid.; Brown, op. cit., p. 123.

citizens of Monrovia to arrest and fatigue work.[37] Native Africans were not regarded as citizens, although in 1841 provision was made whereby they could obtain citizenship if they had remained in the colony more than three years and

... exhibited an uniform course of civilized life and ... abandoned all the forms, customs and superstitions of heathendom.[38]

However, it seems that few took advantage of this provision. George Brown, an American Negro whose economic history of Liberia was published in the 1930's, has this to say of the situation during the first decades:

The older [tribal] children were soon doing the domestic work, thereby relieving the colonial women of drudgery. The men were taken to help on the farms, when it was learned that what seemed an inexhaustible supply of native labour, could be tapped for a small remuneration. ...

And he concludes from this

As the psychology of many of the settlers closely resembled that of their former Virginia and Cotton-belt masters, the Africans were regarded as a peon class. Such settlers immediately planned to dominate Africans as the white planters in America had dominated them. ... Having come to Africa to escape the strictures of slavery, many of the colonists did not want to engage in the manual labour with which they had been so closely associated.[39]

While this was undoubtedly one facet of the situation, the history of relations between Liberia's black colonists and the tribespeople in the early years is not markedly different from that of the relations between white colonists—who were not ex-slaves—and tribespeople in other parts of Africa. Historically, it has been rare for people to choose to carry out manual labour where others were available to do it for them. Many judgments on Liberia have, indeed, been vitiated by the implicit assumption that the black colonists, because they were black and despite their extremely unpropitious background, should have reacted in a more generous fashion than the white colonists elsewhere. In fact, the colour of their skins made it *more* important for them to stress the social distance between themselves and the local Africans. The fact that they were not obviously physically different accentuated the fear—

[37] Huberich, op. cit., p. 508.   [38] Ibid., p. 724.   [39] Brown, op. cit., p. 117.

shared by other colonial communities—of being submerged in
what was to them a barbarous and heathen society. This fear is
still basic in America-Liberian psychology, and to understand many
of the features of America-Liberian culture one must take this
situation into account. Thus, to distinguish themselves in appearance from the tribespeople, they adopted a formal, Western style
of dress, inappropriate to tropical climates, which has been described by every writer on America-Liberian society, and which
later became, for similar reasons, a characteristic of élite groups in
other parts of Africa. Towards the end of the century, Sir Harry
Johnston was to write:

> The America-Liberian still worships clothes as the outward and
> visible manifestation of Christianity and the best civilization; that is to
> say, the European clothes of the nineteenth century . . . No self-
> respecting Liberian would be seen abroad on a Sunday or would pay a
> call or take part in any social function, even under a broiling sun in a
> Turkish-bath atmosphere, except in immaculate black silk topper and
> a long black frock coat.[40]

The colonists also emphasized the social distance between them
and the tribespeople by the type of houses they built: the 'substantial dwellings' turned out to be porticoed mansions built in
the colonial style of the plantation-owners in the southern states.
But only a few were sufficiently wealthy to build grand houses:
materially, the majority of the colonists must have been little
better off than the surrounding tribespeople. Further, although a
few were educated, most had little or no schooling. They were
Christians, though, and this very clearly set them apart from surrounding heathendom. Hence the devout religious observances of
the communities they established. Churches were the first public
buildings erected; laws were passed enforcing Sabbath-keeping; and
the 'psalm-singing' community so often described by later travel-
lers was early established. Baptists and Methodists were the first
denominations in the area. The ministers were all drawn from the
colonists, at least one of whom was appointed a lay preacher before
leaving America. Initially, the churches were supported by American missions, which also operated all schools up to the end of the
Commonwealth period. The 1843 census recorded that 600 children were attending such schools, of whom about a third were of
native parentage. The American Colonization Society received

[40] Johnston, op. cit., pp. 353–4.

much of its support from churches, but carried out no missionary activities itself, neither did it establish schools, either for the settlers' children or for the children of the surrounding tribes.Instead, it advised the colonists to accumulate funds for this purpose.[41]

Towards the end of this period, the society's connexion with the colony was in fact becoming increasingly tenuous. Huberich[42] holds that, legally, Liberia was a sovereign state from the beginning, supreme power having been delegated by the settlers to the American Colonization Society for a period during which they could learn the art of self-government. In effect it remained under the control of the society until 1847. The society governed through its agent, who after the first few years was usually also United States Government agent for the recaptured Africans. Communications were of course poor, so that in practice the agent had almost sole responsibility for the regulation of the settlement's affairs. The agents officially appointed—whose names have been commemorated in many Monrovia street-names—were all white Americans. The fact that eight out of eighteen died within a year of their arrival[43] bears witness to the conditions which they and the settlers met. (The death rate among the latter seems not to have been recorded.) Thomas Buchanan, the last white representative of the society, was appointed first Governor when the Commonwealth of Liberia came into existence in 1838, and he was succeeded by a colonist, J. J. Roberts, who was in 1848 to become first President of the republic.

In the meantime, several independent settlements were being established down the coast, by state branches of the American Colonization Society.[44] Bassa Cove, founded in 1834 by the Pennsylvania and New York societies, became part of the Commonwealth of Liberia (as a section of the county of Grand Bassa) in 1838, the other part at the time being the county of Montserrado, made up of Monrovia and the Upper Settlements. A further settlement, 'Mississippi in Africa', at Greenville joined the Commonwealth in 1842 and became the nucleus of Sinoe County. A fourth colony, 'Maryland in Africa', at Cap Palmas, remained independent until 1856, when it became Maryland County in the Republic of Liberia. (The fifth county, Grand Cape Mount County, was not formed until the twentieth century.) Each of these settlements

41 Huberich, op. cit., pp. 767–70.   42 Ibid., chapter 5.
43 Ibid., pp. 1704–8.   44 Ibid., chapter 15.

enlarged its sphere of influence gradually by making treaties with the local tribes. Sometimes this was as a result of conquest, but more often the tribal territories seem to have been ceded voluntarily. Governor Roberts reported in 1847:

[The natives]... are becoming more and more sensible of the superiority of civilized life over the barbarous customs of their fathers ... They are becoming convinced of the precarious resources of the slave trade and of the sufferings to which many of them are frequently reduced by the wars and wants of savage life, and find it in their interest to dispose of their territories to the government—ceding to it the political control and jurisdiction over all persons and property therein, incorporating themselves with us. . . .[45]

By 1847, 'Liberia' included the coastal area between Cape Mount and Grand Cess, and stretched inland for about forty-five miles. That is, it included much of the territory of the Vai, De, Bassa and Kru peoples, and when Maryland County was added in 1856, of the Grebo. The hinterland was, at the time, virtually unknown.

For some time the Monrovia settlers, in particular, had been agitating for independence from the American Colonization Society, and the society seems to have had little objection to handing over power to them; its actual authority had in any case become rather tenuous. However, the immediate impulse to the declaration of the republic was provided by disputes with the British and French over Liberia's status—in particular over her right to demand customs duties and to lay claim to border territories. In 1847 the settlers took matters into their own hands and declared Liberia a republic. The new state was officially recognized almost immediately by the French and British, and most of the more important European powers followed suit. The United States did not officially recognize the republic until 1862 and had at the time little interest —either political or economic—in the new country. During the second half of the century, it was the European powers— especially Britain, France and Germany—who were most closely associated with Liberian affairs, and who by the outbreak of the First World War virtually controlled her economy.

THE REPUBLIC, 1848–1914

At the time of Liberia's Declaration of Independence, there were 6,100 persons of American origin resident in the republic,

[45] Ibid., p. 813, quoting the message of Governor Roberts to the 9th Session of the Executive Council, 1847.

about 1,300 of them in Monrovia.[46] During the next ten years over 5,000 more emigrants were sent by the American Colonization Society. Africans recaptured from slave-ships were also still arriving, especially in the period 1858–60, when the U.S. Government launched an attack on a fresh outbreak of slave-trading.[47] During the Civil War in America emigration to Liberia almost ceased, and its rate was much slower after the war was over, the attention of freed men being focused rather on new possibilities at home. In 1865, a batch of 356 emigrants was sent from Barbadoes. By 1906 Johnston estimated Monrovia's Americo-Liberian population at 2,500.[48]

The first decade of the republic was a prosperous one for both commerce and agriculture. In the settlements near Monrovia, flourishing plantations of rice, cotton, coffee and sugar cane supplanted the smaller-scale garden cultivation of earlier days. By 1870, about fifty sailing vessels of up to 80 tons had been built in the Monrovia ship-yards. Several of the big traders—who were often also senior officials—were exporting on their own account. One of the wealthiest, who was also Commander of the Liberian Army,

... owned one of the largest stores and mercantile establishments in Monrovia and did a profitable business with England, France and Germany.... One and sometimes two vessels arrived annually from America consigned wholly to him. He had three sea-coast sailing craft and fifteen or more cargo boats which were used to convey merchandise to and from steamers lying off the coast. He conducted a place of business in Water Street, and owned a three and a half storey brick mansion....[49]

Another wealthy trader of the period was Edward Roye, who arrived in 1846 and started business almost immediately. He had a parallel success in the sphere of politics, becoming Speaker of the House of Representatives in 1849, Chief Justice in 1865, and President in 1870, and is remembered as the first pure Negro President of the republic.[50]

But the commercial boom did not continue into the latter part

[46] Johnston, op. cit., p. 228.
[47] Brown, op. cit., p. 135.
[48] Johnston, op. cit., p. 371.
[49] Brown, op. cit., pp. 135 and 141.
[50] Huberich, op. cit., p. 1258; Henries, 1954, p. 101.

of the century. A number of factors combined to end it. The introduction of European-owned steamships, which provided regular and relatively low-cost transport, drove Liberian sailing craft off the sea. The establishment of shipping lines permitted small European traders to operate, in addition to the large companies owning private vessels: these small traders competed with Liberians, and the European-owned shipping lines gave preference to their own nationals. And finally, competition developed among the producing countries: between 1885 and 1900, with rapidly increasing coffee exports from Brazil, Liberia's coffee exports were halved. The introduction of beet sugar cultivation in Europe had an even worse effect on Liberia's cane sugar industry. Most of the republic's trade at the time was with Europe, Germany and Britain being the main receiving countries, and from the late 1860's profits from Liberian trade went increasingly to British, and more especially German, firms. By 1904, Monrovia had no less than twenty trading · houses whose head office was in Hamburg, and Liberians whose fathers had controlled the republic's business were working as agents or employees of foreign firms.[51] Liberia became desperately poor, and its Government was finding it difficult even to pay its officials. It therefore obtained a series of loans—in 1871 and 1906 from British concerns and in 1912 from international funds—but this only led to further disaster. Liberia's credit was low, the terms of the loans far from philanthropic, the loan money was sometimes mishandled, and the actual benefit accruing to Liberia was small.[52]

With the disappearance of Liberian trading concerns, the Monrovians became more and more dependent on Government for a living until, as McCall puts it:

Monrovia took on something of the aspect of a one industry town, government being the industry. Many citizens felt that it was their prerogative to find employment in the government, but it was also true that when the treasury was in difficulty officials went regularly to their offices despite enormous arrears in pay. . . .[53]

For the Monrovians—that is, for the Americo-Liberians in Monrovia—government, politics and law became the only respectable ways of getting a living, and so they have remained until very recently. It is interesting to speculate on the lines Liberia's history

[51] Brown, op. cit., pp. 134 f., 158 f.
[52] For details of the loans, see Brown, op. cit., pp. 139 f.
[53] McCall, 1956, p. 90.

would have taken had her rulers continued to be businessmen. Certainly, the disappearance of the Liberian traders must have greatly decreased social contacts between the Americo-Liberians and the tribespeople—which in turn must have established more firmly the caste system whose general outline was already in existence. The colonists and their descendants ran—and completely staffed—the Government, the foreigners ran the town's business, and the tribespeople worked as domestics or as store-hands and ships' loaders.

During the same period, the territorial sphere of influence of the Americo-Liberians was increasing. At the time of Independence, Liberia had consisted of a coastal strip forty-five miles wide. During the second half of the century, and especially during the explorations in 1868 and 1874 of the Liberian explorer Benjamin Anderson, treaties were signed with chiefs in the 'hinterland', as the stretch of land behind the coastal zone is called.[54] It does not seem to have been very clear, even at the time, how the relationship of these chiefs and their territories with the republic was envisaged. The 1847 constitution had made no provision for the government of the tribal peoples and the Liberian Government certainly had no funds to develop—or even to police—new territories. In fact, apart from putting down rebellions when they arose, it made no attempt to regulate internal affairs within the tribal areas until the end of the century. It seems to have been envisaged that the tribal peoples would gradually become integrated into existing Liberian political institutions, and that there was, therefore, no need for a separate form of tribal administration. President Payne's political platform in 1876 had been

. . . to bring about a closer and more friendly intercourse between the citizens of the Republic proper and the more advanced interior tribes, with a view towards having the latter incorporated into the Liberian political institutions, and forming one people in Liberia.[55]

And in 1904, to French arguments that the absence of Americo-Liberian settlements in the far interior implied a lack of 'effective occupation' on the part of the Liberians, President Arthur Barclay replied that all the Negroes inhabiting Liberia were Liberians, and that he had not the slightest desire to replace native-born Negroes by colonists born on the coast.[56] Johnson commented on this:

[54] Johnston, op. cit., pp. 250 f.   [55] Quoted by McCall, op. cit., p. 94.
[56] Johnston, op. cit., pp. 301–2.

This is a perfectly sound doctrine; but of course the present weakness of the civilized Americo-Liberian government on the coast is that it has no sure means of maintaining law and order between tribe and tribe, and between all these tribes in the hinterland in regard to their relations with the French and British possessions across the frontier. . . .[57]

It was this pressure from neighbouring colonial governments which eventually led to the formulation of a system of indirect rule modelled on British colonial administration—a system which McCall argues, with some justification, tended to slow up development towards unification of Americo-Liberians and tribespeople by regularizing indigenous organization and thus preserving it.[58]

The colonists had established their townships along the coast. Behind and between these townships—that it, within the coastal zone as well as in the interior, were the tribal areas. In 1904, President Arthur Barclay suggested[59] that the tribal districts should be regarded as townships, and should be governed by chiefs who would have a role similar to that of justices of the peace in 'civilized' townships. District Commissioners should be appointed by the President to supervise them and hear appeals from their courts. The Liberian writer Ernest Yancy records that at about the period of the first World War, as a means of providing closer supervision over the tribes,

. . . the government deposed all chiefs and kings who had rebelled against it or were not in harmony with its program. It then instructed the several tribes to select or elect their representative paramount chiefs and submit their names for approval. This was done with some reluctance. The chiefs were commissioned by the President and thus became directly responsible to the government. . . . This also did not work out as well as it was thought it would. Therefore, the interior was then divided into five districts; camps or garrisons were set up, and district commissioners were placed over them. . . .[60]

This formed the basis of the present system of tribal administration. The District Commissioners were sometimes Americo-Liberians, but included men originally from the coastal tribes, especially Kru and Vai. It seems, in fact, to have been the establishment and growth of the Interior Department (the government department responsible for tribal affairs and staffing tribal administration)

---

[57] Johnston, op. cit., p. 304.   [58] In article cited.
[59] As quoted in Johnston, op. cit., pp. 311 f.
[60] Yancy, op. cit., pp. 145–6.

which initially led to the breaking down of correspondence between ethnic origins and occupations in Monrovia. As is implied by their appointment as District Commissioners, individuals from the coastal tribes were being drawn into the cultural orbit of the Americo-Liberians. And within the tribal societies themselves, profound changes were taking place. This was more as a result of the work of the Christian missions—mostly American-supported and staffed—than of the direct influence of the Liberian Government. The missions operated most of the schools in the republic— Johnston records that in 1904 the Protestant and Methodist schools alone (four other missions were already operating) had more than twice as many pupils as had the government schools.[61] Schools and churches were being established in the tribal areas as well as within the townships. On the Kru coast, for instance, it was certainly the missions rather than the Government which gave the impetus to the adoption by the tribespeople of the 'civilized way of life', and to the formation of incorporated 'townships' of educated and Christian tribespeople. The first of these townships was established in the first decade of the present century.

THE REPUBLIC, 1917–39

At the beginning of the First World War, Liberia had declared her neutrality, but in 1917, under pressure from the United States, she broke off diplomatic relations with Germany. This ended the period of German domination of commerce, but it also ruined Liberia's already shaky economy. The Government again looked for outside help. One possibility which offered itself was to link the republic with the 'Back to Africa' movement then getting under way in the United States, under the leadership of Marcus Garvey. The history of the dealings between the Liberian Government and Garvey's Harlem-based Universal Negro Improvement Association indicates the stage which relations between American Negro and Americo-Liberian had reached.[62]

Monrovia, the largest of the settlements, now had an Americo-Liberian population of about 5,000,[63] and had virtually stopped increasing by immigration from abroad. Improved opportunities in the United States had led to Liberia's being practically forgotten

[61] Johnston, op. cit., p. 390
[62] See Cronon, 1955, pp. 124-32.
[63] Strong, 1939, pp. 38 and 46.

C

by the American Negroes. With the appearance of the Garvey movement, interest was temporarily revived. Garvey planned to send 20,000 to 30,000 families a year to Liberia, in addition to providing technical and financial aid. It is not at all sure that so many would have been prepared to go. In his history of Garveyism, Cronon writes

Like their Jewish counterparts, most American Negroes would watch with eager interest the building of a free Negro Zionist state in Africa. They could be counted on for generous financial support and enthusiastic moral encouragement. But only a very few would be ready to undertake the hard and thankless pioneering work required to create a Black Israel in the African Jungle.[64]

Besides, many were critical of the Liberian Government and in particular of its treatment of the tribal peoples. In 1920 Garvey's delegate had visited Monrovia, and on his return had vigorously denounced the ruling aristocracy, warning at the same time that the UNIA

... would have to play down its plans to emancipate the native tribes, at least until the government was well established.[65]

The Liberian Government, for their part, had an ambivalent attitude towards the UNIA and its plans. There was a long tradition of welcoming American immigrants, and it badly needed the money which Garvey offered. On the other hand—quite apart from any suspicions it might have had of the political aims of the UNIA —immigration on such a scale would radically upset the *status quo* by swamping the Americo-Liberian population. Further, what would the relationship of the republic be with Garvey, who had already styled himself 'Provisional President of Africa'? And there was also the question of the shape of future relations with the governments of Britain, France and the United States, all of which were against Garvey's plans. In this situation the Liberian Government vacillated: in 1923 it made a concession of land to the UNIA, but later the concession was cancelled and an advance group of UNIA technicians were deported on the grounds that they would stir up political trouble.[66] Finally, Liberia sent a diplomatic note to the United States Government declaring that the Negro republic was

[64] Cronon, 1955, p. 128.   [65] Ibid.   [66] Brown, op. cit., p. 179.

. . . irrevocably opposed in principle and in fact to the incendiary policy of the UNIA, led by Marcus Garvey.[67]

This negative decision was important in the history of the republic, since it signified Liberia's official choice to identify itself with the powerful metropolitan governments, rather than with movements of protest. The attitudes and interests of the Americo-Liberians, most of whom had left America before the abolition of slavery or were the descendants of such emigrants, and those of the American Negroes, had already moved far apart. Those few Negroes who have come to Liberia in recent decades—many of them as wives of Liberians who have been studying abroad—are 'foreign' in their ways and attitudes and also in their speech. Today even those who have lived many years in the republic and have been naturalized, are commonly referred to as 'Americans', the term 'Americo-Liberian' being usually reserved for the 'sons of the settlers', the descendants of the nineteenth-century immigrants.

During the 1920's Liberia had been negotiating for financial help from other sources, and in 1926 she signed three agreements with American rubber interests represented by Harvey S. Firestone.[68] The first concerned the construction of a deep-water harbour at Monrovia—a plan later abandoned. The second provided for a loan from the Finance Corporation of America—a Firestone subsidiary. The third granted the company the right to lease up to one million acres of land in Liberia at an annual rental of 6 cents an acre for a term of 99 years. The company was to pay a tax of 1 per cent. on the gross value of all rubber exported; it was not required to pay income tax. The agreement saved the country from bankruptcy, but for the next decade did little to effect its economic recovery. Rubber trees take seven years to mature: the first rubber was not tapped until the early 1930's, by which time the price of rubber had fallen drastically as a result of the Depression. Planting operations were also slowed down, and much smaller acreages leased and planted than originally intended, although by 1940, 40,000 acres were in production. Firestone's financial contribution to the republic during the period was small in relation to what had been expected: President Edwin Barclay estimated that in 1938 it amounted to less than 3 per cent. of government revenues, although the company disputed this, claiming that its total financial

[67] Cronon, op. cit., p. 129.
[68] This account is summarized from Chatfield Taylor, 1958, pp. 139 f.

contribution provided a third of government revenues, if its subsidiary activities were taken into account.[69] It had established stores on its plantation and in Monrovia, built a road from Monrovia to its main plantation fifty miles away, and, through a subsidiary company, it had founded the Bank of Monrovia.[70] Most importantly, it was providing wage employment on a scale hitherto unknown in the republic as well as encouraging the development of private rubber farms. But the immediate effect of all this on social relations within the Liberian population was limited by the fact that Firestone's local employees were almost all illiterate tribespeople; clerical, technical and administrative staff were, and to a large extent still are, brought in from America. And, on the other hand, the Liberians wealthy enough to start rubber-farms were almost all Americo-Liberians. The correspondence between ethnic origin and occupation was therefore little affected.

In the meantime, the resentment felt by the tribal peoples towards the Government seems to have been increasing. This was partly because in attempting to impose a system of tribal administration, the Government was inevitably interfering with traditional lines of authority. Again, hut tax, which had been introduced in the first decade of the century, was now being collected more rigorously, and according to Brown it amounted in 1934 to $62,121, providing in that year over 38 per cent. [sic] of total government revenues—and this excluded amounts paid in rice, coffee and palm oil in lieu of money.[71] The tribal areas were getting little in return: schools and medical services, where they existed, were still being provided largely by American missions. And a third major cause of resentment was the labour situation. In the 1920's, reports began to appear in the American press alleging that forced labour practices tantamount to slavery existed in Liberia. The League of Nations took the matter up with the Liberian Government, and it was actually at the latter's suggestion that an international commission was sent out in 1930. The commission was concerned with seeking evidence of forced labour, rather than with making a general study of labour conditions, and, in fact, the accuracy of some of its findings has been questioned by the Liberians. In any case, in fairness to the Liberian Government, it should be said that

[69] Buell, op. cit., p. 151.
[70] The bank has now changed hands and is a branch of the National City Bank of New York.
[71] Brown, op. cit., p. 184.

in the very unlikely event that any colonial power in Africa had invited the League of Nations to investigate labour conditions at that period, practices not dissimilar would have been disclosed. With these reservations, we must rely on the commission's report, *faute de mieux*, for a contemporary account of labour relations during a period which is still very much a part of the memories of Monrovians today.

The commission reported,[72] firstly, that slavery as defined in the Anti-Slavery Convention did not exist in the republic, although domestic slavery existed among the tribes and leading citizens were accepting aboriginals as pawns. The Liberian Government had, in fact, already attempted—without success—to control the system of 'pawning' among the tribal peoples, i.e. the system whereby a relative or other dependent might be offered as security for a loan or debt. After publication of the report, domestic servitude, including pawning, was immediately declared illegal. This ruling was apparently more effective, but it did not do much to improve relations between Government and the tribespeople: on the contrary, President Barclay claimed that the sudden disturbance in the tribal economies which followed was one of the causes of tribal rebellions during the '30's. The charge that leading citizens were accepting individuals as pawns refers to a state of affairs which could have been foreseen from the existence side by side of the tribal custom of pawning and the Americo-Liberian practice of accepting tribal children as wards or servants. The latter practice was obviously open to abuse, and difficult to control. At worst, the children were treated as near slaves. At best, the practice was a singularly effective means of integrating the two sections of the population, and in fact a great many of the educated Monrovians today are tribespeople who were taken into Americo-Liberian families during this period.

Another set of charges made in the commission's report concerned the use of compulsory unpaid labour. At the time, such labour was used for a variety of purposes including road-making and 'porterage', i.e. the provision of carriers for the persons and equipment of various officials. In the tribal areas it was the chief's responsibility to round up men to act as porters. In Monrovia people recall today that when the Frontier Force was sent from the capital to quell the rebellions of the 1930's on the Kru coast, the soldiers

[72] I have quoted the Commission's findings as summarized by Azikwe, 1934.

themselves were permitted to recruit 'porters' to carry their equipment, causing chaos as they chased men all about the town attempting to recruit them by force. In the Monrovia area improved road communications have now made porterage unnecessary, but the system is still remembered with resentment. Porterage—and other public work—is still compulsory in the interior, although porters now receive a small allowance.

From the point of view of the commission, the most important charge was that the shipment of Liberian labourers to Fernando Po and Gabon was associated with slavery because the method of recruiting carried compulsion with it. Recruitment of local tribespeople for service abroad was older than the republic. The Kru people, especially, had long taken jobs on foreign-owned ships, and in the second half of the nineteenth century the ships started carrying gangs of men recruited to work under contract, usually for a year, in territories down the coast, especially the Gold Coast and the Oil River territory. British recruiting agents were also sending men to work in the West Indies, and the French were recruiting for work on the Panama Canal.[73] The Spanish planters at Fernando Po started sending agents to Liberia in 1900. Their recruiting methods, and the working conditions on the plantations, became notorious both within Liberia and internationally, and after an unsuccessful attempt to control the situation, the Liberian Government informed Spain that further recruiting was prohibited. In 1928, however, it was resumed under an arrangement whereby the recruiting agency was to be composed of Liberian citizens and was to receive a bonus for each labourer shipped. There was evidence that force was used in the recruitment of men for work in what continued to be deplorable conditions: some of the recruits died, others returned seriously ill.[74] A number of Liberian officials, including the President himself, were charged with being involved. When the commission's findings were published, all recruiting for service abroad was prohibited and the President resigned, but the underlying bitterness of the tribespeople remained and was one of the factors underlying revolts which broke out on the Kru coast a few years later.

The League of Nations drew up a plan of assistance which was intended to remedy the conditions described in the report and also

[73] Huberich, op. cit., p. 909; Brown, op. cit., p. 149.
[74] Brown, op. cit., p. 150.

to provide economic aid. It required, among other things, that European or American officers should replace Liberian district commissioners. The plan would virtually have deprived the Republic of her sovereignty, and she refused to accept it. The new President, Edwin Barclay, instead attempted a number of internal reforms, including reorganization of the system of tribal administration.

In the meantime, Monrovia was growing very slowly. In 1934, her total population was estimated at 10,000,[75] by the beginning of the Second World War at 12,000.[76] The town remained poverty-stricken, with no electricity, telephone installations, sanitation, or paved streets. Commercial activity was however gradually increasing: the Lebanese had started trading in Liberia in the 1920's, and several new European trading concerns, including German ones, had opened up. Firestone's centre of employment was on its plantation fifty miles away, and although in the 1930's it was employing 6,000 men,[77] the effect of this on the Monrovia population seems to have been remarkably slight, possibly because Firestone labour is partly seasonal, and is drawn mostly from hinterland tribesmen who move between their home villages and the plantation. In any case, there was little new opportunity for employment in Monrovia. Since there were few public facilities to be maintained, government did not require a large labour force. In general, the Americo-Liberians staffed the Government, and the tribal people—the long-established Kru, Vai and Bassa—worked as domestics, ships' loaders, and store-hands. Except in the case of the domestics, they did not even come into contact as employers and employees, since the shipping companies and trading concerns were operated by foreigners. Nevertheless, there was upward mobility from the tribal section of the population; intermarriages had taken place intermittently throughout the republic's history. Extra-marital unions between Americo-Liberian men and tribal women seem to have been even more frequent, and the children of such unions were sometimes taken into the household of their fathers and became accepted as Americo-Liberians. And some individuals of tribal origin were getting government posts. This did not, however, imply a general breaking down of social barriers between the two sections of the population, because the mobile individuals usually passed into the Americo-Liberian group and

[75] Ibid., p. 41.   [76] Lelong, 1946.   [77] Greene, 1957.

lost contact with their kinsfolk. Usually they adopted 'civilized' names, often that of the patron or guardian who had taken them in as children, and some refused to admit their origins. If anything, mobility of this nature tended to increase tension between the two sectors of the population: resentment of the 'superior' attitudes of the Americo-Liberians was far surpassed by the fury aroused in people refused admission to the houses of their educated relatives. In time, however, the cumulative effect of the process of 'passing' would probably have broken down the ethnic dichotomy in the population, as the actual Americo-Liberians became more and more rare. As things turned out, the process was enormously accelerated by the economic impetus that Liberia, like other African territories, received in the years following the Second World War.

ECONOMIC AND SOCIAL DEVELOPMENTS SINCE 1940

Soon after the war broke out it became apparent that Liberia was of strategic importance, both because of her geographical situation and because of her rubber crop. Economic change in the next few years went at a pace undreamed of in the first long century of isolation. Before this could happen, some improvement had to be made in communications: vessels were still being loaded offshore by surf-boats at Monrovia, and there were virtually no roads other than the fifty-mile stretch from Monrovia to the Firestone plantation. In 1942, an airfield was built under an arrangement with Pan-American Airways, next to the main Firestone plantation, and later 5,000 American Army Air Force troops—mostly Negroes—were garrisoned in the area. A modern port whose construction was financed by Lend-Lease funds, was opened at Monrovia in 1948. And finally, United States funds provided for the construction of a road linking Monrovia with Ganta on the Liberia-Guinea border, thus opening up the hinterland. Since the end of the war, United States aid has included two Export-Import Bank loans totalling $6.3 million, and a credit of $15 million for road-building has been established. Another $9 million has been granted under the Technical Aid Program. In addition it was estimated that in 1956 private American capital invested in Liberia amounted to more than $50 million. In the same year, European and Lebanese capital was thought to be between seven and ten million dollars: all these figures have doubtless been outdated since.[78] International organizations like FAO, WHO and UNESCO, have also been providing technical assistance.

At present rubber is still the main export. By 1958, Firestone had 90,000 acres under production, and was employing about 25,000 men, mostly in her larger plantation near Monrovia. The rubber is exported in latex form from the Freeport in Monrovia: in 1956, exports totalled 80 million pounds. In 1951, when Liberia first introduced income tax legislation, the Firestone company agreed to pay income tax at 25 per cent.; in 1959 the rate was increased to 35 per cent.[79] Firestone's contribution to the republic's economy was very greatly increased both proportionately and absolutely. And other companies, potentially equally large, are planting rubber: the Goodrich Company in the Western Province, and a Dutch-German group, whose interests were formerly in Sumatra, near Salala in the Central Province. Finally, there are now nearly a thousand Liberian rubber planters with plantations of up to 3,000 acres,[80] who employ altogether some 8,500 labourers.[81] The majority of these planters are absentee landlords, many of them officials in Monrovia. Their 'rubber-farms' are mostly strung out along the new Monrovia-Ganta highway.

But Liberia no longer depends so heavily on rubber. Iron ore, said to be of the highest grade in the world, is becoming at least as important in the national economy. The Liberian Mining Company (with Liberian and American capital) has for several years been exporting about $2\frac{1}{2}$ million tons of ore annually, bringing it to the port of Monrovia from its mine about fifty miles to the north, by its own private railway—the first and only railway in Liberia. In 1958, the company was employing nearly 3,000 Liberians. Another company, LAMCO, with American, Swedish and Liberian capital, has a vast project to mine ore in the Nimba Mountains in the far interior, and it is constructing a port, larger than Monrovia's, at Lower Buchanan in Grand Bassa, and linking mine and port by a railway. The future exports of these two companies and several smaller ones are expected to make Liberia one of the world's main iron-ore producers.[82] There are also a number of foreign companies —German, Swiss, Israeli, Italian, French, Spanish—and a few Liberian ones, operating smaller-scale agricultural, forestry or

[78] Figures in this paragraph are from Chatfield Taylor, op. cit., pp. 14 and 16.
[79] *The Listener*, 18.2.59.   [80] Macrae, 1958, p. 22.   [81] *This is Liberia*, p. 38.
[82] Macrae, loc. cit., and *Liberian Age*, 8.9.58 and 22.1.59.

mining concessions, or carrying out development work under contract with the Liberian Government.

Some of these economic ventures were still in their infancy when the field research for this study was carried out in 1958-9, and they had not yet made their full social impact. But the direction of social change was already apparent. Many thousands of people— from the hinterland as well as from the coastal region—have been drawn into the money economy for the first time, and employers are, in fact, complaining of a labour shortage. The focus of economic development has moved away from the relatively isolated settlements strung out along the coast, towards the main Monrovia-Ganta road and its extensions into the Eastern and Western Provinces. Between the coastal towns, communications are still by sea, by air, or on foot: as so frequently in West Africa, the topography of the country makes the construction of coastal roads a difficult undertaking, and strips of coastline away from large centres therefore become more isolated than the interior. Men and women— both Americo-Liberians and tribespeople—have been moving away from the smaller coastal towns, and there has also been an exodus from the Montserrado settlements (the former 'Upper Settlements'), whose farms are now overgrown and whose mansions have today a derelict—though picturesque—appearance. Generally, and especially for the educated, the direction of this migration has been towards Monrovia. In the hinterland, however, large numbers are now finding employment with the mines and plantations being established locally.

All this has important implications for social relations. Geographic mobility has brought many thousands of 'Liberians' into contact for the first time, tribe with tribe as well as tribe with Americo-Liberian. There is now a wider range of economic opportunities, for both the educated and the uneducated. This means that competition for places in the administration has relaxed, since Government is no longer the sole provider of non-manual employment. There are now some people of tribal origin in the highest ranks, and in junior administrative posts they probably predominate. And for the first time since the commercial boom of the first decade of the republic, there is for the Americo-Liberian (and the educated tribesman) an acceptable alternative to 'politics, government and the law' in the possibility of becoming a rubber farmer or working for one of the foreign or international organizations.

In the 1930's, the correspondence between ethnic origin and occupation was already beginning to break down because of the assimilation of tribespeople into Americo-Liberian society. Today, this process has gathered so much momentum that among the educated—the 'civilized' as they are called in Liberia—actual Americo-Liberians, i.e. persons descended from the nineteenth-century immigrants—are now a small minority. Some of the older people still attempt to conceal their tribal origins, but increasingly younger tribespeople are retaining their tribal identification and tribal names; occasionally they even appear in tribal dress, at 'civilized' gatherings. On the other hand, the Americo-Liberians are beginning to identify themselves as Africans rather than as an outpost of the 'Western world', and in certain circumstances—especially when travelling abroad—have been known to adopt tribal names and tribal dress. The gaining of independence by other countries in Africa, and their receipt of international recognition, has helped this process along. Official encouragement has been given by the 'Unification Policy' of the present President of the republic:

All the people must be united into one civilized whole. It has been proved in our lifetime that the civilized population cannot get along without the uncivilized; neither can the uncivilized get along without the civilized. . . . For more than 80 years since the Founding Fathers settled here, we have tried to destroy each other by internal wars. Both sides have failed. Now let us for all time bury the hatchet. . . . Americo-Liberianism must be forgotten and all of us must register a new era of justice, equality, fair dealing and equal opportunities, for everyone from every part of the country, regardless of tribe, clan, section, element, creed or economic status.[83]

In practical terms, this has meant, firstly, an increase in schools and official blessing on the entry of tribespeople into government posts. Secondly it has involved an explicit attempt to 'forget Americo-Liberianism' to the extent of even discouraging the use of the *term* 'Americo-Liberian', although the national symbols remain: the exploits of the 'founding fathers' from America; the national motto 'The love of liberty brought us here'; the celebration of Matilda Newport's Day, symbolizing the decisive rout of the local tribespeople by the Monrovia settlers, and so on. And thirdly, the Unification Program has involved an attempt to bring the tribal societies directly into republican affairs by providing for

[83] *Report of the Executive Council Meeting*, Harper, 1954.

direct representation of the tribal areas in the House of Representatives. A fourth, and paradoxical, effect of the Unification Program
has been a renewal of interest in tribal societies and cultures. The
result of the programme, and of the economic growth which has
made it possible, has been, if not yet 'unification', a breaking
down of the caste-like rigidity of the earlier social system.

CHAPTER II

MONROVIA TODAY

ODERN Monrovia—the Commonwealth District of Monrovia, to give it its official title—is not really a town in the generally accepted sense of the word, but a conglomeration of settlements and communities which participate in varying degrees in a common social and economic structure. Its population includes a core (but not a homogeneous one) of long-established Monrovians, and a large number of people who have come to the capital during the post-war economic boom.

POPULATION GROWTH AND ETHNIC ORIGINS

When the first census was taken in 1956, the population was found to be 42,000,[1] and an official estimate put it at 53,000 by 1959.[2] Since no other attempt at census-taking had been made since 1843, its rate of growth over the intervening period can only be roughly estimated. At the beginning of this century, Johnston estimated that Americo-Liberians in Monrovia numbered about 2,500,[3] and the total population was probably less then 4,000. That is, Americo-Liberians were still in the majority. At this time, Monrovia was divided into two sections: the original Americo-Liberian settlement on the hill, and Krutown at its northern base. In 1926, Americo-Liberians in the town numbered about 5,000, but it was already becoming difficult to distinguish them.[4] The beginning of operations at the near-by Firestone plantation seems to have led to a slight increase in the rate of growth of the population of the capital, which by 1934 totalled about 10,000,[5] and by the outbreak of the Second World War about 12,000.[6] The

[1] *Census of the Population of Monrovia*, 1956, Bureau of Statistics, Department of Agriculture and Commerce, RL.
[2] *This is Liberia*, Bureau of Information, RL, 1959.
[3] Johnston, 1961, vol. i, p. 371.
[4] Strong, ed., 1939, pp. 38 and 46.
[5] Brown, 1941, p. 41.
[6] Lelong, 1946.

boundaries of 'Monrovia' were changing during this period, therefore these estimates may not be strictly comparable. However, it seems likely that the population increased fourfold within the twenty years up to 1959. Some confirmation of its rate of growth is given in Table 2, which analyses the length of residence in Monrovia of adults interviewed in the course of a sample survey of eight residential areas, which I carried out in the first quarter of 1959. My methods of sampling and interview are described in an Appendix.[7]

TABLE 2. *Length of residence in Monrovia*

Adults—over 15 years of age in 1959 sample survey

	%
Born in Monrovia	11
Resident at least twenty years	12
Resident ten to nineteen years	20
Resident less than ten years	57
Total	100
Effective sample	1720

Out of every ten adults one was born in Monrovia and another had lived there for at least twenty years. But six had come into the town since 1948, when the economic boom was starting. The newcomers have included Americo-Liberians from the other settlements, but the large majority of the immigrants have been tribespeople, particularly the coastal Kru, Bassa and Vai, who have had longer contact with Christian missions, with Americo-Liberians and with the money-economy, than have the people of the interior. The coastal Grebo and related tribes of the Eastern Province are relatively few among Monrovians, partly because their home territories are far distant and communications poor, partly because local

[7] See p. 230. This survey was not originally designed to determine the characteristics of the total population, and the areas selected cannot, on the face of it, be regarded as 'typical' in a town of Monrovia's residential complexity. However, I was fortunate enough to be permitted to analyse the results of an official sample survey with a quite different basis, carried out three years previously, and the broad correspondence of the two sets of figures suggests that my 1959 results do indicate the population's general features, except on several points of detail which I shall note as they arise.

employment is available at Firestone's second and smaller rubber plantation, near the Cavalla River, and also at Harper, Liberia's second largest city and port. On the other hand, for the peoples of the Central and Western Provinces, the main Firestone plantation at Harbel, near Monrovia, has until recently been the main source of employment, and the plantation labour force is still drawn largely from the Kpelle and Loma tribes.[8] About 80 per cent. of Firestone's workers are unskilled, and among these only about a third settle permanently on the plantation;[9] the remainder work only intermittently, returning home at intervals and especially for the planting season. For this reason, the influence on Monrovia of this vast plantation nearby is less than one might expect, and only a very small proportion of the population of my 1959 sample had worked for Firestone. But lately Monrovia has been attracting immigrants from the interior, especially young Kpelle and Loma, who come in the hope of getting a higher education.

Americo-Liberians are now a small minority among Monrovians, in spite of the recent increase in their numbers by migration from other settlements. Their exact proportion in the total population would be difficult to assess, since there has been a high rate of intermarriage and of extra-marital unions between them and persons from the tribes (especially the coastal tribes). Children of such unions customarily adopt the ethnic identification of the father— more usually the Americo-Liberian. The 1956 census did not cover the question of ethnic origins, on the grounds, I was told, that such an inquiry would be contrary to the precepts of the Unification Policy and—significantly—that it would arouse resistance among the educated population, or at least among some sections of it. My own survey did include this question, but the sample was weighted towards tribal, especially Kru, communities and the results cannot therefore be regarded as a reliable indication of overall ethnic distribution. In passing, it may be noted that I encountered no resistance to the question about ethnic origins, possibly because the interviewers were in most cases residents in the localities concerned. In the course of another inquiry,[10] however, several people objected to the question, notably one senior government official who feared that the question was designed to

[8] Information from the Director of Personnel, Firestone Plantations Co.
[9] Chatfield Taylor, 1956, p. 70.
[10] Concerning membership of voluntary associations.

'make a laughing stock' of persons of tribal origin. In this case, the interviewer was an Americo-Liberian, the interviewee a person whose tribal origin is, in fact, public knowledge today, but who in the 1930's had successfully 'passed' for Americo-Liberian in the area where he worked as an official. The fact that some considered it tactless to make such inquiries indicates the strength of persistence of old attitudes and prejudices, which in turn underlines the significance of the inquiry. In Table 3, I give, for lack of a more reliable figure, my own estimate of ethnic distribution in Monrovia today. Persons socially identified as Americo-Liberian probably account for not more than 16 per cent. of the population, while 'pure' Americo-Liberians are probably much fewer.

TABLE 3. *Ethnic distribution in Monrovia*
Estimated 1959

	Per cent.
Kru and Grebo	25
Bassa and De	20
Vai, Mende and Gola	15
Kpelle and Loma	10
Other Liberian tribes	7
Americo-Liberians	16
Foreigners	7
Total	100

The presence of a substantial proportion of foreigners is also a new development. In the republic as a whole, just over 6,000 aliens were registered with the Bureau of Immigration in June 1958. Of these, the largest national groups were the Lebanese (1,222), Ghanaians (1,193) and Americans (1,132).[11] The Lebanese are almost all traders or shop assistants, the Ghanaians mostly fishermen or carpenters, but also clerks, drivers and teachers—although to work in Government they must take on Liberian nationality. The Americans and Europeans are employed by commercial firms, embassies, missions and organizations like UNESCO and ICA, and a few are employed directly by the Liberian Government as advisers or technicians. The majority are professionals, administrative or clerical staff or businessmen, but they include skilled

[11] Information from Director of Bureau of Immigration, RL.

FIGURE I. *Age-sex distribution*

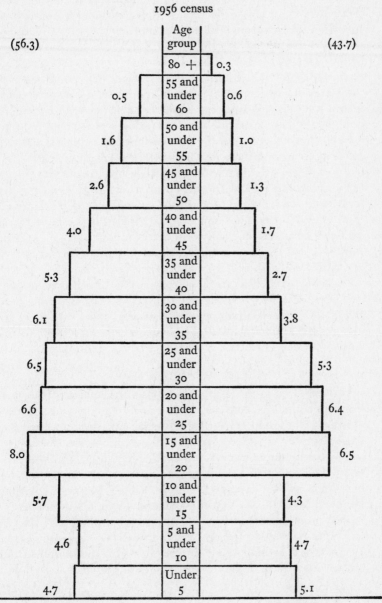

1956 census

(56.3)   Age group   (43.7)

Per cent. male	Age group	Per cent. female
	80 +	0.3
0.5	55 and under 60	0.6
1.6	50 and under 55	1.0
2.6	45 and under 50	1.3
4.0	40 and under 45	1.7
5.3	35 and under 40	2.7
6.1	30 and under 35	3.8
6.5	25 and under 30	5.3
6.6	20 and under 25	6.4
8.0	15 and under 20	6.5
5.7	10 and under 15	4.3
4.6	5 and under 10	4.7
4.7	Under 5	5.1

Per cent. male   Per cent. female

D

workers, especially among the employees of the construction companies. There were probably about a thousand Americans and Europeans in Monrovia in 1958. These included a number of American Negroes, notably, at that time, the American Ambassador and the heads of several missions and schools. On the other hand, I met no instance of employment of American Negroes on the foreign staff of the commercial companies, including Firestone.

The age-sex structure of Monrovia's population, as discovered by the 1956, census is illustrated in Figure I (p.37). There is a disproportion between the sexes: 129 men for every 100 women, but not the marked disproportion which has developed in other rapidly expanding towns elsewhere in Africa.[12] There are considerable differences in age-sex structure between the several tribal components of the urban population. Disproportion is least marked among the Kru, Bassa and Vai, who have long-established communities in Monrovia. Moreover, for some of the Vai and Bassa immigrants, the home areas are sufficiently near to let the women move between Monrovia and the home village, maintaining ties with both urban and rural branches of their families. A striking feature of the age-sex diagram (Fig. I) is the small proportion of children, despite the presence in Monrovia of many who have been sent from outside to live with relatives or guardians and attend schools. This may be due to an apparently high rate of either infertility or infantile mortality, or both—a point to which I return later.

ECONOMIC STRUCTURE

Up to the end of the 1930's Monrovia's economic structure was relatively simple: Government was virtually the only source of employment for the educated—that is, for the Americo-Liberians and those assimilated by them—and the tribespeople worked for foreign companies as ships' loaders and deck-hands, or as domestic servants. Today there is a much greater variety of jobs available, and many more sources of employment. In Table 4, I give the distribution, according to types of employment, of the adult men interviewed in my sample survey. The figures are broadly indicative of the general situation, except that port-workers were somewhat over-sampled because of an emphasis on Kru communities, and on the other hand domestic servants—and therefore those listed

[12] See UNESCO, *Social Implications of Industrialization and Urbanization in Africa*, 1956, p. 211.

in Table 4 as employed by private individuals—were somewhat undersampled.

One in five of the men was on government payroll at the time when the survey was made, and Government was still the largest single employer. In 1958, civil servants and officials in Monrovia numbered about 3,000, and others on government pay, including labourers, a maximum of 2,000 in peak periods, making in all about 5,000 male and female employees of Government.[13] Of the government departments, the largest employer is the Department of Public Works and Utilities, which now has a large daily-paid labour force, working mostly on road construction and upkeep, in addition to clerical and administrative staff.

TABLE 4. *Types of employment*

Adult males in 1959 sample survey

Employer	Numbers employed as percentage of adult males in sample
Government	22
Port and shipping companies	13
Other companies, missions and embassies	18
Private individuals	8
Self-employed	23
Students	8
Unemployed, retired	8
Total per cent	100
Effective sample	932

Taken together, the private companies—mainly commercial and construction enterprises, usually foreign-owned—employed nearly as many persons as did the Government. At present, Liberians working for such companies are largely unskilled, most of the administrative, managerial and technical work being done by foreigners, although some firms have introduced local training schemes. Individual labour forces are not large. Some of the more important of the private employers are: the Liberian Construction Company, an Israeli firm employing about 1,500, which has had a number of

[13] Information from the Commissioner for the Civil Service, RL.

important government contracts including those for the City Hall, the new Executive Mansion, and a luxury hotel;[14] the Munaritz Industrial Works Corporation, a Spanish-Liberian company which operates a small brick and tile factory and a soap factory, employing several hundreds of Liberians and thirty Spanish technicians;[15] Vianini's, an Italian firm engaged on road construction under government contracts, which in 1958 employed a maximum of 250 Liberians at peak periods, as well as forty European skilled workers;[16] and LISCO, another Italian firm engaged in building construction, which was employing about 200 Liberians and six European skilled workers.[17] There are, in addition, a large number of garages and car repair shops, of which the biggest employer is probably the Firestone Garage in Monrovia, with about 100 Liberians and ten foreigners working in the garage and the Coca-Cola warehouse next door to it.[18] Liberian-owned enterprises are few and on a smaller scale: the largest employer among them is probably the Mesurado Corporation, which runs a fishing company, a cold storage plant, and an hotel.

Operations at the port are directed by the Port Management Company, an American firm acting as agent of the Liberian Government. An average of 430 dock-workers, again on daily rates, are employed more or less continuously, as well as thirty-six Liberian skilled and clerical staff; one Liberian is on the managerial staff. In addition, a maximum of eighty men may be taken on in special circumstances, for example, when an unexpected ship comes in.[19] The labourers work under eight dock headmen, with roughly fifty to sixty in a gang, and provide the largest locally concentrated labour force in Monrovia. Some of the men move between dock-labour and the occupation known as 'stevedoring'. The stevedores —I follow the local usage, although it is not the conventional one— travel down the coast, sometimes as far as Luanda, on deck, loading and unloading at the various ports of call. Shipping companies which adopt this arrangement do so partly because of a preference for employing Kru men, who have a long tradition of this type of work and are considered the most adept at it, partly because of the

---

[14] *Liberia, Trade, Industry and Travel*, No. 7, 1959, p. 19, Bureau of Information, RL.
[15] *Invest, Trade and Prosper in Liberia*, 1957, p. 33, Bureau of Information, RL.
[16] Information from the Director of the company.
[17] Ibid.
[18] Information from the chief of the garage.
[19] Information from the Assistant Director of the Port Management Company.

advantages of working continuously with the same gang rather than taking on separate gangs at each port. But there are today Kru communities in most other West African ports, and not all the shipping lines take gangs from Monrovia: of those which do, two are American and two West German. Each company employs a 'shore headman' who selects 'ship headmen' for the company's several ships and acts as general liaison officer. The ship headmen select their gangs, and direct their work on board. Often, the same headman and basically the same gang work over long periods exclusively with one particular ship: that is, they go on board when it reaches Monrovia, travel down the coast and return with it, disembarking at Monrovia, to await its return on the outward voyage again from Europe or America. Normally a trip lasts about a month, but may take six weeks or longer. Between trips, the stevedores 'rest', or work intermittently on the Monrovia dock or as fishermen or painters. The total number of men who work as stevedores is therefore not easy to ascertain. According to Bureau of Labour records,[20] in the first six months of 1958 fifty-one ships calling at Monrovia took on gangs varying in size from fifteen to fifty, and containing 1,631 men altogether. But some of the ships called more than once, taking on the same gang each time. If one reckons that each ship called at least twice, a total of about 800 stevedores were involved. The number is higher during the dry season, when conditions are better for loading and more ships call.

Nearly one in four of the men in the sample was self-employed. They included not only traders, fishermen and craftsmen, but also a considerable number of artisans—painters, masons, carpenters— some of whom undertake work under private, usually verbal, contract with individuals, in between periods on the payroll of Government or one of the companies. As one might expect during the boom period in construction, a large section of Monrovia's labour force is casual, daily-paid and seasonal. All employers reported a high rate of turnover, and there is a great deal of intermittent unemployment. The bulk of interviewing for my sample survey was carried out in January and February, during the dry season, when plenty of work was available both at the port and in road and building construction. Had the interviewing been done during the rainy season, from May to October, the proportion of

[20] Computed from payroll sheets, by kind permission of the Commissioner of the Bureau of Labour, RL.

unemployed would have certainly been greater than the 8 per cent. shown in Table 4.

Monrovia has by far the largest concentration in the republic of skilled and administrative personnel, but its population is nevertheless predominantly unskilled and about 80 per cent. are illiterate. The distribution of the adult men in my sample, according to their occupations, is shown in Table 5. 'White collar', administrative, or professional work employed just under one in five. Over half of

TABLE 5. *Occupations of adult males*

Adult males in sample survey

Occupational category	Percentage of adult males
Professional and clerical (official, lawyer, legal agent, minister of religion, clerk cashier, typist, bookkeeper, accountant, auditor)	18
Traders (diamond-dealer, butcher, baker, shop-keeper, market-seller, hawker)	5
Skilled and semi-skilled workmen (mason, carpenter, painter, plumber, bricklayer, mechanic, electrician, technician)	21
Driver	9
Port-workers (stevedore, dock-worker, ferry-boy)	13
Domestics (cook, steward, houseboy, waiter, washman, watchman)	5
General unskilled labour	8
Police, Army, Coast Guard	5
Fishermen	4
Craftsmen (tailor, barber, weaver, smith, shoemaker, with apprentices)	9
Others (including rubber tappers, tribal doctors, and farmers)	3
Total occupied men in sample	100 per cent = 793

these were working for Government, although the dependence of the educated on Government for jobs is decreasing. A slightly larger number fell into the category 'skilled and semi-skilled workers': these certainly included many whom their employers would class as unskilled, for we accepted a man's own evaluation of his job. Actually, really skilled Liberian artisans are rare, and most men have to be trained on the job, since this type of work, on a large scale, is new. Most men in this category were employed in one aspect or another of the thriving building trade. The motor-car has also boomed, as indicated by the fact that 'driver' was the most frequent single occupation among the men; this was no accident, since the same phenomenon appeared in the 1956 survey. Government provides a large fleet of cars, with drivers, for its officials; there are several taxi firms and private individuals purchase cars for use as taxis, as a form of capital investment. The category 'trader' in Table 5 was an omnibus one, including Mandingo diamond dealers reputed to be the wealthiest men in the town, and market sellers making a meagre living. In fact, the bulk of the petty trade, as in most parts of West Africa, is carried on by women, and such trading is almost the only occupation open to uneducated women. Among the educated women, a large proportion are employed as clerks, teachers, nurses, and so on, and there are several senior officials who are women.

Despite the economic boom and the alleged shortage of labour, wage levels are generally low, and poverty—by any definition— widespread. In Table 6, I show the distribution of men in my sample, according to their monthly wage or salary, or, in the case of the self-employed, their estimated average monthly income. The effective sample for this table was low: there were nearly a hundred employed men whose wage or income was not recorded. These included some illiterate traders or casual labourers who were unable to answer the question, and some men of wealth and/ or seniority in office who were unwilling to do so: that is, the 'unknowns' were concentrated at the extremes of the distribution scale. For the wage-earners, the wage is the *total* emolument for the job: at Firestone plantation, labourers are provided with housing and subsidized rations, but this paternalist system is unknown in Monrovia except in the case of stevedores, who get food while on trips. The legal minimum wage is 4 cents an hour, but hardly anybody gets as little as this, and the normal *de facto* minimum for unskilled labour is 7 cents an hour, or about $13 for a full month's work. In the absence of cost-of-living figures, the significance of Table 6 can be only roughly indicated. One may safely say that it is extremely difficult for a man to support a family on less than $30 a month, and one out of three of the men in the sample were in

fact earning less than $30. This combination of low wages and
casual employment makes life in Monrovia a hazardous and in-
secure affair for a large section of the population. Partly for this
reason, large households whose members pool at least a part of
their resources and support members in times of need are common,
especially in the long-established communities. Of the 400 households interviewed in the course of the survey, over half had at
least two people bringing in wages or other earned income such as
trading profits.

TABLE 6. *Monthly wage or income*

Adult men in 1959 sample

	Percentage of effective sample
Under $20 a month	12
$20–49 a month	54
$50–99 a month	26
$100 a month or more	8

Total effective sample   100 per cent. = 696

A further point which emerged from the inquiry into incomes
was that there was a considerable range of incomes within each
occupational category. Of those getting $100 a month or more, 80
per cent. fell within the occupational categories 'professional and
clerical' or 'trader', but in both these categories there were also
men getting less than $30 a month. And wage differentials between
one occupational category and another, at least on the junior levels,
were not large. Thus, an elementary school teacher, who has not
himself completed the elementary school grades (and there are
many such teachers), gets $30 a month,[21] an ordinary private in
the Police Force $22 a month,[22] a headman stevedore about $26 a
month during a trip,[23] a civil service clerk on the lowest grade $25
a month,[24] For the 'skilled' workers, the definition of 'skills' differs
from one firm to another: the lowest paid men in this category
(those working for the Department of Public Works) get about $20

[21] *Acts of the House of Representatives*, RL, 1956, pp. 40–41.
[22] *Annual Budget for 1958*, RL, p. 66.
[23] Information from Director, Bureau of Labour, RL, and two shipping
companies.
[24] *Code of Laws*, RL, 1956, 30:9.

a month,[25] the highest paid (those working for one of the private companies) about $52[26] assuming a full month's work in each case. On the other hand, fully qualified teachers—with high school certificates and teacher training—get $80 a month,[27] and middle-rank officials such as assistant secretaries of heads of bureaux $200 to $300,[28] in addition to certain privileges of office, for example, the use of a motor car, and, in certain cases, the provision of a house. On lower levels, however, the economic advantages of one job over another lie in continuity and security of employment rather than in actual wage differentials.

A note on literacy

Except in the case of the traders, the amount of education a person has relates directly to the possibility of his reaching the higher income brackets. The proportion of literates, and of those who have completed elementary education, to the total population, is one of the basic social facts to be taken into account in discussing the characteristics of urban areas in Africa. Figures are, however, seldom available, because of the difficulties of collecting them. The 1956 census of Monrovia did make such an assessment. The great majority of the population is illiterate. English is the official language of the republic, and is, at least in its local form (which has some affinities with Sierra Leone Krio), the *lingua franca* in Monrovia. According to the Census Report, only 33 per cent. of the total population could not speak English. But of those over 5 years of age, 70 per cent. could not read and write in English—and this implies that they were illiterate,[29] since the vernacular languages are not used at all in the Liberian educational system. Indeed, some of them, including Kru, have not been reduced to writing. The census further distinguished 'functional literacy', that is, the ability to read and write simple written instructions with comprehension, for which, it was found, Grade 6 or its equivalent level was necessary, and on this definition, 80 per cent. of the population over 5 years of age were functionally illiterate. These census figures are summarized in Table 7, the distribution among males and females being shown separately. The literacy figures

25 Information from personnel officer, Department of Public Works.
26 Information from the Director of the company (Vianini's).
27 *Acts of the House of Representatives*, RL, 1955–6, pp. 40–41.
28 Actual salaries as estimated in the *Annual Budget for 1958*, RL.
29 Apart from a few who were literate in Arabic.

ST. PAUL RIVER

NEW KRU
TOWN

To Bomi
Hills

ATLANTIC
OCEAN

LOGAN
TOWN

NEW GEORGIA

FREEPORT

Port
Area

BUSHROD
ISLAND

OLD KRU
TOWN

CLARA
TOWN

Stockton
Creek

VAI
TOWN

Snapper
Hill
Lighthouse

TOWN

MESURADO RIVER

MAMBA
POINT

Mansion

Crown
Hill

CENTRE

BISHOPS
BROOK

CAMP JOHNSON ROAD

LOMA
Quarter

BASSA
Community

ATLANTIC
OCEAN

Capitol

University

SINKOR

To Firestone

AIRFIELD

REGMARAD

0   ¼   ½   ¾   1   ¼   ½   ¾   2
MILES

MONROVIA

Bomi Hills

Suehn

Arthington

ST. PAUL RIVER

Ganta

Roysville

Millsburg

Brewer-
ville

Whiteplains

Crozierville

Benson²
ville

Careysburg

New Georgia

Caldwell

FIRESTONE
PLANTATION

MESURADO R.

Johnsonville

Harbel

MONROVIA

Paynesville

MONROVIA AND SURROUNDING AREA

from my own sample of the population were almost identical with the census figures in the case of females, but there was a considerably *higher* degree of literacy among the males: only 44 per cent. were illiterate and 61 per cent. had not passed Grade 6. The discrepancy is probably accounted for, very largely, by the fact that my figures were based on the population aged 15 years or more. A very small number of women, but a great many men, continue or even start their schooling after the age of 15 years.

TABLE 7. *Literacy in Monrovia*

Persons over five years of age (1956 census)

	Percentage of males	Percentage of females	Percentage of total population
Reading and writing no English	65	76	70
Not passed Grade 6	77	84	80

GEOGRAPHIC GROWTH AND RESIDENTIAL PATTERN

Büttikofer in 1879[30] and Johnston in 1904[31] described Monrovia as being made up of two sections—Monrovia proper on the ridge of Cape Mesurado, and Krutown by the lagoon at its northern base—corresponding with the broad dichotomy of the population into the Americo-Liberian element on the one hand, and on the other hand the tribal people, at that time mostly Kru, although there were also Bassa and Grebo clusters in Krutown. There were other tribal villages in the vicinity: Vaitown, notably, was already established on its present site on Bushrod Island, and some of their present residents claim that the Vai villages in Sinkor (see map opposite) have an even longer history. In the 1920's, a section of the Bassa left Krutown to form their own community to the south-east of the cape, on the other side of the old Monrovia settlement. In 1945, when the building of the breakwater for the new port was being undertaken, Krutown was evacuated prior to the inundation of a large part of the land on which it was built. New Kru communities, of which New Krutown and Claratown are the largest, have since been formed on Bushrod Island near the port, but the destruction of the original Krutown decisively broke up the dichotomous pattern of residence, which

[30] Büttikofer, 1879, i. p. 35.   [31] Johnston, op. cit., vol. i, p. 444.

was already becoming less marked during the 1930's with the absorption of more and more tribespeople into what is today known as 'the civilized element'.

By 1959, Monrovia's official limits had been extended so that they now engulf all the outlying communities I have mentioned, and also include areas which can hardly be described as 'urban'. There are, for example, several small private rubber farms on Bushrod Island, and in the Sinkor area and beyond are a number of villages whose economy is based partly on subsistence-, partly on market-farming. The capital's boundaries now contain, in addition, several old America-Liberian or Congo farming settlements:[32] Virginia and Brewerville about seven or eight miles north of the cape, across the St. Paul River, and Paynesville about the same distance to the south-east. Along the fourteen-mile stretch of coastal road connecting Brewerville and Paynesville is a series of neighbourhoods and communities strung out like beads on a chain, becoming more widely spaced the farther one gets from the centre. This ribbon development has been determined by the lay-out of land and water (see map). To the north, the cape is connected by a bridge with Bushrod Island (a narrow strip of land bordered inland by a swamp-lined creek), and by a second bridge with the mainland beyond. To the south-east of the cape, Monrovia is separated from the mainland by the Mesurado Lagoon, and later by extensive mangrove swamps. Thus, even the more heavily built-up strip, which stretches for about eight to ten miles, seldom has a depth of more than a mile or so on either side of the main arterial road. This, combined with the absence (up till 1959 at least) of public transport, has contributed to the relative isolation of some of the residential areas—especially the poorer ones whose inhabitants travel on foot—and the retention of diverse ways of life within them.

For the majority of Monrovians, however, social and economic activities centre on the oldest part of the town on the tip of the cape, which is still the commercial and administrative centre, housing about a third of the total population. Locally, this area is often referred to as 'Town', or 'Monrovia', as distinct from suburbs like Sinkor, New Krutown, etc., or sometimes 'The Hill'. The Kru call it the *kwiklo*, the 'white man's town', i.e. the town whose way

---

[32] There seems to have been a tendency for Congo families to move in to these settlements as America-Liberian families move to Monrovia.

of life resembles that of the white man, and the phrase has spread among other tribes. Here, to avoid confusion, I have called it the Town Centre, although this is not a local term. People come into this area to work—especially in government offices—to shop, to go to school, to church, or to the cinema, to attend clinics or court hearings, to take part in the city's numerous public celebrations, and so on, although some of these activities can, of course, also be carried out elsewhere. The main shopping street is still Waterside, today a narrow and congested thoroughfare at the edge of the lagoon. The shops—mostly Lebanese general stores but also the larger Dutch, British, American and West German establishments —are one- or two-storied, dilapidated and cramped, characteristically displaying goods ranging from cheap enamel basins and 'country cloth' to refrigerators and expensive photographic equipment, in one large room. The frontier-town appearance of Waterside is, however, deceptive: the Dutch OAC, for example, has been established there for a hundred years and still does business in what is reputed to be the original zinc shed. The shabby appearance of Waterside is a frequent subject of discussion and complaint among Monrovians. Under Liberian law, only citizens may purchase land, and foreign commercial firms, however succesful, have not been prepared to erect permanent shop buildings on leased land, probably because such buildings could not easily be sold. The Liberians have not returned to trading in the present period of prosperity, some saying that foreign, especially Lebanese, competition is too great. There are one or two small Liberian-owned stores on the Waterside, but local enterprise has recently been more successful in opening up new commercial fields where there is less competition—a taxi company, a laundry and dry-cleaning business, boutiques, beauty parlours and so on. Petty trade, of course, is mostly in Liberian hands, and there are tiny stores all over Monrovia selling such articles as paraffin, matches, tinned goods, rice, and fruit. These petty traders often purchase imported goods retail on the Waterside, and their prices may therefore be higher than in the big stores.

Behind Waterside, the land rises steeply to a spur between two hills, which are connected by a grid pattern of five wide, macadamized roads intersected by four, with minor dirt roads and paths behind. Within this area are the Executive Mansion (the home and offices of the President and the official reception pavilion), the headquarters of most government departments, the government hospital and several private clinics, three banks, seven hotels and numerous bars, three cinemas, a mosque, and sixteen of Monrovia's forty or so churches. Between and behind the public buildings are private residences ranging from imposing three- or four-storied mansions to huts made of pole and daubed clay, or of mats and tarred paper. Contrasts are striking. The main, macadamized roads have traffic lights, while the side roads are often impassable to motor vehicles, because they have not yet been levelled or cleared of outcrops of rock. There are concrete office buildings and cinemas of modern anonymous style, but older constructions of peculiarly Liberian architecture predominate. A century ago, the more wealthy families built in brick, while the more modest used wooden 'shingles'. Later, 'zinc' (corrugated iron) sheets became popular for walls as well as roofing. But the style has retained basic similarities. Characteristically, houses have a wide veranda on the first floor, used as a general living-room and for entertaining. Sleeping and smaller living-rooms open off behind it, and the kitchen is at the back. Often the dwelling is built on piles—sometimes Doric columns, sometimes towers of unwrought stones which have balanced precariously one on another for decades—and the area under the house is sometimes occupied by petty traders during the day, by domestics, night watchmen, and general hangers-on at night. There are many trees—flamboyants, mangoes, breadfruit—and the combination of red- or green-painted, but often peeling, corrugated iron with this lush vegetation has a seedy attractiveness. Physically, the boom town of the post-war period has overlaid the older town but has not replaced it. The streets illustrated in Johnston's photographs at the turn of the century are still quite recognizable. The population inhabiting them is, however, much more diverse—in one main street, for example, one finds in addition to wealthy and poor Liberian families of Americo-Liberian or tribal origin, a Haitian doctor's surgery, a Lebanese merchant's house, a Swiss jeweller's shop, Mandingo curio stores, a French hotel, and so on. A large number of the plot owners along such streets have tenants occupying huts or inferior-type houses in the back yards. This means that the Town Centre is no longer one community, but a complex of different social networks. Its dominant pattern of living is however the 'civilized' one for which standards were set by the Americo-Liberians.

But by no means all of Monrovia's Americo-Liberians live today in the Town Centre. On the contrary, officials and others with motor cars often move out to the newly developing residential areas in Mamba Point, Sinkor or on Bushrod Island, while clerical staff and those in the junior ranks of the administration, who are more often tribespeople, tend to move towards the Town Centre.

Land and housing

In the first chapter I have mentioned that the Americo-Liberian settlers were allocated plots—both 'town lots' and 'farm lots'—in areas which are today a part of Monrovia, and that they could purchase further land if they wished. In a few cases, the descendants of the settler family remain on the original plot of land, but most plots have changed hands frequently and land-owners today include tribespeople, in just what proportion I was unable to discover. By now, practically every acre of land within the city's limits is owned by one private individual or another, including even the land on which many of the government departments and public buildings stand. Land changes hands at anything up to $600 a quarter-acre plot; its official price is $30 for such a plot, but there is virtually no unallocated land in Monrovia so this has little significance. Since original deeds have not always been filed, nor records of sale kept up to date, there is much litigation over land titles and boundaries. Quite modest families may own a number of lots in different parts of the town, and some own large tracts of urban land: the 52-acre site on which New Krutown is being built, for example, was purchased from a Vai family, while most of the area known as Loma Quarters belongs to an Americo-Liberian landlord to whom the house- and hut-owners pay rent. Most of the land in Sinkor has now been privately purchased, including the sites of the old Vai villages, whose residents pay rent in cash or produce. Many land-owners permit 'tenants' to build houses or huts on lots which they have not built on themselves, or behind their own houses. As a more profitable form of investment, those who can afford it build houses for leasing to Government or to private individuals. A few of the larger, old-style mansions are now let out as separate apartments or offices, and one large privately owned block of flats had been completed by 1959.

Despite the population's very rapid increase, there is complete laissez-faire in housing policy. That is, there is no official attempt to provide or control housing; the only government housing scheme consists of three small houses built in New Krutown as an experiment which was not continued. Neither are employers under any compulsion to provide housing for their employees, although most foreign concerns lease houses for their foreign staff and the Government provides houses (leased from private individuals) for its senior officials whose homes are outside Monrovia. Apart from this, the newcomer to Monrovia lives wherever he chooses, or, more usually, wherever he can find a place. The result of all this is a great deal of poor-quality housing, much overcrowding, a rampant landlord system, and high rents—one small room may cost anything from $2 to $60 a month, depending on area and type of house, while a simple three- or four-roomed bungalow is likely to cost the lessee $200 to $300 a month. A more positive result has been the encouragement of small-scale building enterprises, and the provision of a great deal of work for the independent artisan.

At present there is no 'industrial' area, although Bushrod Island, being the site of the port and the terminus of the Bomi Hills railway, has attached several small industrial establishments. Most of the dockworkers and stevedores live on Bushrod Island or in its vicinity, although some come from the other side of the town. Apart from this particular factor of proximity to working places, two general factors influence the residential pattern: one is membership of particular tribes, and the other is social status.

Tribe, social status, and residence

In three areas—Vaitown, New Krutown, and the Bassa Community—land is, in a sense, owned corporately rather than by individuals, although the system differs in each case, being bound up with the history of the three communities. Each has, in addition to a form of corporate land-ownership, its own internal system of administration, and a corporate social life based on the common tribal membership of the majority of its inhabitants but also arising from a correspondence between tribe, occupation and adherence to particular religions or religious denominations. There are several other areas which have most of these characteristics, with the important exception of corporate land-ownership: Claratown (the other large Kru community on Bushrod Island), Loma Quarters, the Vai villages in Sinkor (which are administered as one unit), and a number of smaller villages which are sometimes little

I. Housing: Monrovia Town Centre

II *a*. Monrovia: back yards in the Town Centre

II *b*. Housing: Logantown

more than extended family compounds. Logantown, which is built
on the Bushrod Island site of the village of the Bassa/De 'King Peter'
who made the original sale of land to the American immigrants, and
which is named after its present chief, a descendant of King Peter,
has some of these characteristics, but is today tribally mixed, including Bassa, De, Kru and Vai among its residents. Persons from
these several tribes are not obliged to live in these communities,
and in each case there are probably at least as many living *outside*
the tribal community as within it. However, a newcomer to Monrovia tends to come for assistance to relatives or other people from
his home village or town, or at least to fellow-tribesmen, and this
has led to a considerable recent increase in the population of the
tribal communities as well as to the formation of tribal clusters in
other parts of the town. In all, probably about 10,000 persons,
possibly about a quarter of Monrovia's population, live in one or
other of the tribal communities.

The remainder live in areas which are mixed in terms of tribe,
occupation and social characteristics—about 17,000 in the Town
Centre, 13,000 in the Camp Johnson area, and a few thousands
each on Bushrod Island and in Sinkor.[33] Within these areas, localities are distinguished by names referring to geographical or historical features: Snapper Hill, Cooper Farm, Bishop's Brook,
Soneh Wein, Mamba Point, and so on. But these are in no sense
administrative units and their boundaries are not defined. Here,
neighbours are generally related simply by being neighbours, and
are much less likely to meet one another at work, in church, or at
social gatherings than are neighbours living in the tribal communities. They may not even know one another. No area is exclusive,
and poor, illiterate families may be found living next door to (or
more often behind) wealthy, civilized ones. Nevertheless, there is
a correlation between neighbourhood and social status. Areas in
which the civilized dominate on the one hand, and those where
the illiterate dominate on the other, are easily recognizable by the
type and quality of housing and by the dress of the inhabitants,
more especially the women—since educated women almost never
wear the 'lappa'. In one or two areas, residence alone bestows
prestige. On the other hand, it is unusual to find 'civilized' people
living in tribal areas like New Krutown or Claratown. Those who
do so are normally persons who have fallen out of line—through

[33] Figures computed from the 1956 Census Report.

E

losing their jobs or falling into political disfavour—or who have not been able yet to accumulate capital to build elsewhere; occasionally they have more positive reasons, like wishing to be near their kin, to have their children grow up speaking the tribal language, and so on.

Of the eight residential areas covered by my sample survey, five could be classed as tribal communities although they differed considerably in their degree of homogeneity and also in the manner in which they were administered. The other three were localities of mixed population: none was predominantly 'élite' but one—which I have called Kwi Street—was dominantly inhabited by

TABLE 8. *Social status and residential area*

1959 sample survey

	Professional or clerical occupations	Education to Grade 9 or more	Income of $80 a month or more
	Percentage of adult men in each area		
Kwi Street	37	47	40
Bishop's Brook	31	39	20
Old Krutown	17	26	20
Bassa Community	13	22	13
Claratown	9	23	5
Vaitown	8	14	5
New Krutown	9	7	2
Loma Quarters	6	11	2

civilized people and could be categorized as 'middle class.' I illustrate in Table 8 how these eight areas fall into a fairly consistent order on the criteria of the occupations, educational levels, and wealth of their inhabitants. *Kwi Street* is one of the back roads in the Town Centre, not yet macadamized but negotiable by motor traffic. Most houses along it are permanent and of solid but unpretentious appearance, made of brick or concrete blocks with zinc roofs. Some are built on piles, some are two-storied, and several have gardens at the front. The residents included the largest proportion of educated people, of white-collar workers, and of the relatively wealthy, in the sample. In fact, the proportion of the 'well-off' was probably higher than the 40 per cent. shown in Table 8, since, particularly in this area, there were a number of apparently wealthy who were unwilling to divulge their incomes. Over 80 per cent. of the adults were Christians, nearly all of them members of the Methodist, Protestant, Episcopal, or Roman Catholic churches: while Christianity *per se* is no longer an index of social status in Monrovia, membership of these long-established churches is. The main tribes were Kru and Bassa—this happened to be one of the areas where a number of ex-Krutowners bought land when Krutown was demolished—but there were also Vai, Mandingo, Fanti, Americo-Liberian and Lebanese households. Many households contained persons drawn from different tribes, and half the married women —twice as many as in any other of the sample areas—were married to men of tribal groups other than their own; there were also a few instances of tribal-Americo-Liberian marriage. All the adults of Americo-Liberian or Congo origin in the sample were in fact living in one or other of the first four areas listed in Table 8.

Both Bishop's Brook and Old Krutown have a more mixed composition. *Bishop's Brook* is an area which has been densely settled only within the last decade or two, and its population includes many newcomers to Monrovia. It has a largish cluster of Kru people, another of Mandingo, and a third of Kpelle: the Kpelle urban tribal chief lives in this area. Physically, its general appearance can be summed up as 'slummy', but it has nevertheless a number of large, prosperous-looking houses. The locality known as *Old Krutown* is built partly on the site of the Krutown demolished in 1946, partly on a newly formed sandbar, on which stands the main Monrovia market, and, seawards, a Fanti fishing community. Houses are of mixed types, and there is evidence of misplaced optimism in the sight of several half-completed, concrete block houses already slipping back into the sea. Some of the old houses remain clinging to the side of the hill. But Old Krutown is no longer a Kru community, nor is it today an administrative unit. The Kru are probably still the largest single tribe, but the Mandingo, Vai and Fanti taken together are just as numerous. On criteria of occupation, education and wealth, Bishop's Brook and Old Krutown fell below middle-class Kwi Street, but clearly above the tribal communities. Of the latter, however, the *Bassa Community* had a relatively high proportiom of the educated. This, it must be made clear, arises not from any necessary difference in educational level between the Bassa and the other tribes, but rather from the fact that the community is situated very near to the university, the maternity hospital, and several high schools, and it is also relatively near to the Town Centre, so that it is a convenient residential area for students, nurses, and clerks of both Bassa and non-Bassa origin. Its characteristics, and those of the other four tribal communities included in the survey, are discussed more fully in the next chapter. Here, I have simply indicated that place of residence is one indicator of social position.

URBAN ADMINISTRATION

Local government, in the sense of participation by the residents of the town in its government—either directly or through the election of officials—does not exist in Monrovia except, in a limited sense, within some of the tribal communities. The capital is the seat of power in Liberia's highly centralized system of administration. It is the headquarters of the President, whose formal role and personal authority are far-reaching, and it is also the headquarters of all the government departments which carry out the administration of the republic. The Liberian author, Ernest Yancy, has put it:

No county has any authority to formulate its own scheme of local government. Everything flows from Monrovia. The counties, cities, commonwealths and villages depend on the nation for their existence. Created by acts of the legislature, they are agencies of the nation for the enforcement of its laws, the collection of its revenues, and for other administrative functions.[34]

Paradoxically, Monrovia's citizens play an even smaller part in urban administration than do those of other townships and cities.

For administrative purposes, the coastal counties are divided into, on the one hand, districts inhabited wholly by tribespeople (that is, by tribespeople living a largely traditional life on tribal lands), and, on the other hand, into a number of settlements which are known, according to their size, age and status, as townships, municipalities, cities and commonwealth districts. To the outsider, these titles are rather misleading, since the towns other than Monrovia are all very small and some are rural in character. Apart from Monrovia, the only town in which a census has been taken is Greenville, which is the capital of Sinoe County, has the status of 'city',

[34] Yancy, 1954, p. 138.

and a population of only 3,600.[35] I was informed by persons from
Harper, which is said to be Liberia's second largest town, that its
population was not more than 10,000. Each of these smaller 'urban'
areas is administered by a township commissioner (or municipal
commissioner, or mayor) who is appointed by the President. All
township monies are collected directly by the national Bureau of
Revenues,[36] and grants for the operation of the towns are made out
of the national budget.[37] Legislation does, however, provide for a
minimum of urban local government: the citizens are empowered
to hold an annual town meeting at which they may make local
regulations which do not conflict with the laws of the republic,
and levy local taxes—although the latter are also collected by the
Bureau of Revenues. At this meeting they may also elect a town
clerk, a treasurer, three road overseers, and three constables [sic],
who are paid proportionately to the size of municipal expenditure,
the town clerk, for example, receiving 5 per cent. of all monies
paid out by the township.[38] How effectively this system operates
I do not know; the slowness of communications probably makes for
more de facto local government than this suggests. It is clear that it
could operate only in small communities.[39] Monrovia has long out-
grown this situation, and the problem of administering its large,
heterogeneous, and scattered population has been met by distri-
buting the entire authority for day-to-day urban affairs among
the various departments of the national Government. The city has
a mayor, but his role is largely a formal one, and he has, in fact,
less authority than have the equivalent officers in the smaller towns.
As a first step towards providing some sort of co-ordination, a city
council has recently been formed, but it is not so far very active.

The role of the President
   In effect, the President of the republic is the central figure in
the affairs of the capital, and it is in his office at the Executive
Mansion that the activities of the various departments, of the tribal
communities, and of the private commercial and philanthropic
organizations, are informally co-ordinated. It is not easy to distinguish his powers and duties *ex officio* from the personal leadership

[35] *Census of the Population of Greenville*, Bureau of Statistics, RL, 1958
[36] *Code of Laws*, RL, 1956, 21:80 and 35:630.
[37] *Annual Budget for the Year 1958*, Bureau of Budget, RL.
[38] *Code of Laws*, RL, 1956, 21:82–89.
[39] C. L. Simpson in his *Memoirs* describes how the system operated in Royes-
ville in the early twentieth century.

and authority of the present incumbent, President William Vincent Shadrach Tubman, who has been in office since 1943. One cannot hope to understand Monrovia's administrative framework without reference to his multifarious functions.

The formal structure of government in the republic in principle follows the tripartite American system, but in practice the powers of the President are much more far-reaching. As Head of State, he is responsible for making appointments on many levels, including almost everyone directly concerned with urban administration: the officials of the various departments of the executive, and all members of the City Council except the representatives of the Chamber of Commerce and the (Church) Ministers' Union. He also appoints the members of the judiciary, from the Chief Justice (who, however, is appointed for life) to clerks of court and justices of the peace. These appointments are made by him, in a real, and not only a formal, sense. Some he makes personally, others 'with the advice and consent of the Senate'. However, as Leader of the True Whig Party, he also has control of both the Senate and the House of Representatives, which together make up the legislative branch of Government; all Senators and Representatives in the Legislature are members of this Party, which has been in power since 1870. So also are all civil servants, a half-month's salary being deducted annually from their pay as their membership dues. Theoretically, such contributions are voluntary, but in the President's own words: 'Without such loyalty, political patronage might be withdrawn.'[40] Once in power, then, he has little difficulty in getting legislation passed, and, in addition, he has the power to issue 'executive orders' and proclamations which have the effect of law.[41]

As Chief Executive, he is ultimately responsible for the operation of the government departments, and his specific approval is a prerequisite for a great many of their activities. He attends to their operation in great detail. For example, he personally countersigns all government cheques for sums of $100 or over, and he must approve all city ordinances prepared by the mayor. His attention to the details of administration is illustrated by the following extract from the local press:

[40] Reuters: report from a press conference given by President Tubman, 12.8.60.
[41] Konvitz, Introduction to Code of Laws, RL, 1956, p. viii.

President Tubman is up again with another of his great moves that have always endeared him to the heart of his people. He has ordered that both big shots and low employees of government must be paid at one and the very same time. The Chief Executive, Liberia's Number One Humanitarian, has condemned the selfish practice of certain departmental heads ... Mr. Tubman instructed the gentlemen of the Bureau of Audits never to honour any payrolls made separate for big shots alone, unless those of the ordinary members of the same Department are included.[42]

He is probably more in touch than any other official with affairs in the various sections of his capital. To a large extent, this contact is on an informal, paternal basis, as may be illustrated in the range of problems of those who attend his daily sessions at the Executive Mansion. Here, each morning, up to sixty people wait on the wide veranda which spans the first floor for admission to his office. During one such session which I attended, those waiting included several members of the Cabinet and a number of minor officials, a foreign businessman making arrangements for a concession, a junior woman official needing the President's signature on her deed of purchase of land on which to make a rubber-farm, a typist wanting a transfer to another government department, two women of the élite class, just returned from abroad, who had come to pay their respects, and a group from one of the urban tribal communities wanting to give the President their views on the appointment of a new chief. 'They come to tell him their cat has died' explained a woman sitting next to me. Not all, of course, are fortunate enough to get entry to the Mansion, and of those who do, some return daily for weeks on end, patiently awaiting their turn to see 'the Old Man'. But in keeping in touch with what is going on—in the capital as in the republic—the President does not depend only on such face-to-face interviews. He is assisted by legislation which empowers him

... to appoint as many Liaison and Relations Officers in the respective counties, provinces and districts of the Republic as may be required for the prevention of subversive activity and dissemination of dangerous propaganda.[43]

In 1958, an amount of $250,000 was allocated to him in the national budget for the appointment of such Relations Officers. The legislation lays down that their duties and functions are 'to be prescribed

[42] *The Listener*, Monrovia, 5.2.58.　　[43] *Code of Laws*, RL, 1956, 13:12.

and assigned to them by the President'. The system provides a pension scheme operated personally by the President, in so far as *some* of the Relations Officers appointed are aged or retired persons who thus qualify for a stipend, and whose duties seem to be little more than the purveying of local gossip. Others are regarded with considerable suspicion by the general public, and are considered to form a private investigation service.

His authority is much more direct and personal than is usually associated with the head of a modern bureaucratic state; he has not only the political and economic power more often associated with tribal chiefs, but also something of the latter's mystical authority. There are stories to the effect that his personal 'ju-ju' [*sic*] will cause the glass to break in his hands if anyone proffers him a poisoned drink; that it also deflected the bullet of a would-be assassin during the 1951 elections; that he has a magical television set which enables him to see what is going on in distant communities. It is also said that as a leader of the Masonic Order, he has powerful medicines which, for example, make it inevitable that he should win elections: leadership of the True Whig Party and the Masonic Order in fact more or less coincides. Individuals and organizations vie one with another in eulogizing the President in a manner reminiscent of praise-songs. He has been given an extraordinary variety of honorary titles, illustrated in the following examples chosen at random from the scores of tributes which appear in the local press:

Right on the birthday of his devoted wife, February 24th, the President of the Nation, Dr. William V. S. Tubman, will be honoured by the workers of Liberia when he receives the title of Most Exalted Grand Chancellor and Defender of the Knights of Labour, an Order instituted by resolutions of the Labour Congress of Liberia. . . .[44]

Smallpox patients at the Congotown isolated hospital have conferred a new degree of 'Doctor of Citizens' in absentia on the President of Liberia. . . .[45]

President Tubman has been made by the Porror Zoes Society and Dazoes of the Hinterland, Grand Master of the Ancient Porror Society and had been given the traditional token of authority.[46]

Sometimes the eulogies appear a little ambiguous. One contribution to *The Liberian Age* reads:[47]

[44] *The Liberian Age*, 10.2.58.
[46] Oscar S. Norman, oration.
[45] Ibid., 25.8.58.
[47] *The Liberian Age*, 2.2.60.

Ten Commandments of Tubmanism

I am thy President who brought thee from the end of the first to the beginning of the second centuries of our national existence as a result of which the people have been regenerated and rejuvenated to a new way of life and are now breathing the new life of liberty, freedom and happiness. . . .

1. Thou shalt have no philosophy whose dogmas are to all intents and purposes diametrically opposed to the accepted standard set by the absolute majority of the sovereign people who are ardent and potent adherents to Tubmanism.
2. Thou shalt not indulge in any kind of malfeasance, misfeasance, and nonfeasance, nor conspire with any clique within or without the Republic, for a true Tubmanist will not hold him guiltless who plays the sycophant and the hypocrite.
4. Remember the 29th day of November of each and every year, so as to celebrate the same, though Tubmanism does not cherish nor favour much gaiety and display of pomp on such a day. [The date is, of course, that of the President's birth].
5. Honour not only thy father and thy mother but all those highly placed in Church and State, and in all walks of life, that thy days may be long upon the land which the Lord thy God giveth thee. . . .

Approval of his administration is by no means universal, although criticism is seldom openly expressed. But there is no doubt that the President is personally popular, partly because of his direct approach and his generosity. 'If only I could get to see the Old Man . . . Tubman is kind' is a sentiment often expressed by those in trouble, and he is also credited with responsibility for the general increase in prosperity.

> Inauguration, President Tubman,
> Inauguration is a time for rejoicing.
> He give me a house,
> He give me good water,
> President Tubman thank you for your kindness
> He give me good roads,
> He give me good food
> President Tubman thank you for your kindness,

runs one popular song. And another sums it all up:

> Tubman is a father to his people
> Big or small, rich or poor, whomsoever you may be,
> Tubman is a daddy to his people.

Public utilities and social services

Bearing in mind, then, the President's role in making appointments and decisions, we may turn to an outline of the day-to-day organization of the capital's affairs.

(*a*) The provision of light and power, water supply and sewerage, road maintenance, and so on, falls into the province of the Department of Public Works, although the actual installation and operation of public utilities is sometimes carried out by foreign firms working on government contract: for example, the Liberia Company, an American concern, manages the Division of Light and Power. Most of these utilities have been introduced since the war, and their coverage is better for areas nearer the Town Centre and for those of higher average income. In New Krutown and Vaitown, on the other hand, water is drawn from pumps installed and kept up by the residents; electric power has been taken as far out as the edge of New Krutown, but only a handful of householders have been able to afford installation and running costs. As an example of the general informality of affairs in Monrovia, I may mention that those who wish to have electricity in their houses and happen to be near enough to a power pole sometimes wire up their own houses and also fix the wires on to the pole; there are no meters, and accounts are worked out by counting the number and strength of electric bulbs which happen to be in use on the day when the assessors call: with 'good friendship' some agreement can usually be reached.

(*b*) Taxes are collected and licences issued by the Bureau of Revenues. All adults are liable for an annual *per capita* tax of $5.00, made up of: water tax ($2.00), health tax ($1.00), development tax—for street-lighting, cleaning, etc. ($1.00) and coast guard tax ($1.00).[48] This gives rise to some resentment in areas where facilities are not yet provided. In addition, those with gross incomes over $2,000 are required to pay income tax on a graduating scale which starts at 2 per cent. and reaches its maximum of 25 per cent. at $50,000. Land-owners are required to pay real estate tax at a rate of $2.00 a lot plus ½ per cent. of all the buildings thereon, excluding huts.[49] Hut-owners pay a hut tax of $2.00 annually, a hut being defined as 'any small habitable domicile of a man, his wife or

[48] Information from the Superintendent of the Bureau of Revenues, RL. In fact, 'adults' are differently defined for the purpose of different taxes
[49] Information from the Superintendent of the Bureau of Revenues, RL.

wives, and minor children'.[50] Statistics on the numbers who pay real estate tax on the one hand, and hut tax on the other, might be interesting as a rough guide to the proportion of 'civilized' persons in the population. They are, however, not available, and if they were would be misleading, since taxes seem to be not very rigorously collected. Persons paid by or through Government—and this, by arrangement with the shipping companies, includes stevedores—have their tax deducted at source. Others are expected to pay directly to the bureau. Within some of the tribal communities—Vaitown for example—the local chiefs are said to be responsible for collecting taxes and passing them on to the Bureau, retaining a proportion as compensation, as do rural chiefs. However, the exact limit of their responsibilities seems never to have been clearly defined.

(c) Labour registration is the task of the Bureau of Labour. All men seeking work are required to register at the bureau, and employers are required to take on only men who have their registration forms. But since the forms are not recorded nor copies made, and since employers do not have to inform the bureau when they take on men, the ruling has little effect on the general direction of labour. The bureau also, through its Labour Court, arbitrates in labour disputes, although major disputes are in fact usually settled by reference to the President.

(d) Hospitals, clinics and sanitary services are managed by the National Public Health Service. Monrovia has two hospitals—the government hospital in the Town Centre, and a maternity hospital, operated jointly by the Government and the (Negro) National Baptist Convention of the USA, in the Bassa Community area. Free treatment is officially provided for 'all students and indigents';[51] others pay. There are no clinics in the outlying residential areas. Most of the doctors are foreigners, and several of these operate flourishing private practices in the Town Centre. In addition, tribal doctors, herbalists, and bonesetters—and of course midwives—have extensive practices, as do, unofficially, a number of quite unqualified persons. The élite do not normally patronize local hospitals, but go to those operated by Firestone or the Bomi Hills Mining Company, or travel to Europe on 'health trips'.

[50] Ibid.
[51] *This is Liberia*, Bureau of Information, RL, 1959, p. 24.

(e) Schools are regulated by the Department of Public Instruction. Education is compulsory between the ages of 6 and 16,[52] but this is not enforced—it would be difficult to enforce because there is a shortage of school places. According to the 1956 census, only about half the school-age population of Monrovia was attending schools, including 70 per cent. of the boys and 30 per cent. of the girls.[53] Monrovia has about a dozen elementary schools, half of which are run by Government, the remainder by Christian missions. These provide the first eight years of schooling. High schools provide for the remaining four years: the missions operate four such schools, the Government one, in addition to the University of Liberia. Tuition is free in government elementary schools. It is generally agreed that the standard of schooling is low; the reasons for this and the means for improving it are under discussion. Many of the wealthy send their children to schools in Europe and America, and in the past Government has given such students generous grants, although selection has been more often on the basis of family connexions than merit.

(f) The maintenance of law and order is the task of the National Police Force, the hierarchy of courts which make up the judiciary, and the tribal courts which fall under the Department of the Interior. Judicial institutions follow the dual lines of authority inherent in the general administration of the republic, and are illustrated in Figure III (p. 99). Liberian criminal and civil law is administered by the courts which make up the judiciary: in Monrovia, cases are first heard in the City Magistrates' Court, from which appeal lies, in turn, to the Circuit Court for Montserrado County, the Supreme Court and finally to the President. But tribal law is administered by the courts of urban tribal chiefs and governors, from whom appeal is to the Native Appellate Court and then to the President— although in some cases appeals are made directly to the President. The two types of court—criminal and civil on the one hand, and tribal on the other—are distinguished both by the degree of 'civilization' of the litigants, and by the nature of the cases with which they may deal. The distinction is a complex one which I discuss more fully later.

(g) Welfare activities are sometimes subsidized by the Govern-

[52] *Code of Laws*, RL, 1956, 11:1 and information from the Assistant Secretary of Public Instruction.
[53] *Census of the Population of Monrovia*, 1956, p. 26.

ment (or by gifts from the President) but are carried out by private organizations. No provision is made by Government for the aged, unemployed or incapacitated, although for government employees of long standing, or their widows, annuities are sometimes provided by the passing of a separate and special Act of the House of Representatives in each individual case. Some of the foreign companies are now introducing pension schemes. An unofficial form of dole for beggars and the incapacitated is provided by the President; one beggar of my acquaintance was 'earning' $1.00 a week by attending the weekly gathering of beggars outside the mansion. There is a story that the beggars, infected by the general climate of eulogy, clubbed together to buy the President a goat as a token of appreciation: seeing that they could afford a goat, the President reduced the weekly 'gift' to 50 cents. How true the story was I do not know: one acquaintance of mine certainly had his weekly 'gift' reduced.

The mayor and the city council

The office of the Commonwealth District of Monrovia is a section of the National Government, but unlike other departments it is concerned solely with the affairs of the capital. The mayor was its only executive officer until 1958, when the post of Director of Social Welfare was created. The Mayor is a salaried government official, appointed by the President and, unlike other Mayors and town commissioners, responsible directly to him. A great deal of the Mayor's time is taken up with his formal duties as representative of the city at official functions. His administrative duties, in practice, have been more or less confined to areas of urban government which do not happen to be controlled by other government departments: thus, the present incumbent has been responsible for the operation of the markets, and has made attempts to improve the organization of the city's food supply. He also prepares city ordinances, again usually concerning matters outside the control of other departments: Sunday observance, the control of night noise, and so on: all such ordinances have to be approved by the President. Newspaper editorials sometimes ascribe to the Mayor responsibility for such problems as slum clearance and the control of juvenile delinquency, but his effectiveness in this field is limited by the absence of personnel, funds, and public land. In short, the formal, ceremonial aspects of his office are the most important ones.

Recently, however, he has been concerned with an attempt to form a functioning city council.

In the pre-war period, when Monrovia was much smaller and the residential pattern less complex, Monrovia had a city board composed of the Superintendent of the Police Force, the Director of Public Works, and a representative of the Health Department, under the chairmanship of the City Commissioner (whose title was later raised to that of Mayor).[54] The Kru, Bassa and Vai communities were administered as separate units through their governors or chiefs, who were responsible not to the City Commissioner but directly to the President. The limits of the authority of these tribal heads are not very clearly remembered and it is, indeed, likely that they were not very clearly defined. (No records survive.) As persons of other tribes became more numerous in the urban population, new tribal heads were appointed. By the 1950's, it had become apparent that a co-ordinating body which would provide liaison between the departments on the one hand and the tribal heads on the other, was necessary. In 1956, legislation was enacted for the formation of an Advisory City Council under the chairmanship of the Mayor.[55] It seems to have been conceived primarily as a means of explaining and communicating various aspects of government policy to the tribal heads. Hence its composition: it is made up of representatives of the Departments of Public Instruction, State, Justice, and Public Works, the National Public Health Service, the Labour Bureau, the National Police Force, the Sports Commission (another government department) and two non-governmental organizations—the Chamber of Commerce and the (Church) Ministers' Union—and, in addition, the Kru and Bassa governors, the Muslim chief [sic] and fourteen of the urban tribal chiefs. These tribal heads represent the less-educated section of the population: the 'civilized'—tribal or Americo-Liberian—are not directly represented. So far, the Council's meetings have been few, and those which have taken place have been mainly concerned with the organization of public celebrations—the reception of Dr. Nkrumah, the programme for parades on national holidays, and so on. The Council has no authority to make by-laws or to levy taxes.

---

[54] Information from the Mayor of Monrovia.
[55] *Acts of the House of Representatives*, RL, 1955–6, chap. xix, p. 38.

' In summary, then, Monrovia's population has increased four-fold within the last two decades, and Americo-Liberians are now a small but politically and socially important minority. The capital's economic structure has become much more diverse; both Government and the port now provide work for a much larger number and variety of people than in pre-war years, and the present boom period has seen a great increase in private enterprise, especially in construction of roads and buildings. Much of the labour force is employed on a casual, daily-paid basis, wage-levels are low in relation to the cost of living, and there is a considerable amount of intermittent unemployment. There is virtually no direction or provision of housing by government or private employers, and newcomers live wherever they can find places. Geographic growth and social change have combined to break up the old dichotomy between the Americo-Liberian settlement on the hill and Krutown at its base, but a correlation between tribe, social status, and place of residence is apparent. There is no unified system of urban administration, a great deal of the direction and co-ordination of the city's affairs being undertaken personally by the President.

A note on 'civilized' status

In describing Monrovia's demographic, economic, residential and administrative structures I have had repeatedly to refer to the new dichotomy between the 'civilized' and 'tribal' or 'uncivilized' elements. This distinction is made, not only in everyday speech, in government publications and in presidential speeches (such as the one from which I have quoted at the end of the previous chapter), but also in certain legislative enactments. At this point, therefore, it should be made clear that 'civilized' is *not* a status actually defined by legislation, comparable to the French *civilisé* or the Portuguese *assimilado*. Neither is it simply a new term to cover that section of the population made up of those of Americo-Liberian descent and tribespeople assimilated by intermarriage or in others ways, by them. Among the 'civilized', many are today openly—and proudly—of tribal origin. In fact 'civilized' and 'uncivilized' or 'tribal', as the terms are used in Liberia, are not distinct and mutually exclusive statuses, but two ends of a continuum which, as I shall attempt to show, is really an embryonic social class structure. The most important component of 'civilization' is education, but while to the outsider the question immediately arises of how much education a man needs in order to be regarded as civilized, to the Monrovian it does not occur in quite these terms, since 'civilized' has a much wider connotation than 'educated'. Where one lives may, as we have seen, itself influence one's ranking. More generally, 'civilized' status involves the adoption of the outward signs of civilized life—Western dress (more especially by the women), house type and furniture. The question then becomes one of how much education a man needs to get a job sufficiently well-paid for him to lead a 'civilized' life. With the recent increase in schools and school places, the general level of education has risen, so that while among older persons there are many whose civilized status is unquestioned although they had only elementary schooling (or occasionally, if they are rich enough, and Christian, none at all), a young man without a high school certificate now finds it difficult to get a clerical post, unless he has a very influential patron. Again, although there is general agreement on the status of individuals at both extremes of the social scale, the ascription of status to those who fall between the extremes is relative to the position of the speaker. The pigeon-holing of people is done in a matter-of-fact way, as is illustrated in the following two examples chosen from among a great many statements of this kind which I heard daily:

In an old church hall now used as a school, I met a young woman in very smart tribal dress, head-tie and imported shoes, copying lessons on to the blackboard from a text-book. I asked her whether she was the teacher. 'Oh no,' she replied, in the amused tone people use with ignorant foreigners, 'one civilized woman teaches here'.

I was chatting with an elderly Americo-Liberian woman when a visitor arrived bringing news that a group of people had been arrested on a complicated charge which involved witchcraft and an attempt to blow up the Executive Mansion. 'Were any civilized people arrested?,' she asked. 'No,' replied her informant. 'They were all black men.'

But while on the upper levels of the social scale people talk about 'we civilized' and ascribe 'uncivilized' status to others, no one uses the latter term for his own reference group: in similar contexts the illiterate man will say 'we poor people', or 'we tribal people', or, more frequently, 'we Kru', 'we Bassa', and so on.

I am here faced with a semantic problem. I prefer to avoid, where possible, use of the pejorative term 'uncivilized', and use 'tribal' instead. But a large proportion of the 'civilized' are of

III *a*. New Krutown: women gossiping

III *b*. New Krutown: the congregation builds a new church

IV *a*. Housing: Vaitown

IV *b*. Housing: New Krutown

course also of tribal origin. In contexts where the meaning of
'tribal' may not be clear, I therefore distinguish 'educated' and
'uneducated' tribespeople, although this is, as I have explained,
an over-simplification of the actual dichotomy. In the course of
the chapters which follow, I show how, especially for the tribespeople who form the great majority in Monrovia's population, a
man's social status is related to the way in which he seeks legal
redress, to the composition and nature of his household, to the
church he belongs to and the associations he joins. In the final
chapter, I turn to more detailed analysis of the overall social hierarchy and the manner in which mobility takes place within it.

F

CHAPTER III

THE TRIBAL COMMUNITIES AND
TRIBAL ADMINISTRATION

THE large majority in Monrovia's population is, then, made up of tribespeople who have received little or no Western-style education. Among them are many who have come only recently to the town and who do not necessarily regard themselves as permanent Monrovians. Some of the younger people aspire to become educated and enter civilized society. Others come in the hope of earning a better living than they can make in their home areas, or because they want money for some special purpose—to send to their families left behind, to buy land for farming, or a canoe, and so on. For some period of wage-earning is now an accepted part of the life cycle: among the coastal Kru, for example, there are few young men who do not work at least for short periods as stevedores. And many, of course, are motivated by curiosity and a spirit of adventure. But by no means all of the illiterate are immigrants—some are second- or third-generation Monrovians who have in fact never visited the towns and villages from which their families came. Such people still, however, identify themselves first and foremost as members of particular tribes. In many comparable African towns, tribe as a social category becomes less important as people become increasingly absorbed into urban life, since occupational and other categories cut across tribal ones and minimize their significance. In Monrovia, however, there is a tendency for occupational and religious groupings to correspond with tribal ones and so to reinforce them. The significance of tribal membership is further emphasized by the fact that little attempt has been made to impose a unified system of urban administration. The long-established communities have developed their own, urban, traditions and their own forms of internal administration, which have set a pattern for leadership in the more recently arrived tribal groups. The Kru communities, Vaitown, and the Bassa Community are the largest and most important of these focal communities, and of these three the Kru have developed by far the most complex system of urban administration.

THE KRU COMMUNITIES

The Monrovia Kru have a local tradition as old as the Americo-Liberians. Cape Mesurado is some distance from the Kru tribal territories, but it had long been a port of call for European coastal ships, and this probably accounts for the existence of a Kru village at the northern base of the cape, at the time when the first American immigrants arrived in 1821. By the end of the nineteenth century, Krutown, as it had come to be called, had a population of possibly a thousand, but it had not become wealthy and it remained quite distinct from the Americo-Liberian settlement on the hill above. Büttikofer described it in 1879 as a confusion of small square pole-and-mat huts with thatch roofs, whose occupants—men as well as women—were wearing tribal dress.[1] Most of the men were working on coastal ships or in the local Dutch and German trading 'factories'. Some were fishermen and were selling some of their fish to the community on the hill, but apart from this the two settlements apparently had little contact: the Americo-Liberians seem to have been content to leave the Krutowners to run their own affairs, providing that they made no trouble. The Kru, on the other hand, never took with much enthusiasm to domestic service, and, according to present informants, did not, in the past, follow the custom of other tribes in sending their children to live as wards in Americo-Liberian households. Movement of people between the two communities must therefore have been very limited.

Around the turn of the century, there was an increase in shipping activities and in the number of foreign trading concerns operating in Monrovia, and this attracted further immigration to Krutown, whose residents by 1916, at least, included members of other tribes also, especially the Bassa and Grebo, whose languages are related to Kru and are to some extent mutually intelligible. In that year, Governor Davies, who is remembered as the first educated man to be elected Governor, had the 30-acre site of Krutown surveyed and restyled the 'Borough of Krutown', and he created the Kru Corporation. The significance of this survey was that it provided the basis for the issuing of title deeds by the Government to the Kru; the incorporation of the Kru entitled the community to hold

[1] Büttikofer, 1879, i, p. 35.

property under Liberian law. Now, on other parts of the Liberian coast, land surveys have been the first step towards the formation of 'civilized' townships in which land is held individually and which are administered under the Townships Ordinance, as distinct from the traditional towns on tribal land and under the tribal authorities. Such townships are formed by the splitting off from the traditional, tribal town of a number of educated and Christian families who found a separate, but usually contiguous, settlement. The surveying of the land suggests that Krutown itself was in the process of being transformed into such a township, although *vis à vis* the neighbouring Americo-Liberian community its role was comparable rather with that of a tribal town. In any case, as more people started attending schools, Krutowners were becoming more differentiated according to their occupations and their style of living, and by the 1930's they included teachers and lawyers, for example, and architectural styles had become much more diverse. The area was by now also becoming very congested, and some residents were already moving out. However, in 1945, when the construction of the new breakwater led to the inundation of much of Krutown, virtually the entire community was evacuated. House-owners received some compensation for their property: how much, and on what basis, is not very clearly remembered; in any case, it was insufficient to allay resentment. Two new settlements, New Krutown and Claratown, became established on Bushrod Island, the site of the new port, and these two settlements absorbed most of the fishermen, stevedores and dockworkers. The more educated Kru, however, moved up to the Town Centre or to the new mixed residential areas springing up around it. Some of them purchased plots and built houses on Bushrod Island, near but not within the new communities—which suggests that the split in the population represented a split along class lines, and was not simply a question of choosing to live near to working places.

New Krutown is about one mile to the north of the port, and about five miles from the Town Centre (see map, p. 46). It stands on a 52-acre site, which was purchased by the Kru Corporation, with some financial assistance from the Liberian Government, from a private landowner. Any individual of Kru origin may buy land from the Corporation, at a price of $100 for a half-lot—i.e. for one-eighth of an acre. Most of the original lots had been purchased in this way by 1958, although not all had been built on, and at the time of my stay in the community the Corporation was negotiating for the purchase of several other, adjacent, tracts of land. The area in the immediate vicinity of New Krutown is only sparsely settled, and this has permitted the community to expand beyond its official limits and is giving rise to much litigation over land-rights on the periphery. By 1958, there were about 250 houses, well-spaced and built on a street plan, although only one road had been made fit for motor traffic. The majority of houses were pole-and-mat structures, but there were a number of more solidly built ones of pole and daub with cement plaster and corrugated iron roofs. Two-storey buildings had not appeared. Conspicuous in the centre of the town were three houses representing the Government's only experiment, in Monrovia, in low-costing housing. Their prices were $3,500 to $4,000, payable to Government over a ten-year period, but this was far beyond the means of the Krutowners—half of whom were earning less than $30 a month—and the experiment was not followed up. At the time, two of the houses were being occupied by the Governor of the Kru Corporation and his large household, the third by the Member of the House of Representatives for the tribes of Sinoe County. The Governor's house also contains his office and court-room, and the flag of the republic therefore flies over it. The only other public buildings in the community are the three Pentecostal churches and one Methodist church; the latter houses also a small elementary school, but most of the Krutown children who attend schools do so outside the community. Electricity has been extended to the edge of the community, but not more than a dozen householders have been able to afford the installation and running costs. Water is carried daily from three pumps in different sections of the town. Four or five of the householders use one of their rooms as a shop, stocking such articles as rice, matches, paraffin, tea and tinned tomato paste, but most household purchases are made outside the community by women who, in any case, go out daily to sell goods at the market, or along the roadside near the port.

New Krutown and Claratown are the most homogeneous areas in Monrovia, in terms of tribal origins, containing only a handful of persons who are not of Kru descent. The main features of their populations, and also of the other six areas covered by my sample survey, are summarized quantitatively in Table 9, p. 75. In New Krutown, the nucleus of former (Old) Krutown residents has been augmented by new arrivals—nearly half of the adult men had come to Monrovia within the previous ten years. But these were not necessarily newcomers to urban life, since many had lived in other West African ports, especially Freetown and Accra, and had returned to Liberia with improved opportunities for work there. Stevedoring was the main occupation of 37 per cent. of the men in the sample, 14 per cent. were fishermen, and 12 per cent. artisans, mostly painters or carpenters. But there is considerable mobility between occupations, stevedores often working, between trips at sea, as painters or fishermen or on the docks in Monrovia. Many of the women are fish-sellers or petty traders, but hardly any are in other types of employment. Excluding Islamic Vaitown, New Krutown had the least educated population of the eight areas surveyed—nearly three-quarters of the adults had not attended school at all, and only 4 per cent. had gone beyond the elementary grades. Another striking feature of the population was the relatively large proportion of old people in it—proportionately twice as many as in any other of the areas surveyed. The elders—both men and women—wield considerable authority, and this is reinforced by the influence of the churches, so that the community has a somewhat strict and puritanical character: the sale and consumption of alcohol, for example, is disapproved.

Many of the younger people prefer the less restricted life of Claratown, which has grown up unofficially on Methodist mission land on the other side of the port area, and much nearer than New Krutown to the Town Centre. In appearance, size and population, it has a general resemblance to New Krutown, but it is a much less sedate community: it contains, for example, several lively dance-bars and cafés, and it has a reputation for being 'tough'. Of the Claratown men in our sample, two-thirds were between 15 and 29 years of age, compared with one-third in New Krutown. Consequently, levels of education were higher: 39 per cent. had attended school, and 13 per cent. had gone beyond the elementary grades. But there were fewer Christians than in New Krutown, although the local churches—again Methodist and Pentecostal—were well attended.

Residents in one or other of these two communities make up over a third of the Kru population of Monrovia. The remainder, including many illiterate as well as those absorbed into civilized society, are scattered all over the town. There is no direction of

TABLE 9. Main characteristics of the population of the eight sample areas

	New Krutown	Claratown	Vaitown	Bassa Community	Loma Quarters	Old Krutown	Bishop's Brook	Kwi St.
Main tribal groups (percentage of adult population)	Kru 96	Kru 99	Vai 81	Bassa 79	Kpelle/Loma 70	Kru 41 Bassa 10 Vai 10 Ghanaian 10	Kpelle 27 Kru 24	Kru 38 Bassa 26 Vai 10
Sex ratio (M per 100 F)	89	125	96	120	201	110	185	130
Arrived in last 10 years (percentage of adult men)	49	54	72	45	82	35	65	41
Persons aged 45 or more (percentage of total population)	17	9	3	13	1	6	4	8
Main occupational groups (percentage of adult men)	Port. 37 Fisher. 14 Artisan 12	Port. 27 Artisan 14 Profess. 12 Driver 11	Artisan 27 Craftsman 26	Artisan 27 Driver 15 Profess. 13 Domestic 11	Labourer 23 Artisan 17 Police 12	Profess. 18 Port. 16 Artisan 13 Trader 11	Profess. 11 Artisan 15 Labourer 10	Profess. 37 Artisan 10
Illiterate (percentage of adults)	74	61	80	56	66	67	37	27
First-year high school or more (percentage of adults)	4	13	8	17	7	13	28	32
Pagan (percentage of adults)	21	33	27	33	55	18	27	17
Main denominations (percentage of adults)	Pentecost. 36 Methodist 22 R.C. 11	Methodist 32 Pentecost. 23 R.C. 15	Islamic 63	Baptist 51	Lutheran 18	Methodist 34 Islamic 17	Methodist 16 Lutheran 10	Methodist 35 Episcopal 19 R.C. 16

housing, and residence in the communities or outside them is a matter of personal choice. There is, however, a slight tendency for residence in the communities—and in certain other Kru enclaves in Monrovia—to coincide with membership of particular *dako* or sub-tribes: for example, the Jloh and Gbeta sub-tribes, which have traditionally manned ships sailing from Monrovia, predominate in New Krutown. But close ties of kinship bind households within the communities with households outside: to give an obvious example, several polygynous New Krutowners have one wife in New Krutown, one living elsewhere, and on the other hand it is not uncommon for educated Kru living elsewhere in Monrovia in Christian marriage to support 'outside' wives in the tribal communities. And all Kru in Monrovia are bound together in a general sense by the administrative framework provided by the Kru Corporation.

KRU INTERNAL ADMINISTRATION

From the earliest years, the Kru have regarded their Monrovia settlement as something quite different from their traditional tribal towns, and requiring a new type of organization and leadership. Their leaders and spokesmen seem never to have been referred to as 'chief' in English or in a vernacular equivalent, probably because the nearest equivalent title, *koloba* (literally, father of the town), used for the senior official in Kru tribal towns, is linked with ownership of traditional lands. Since the 1880's at least, the headman of Krutown has been known by the English term 'Governor', a title probably borrowed from British colonial practice, with which the seafaring Kru have long been familiar. Similarly, the Kru in the home territories speak of their settlements in Monrovia and other West African ports—as well as London, Liverpool, and New York —as 'colonies'. The Governor is the senior official in a system of administration which has developed to meet the needs of the urban Kru community in Monrovia, but whose structure is nevertheless based on the traditional social grouping of the Kru in the coastal areas.

The coastal Kru divide into six main *dako* (or 'tribes' as the Kru call them) on the basis of dialect and traditions of migration: Jloh, Kabor, Gbeta, Sasstown (or Pahn), Grand Cess (or Siklio), and finally the inhabitants of a group of towns known collectively as the 'Five Tribes'. Behind these, starting about thirty to fifty miles

in from the coast, are the interior *dako*, of which the more important are the Matro, Bolo, Nanke, and Bwa. These are often referred
to derogatively by their coastal neighbours as *kwia* or in English
as 'Bush Kru', and they in turn refer to the Sarpo and Putu, further
in the interior, as 'Bush Kru'. Recently, some of the interior tribespeople have been drawn into the wage-earning economy. But the
bulk of the seafaring Kru are still drawn from the coastal *dako*.
The *dako* was not necessarily a political unit. Traditional political
organization was based on a large number of autonomous towns
with populations often reaching several thousands. Most of the
dako I have listed occupy several of these autonomous towns,
although in two cases (Sasstown and Grand Cess) they correspond
with single towns which have however smaller, segmented villages—
'half towns' as they are known in Liberia—under their jurisdiction.

Each Kru 'colony' has drawn into one community people originating from different towns and different *dako*. But particular *dako*
have come to be associated with particular colonies—the 'Five
tribes', for example, with Freetown, and later with London and
Liverpool, the Grand Cess people with Accra, and so on. Since
the nineteenth century, the Monrovia Kru colony has been dominated by the Jloh and Gbeta, who have in the past more or less
controlled the supply of stevedores from that port. The original
Krutown is said to have been divided geographically between these
two sub-tribes, other residents—including Bassa and Grebo as
well as members of other Kru *dako*—being identified with one or
other of the two sections. From the recollections of former Krutowners, it seems that there was considerable rivalry between these
two sections, that they had little social contact, and that since the
sea-going gangs were selected by ships' headmen, themselves
either Jloh or Gbeta, they did not even work on the same ships.
In the 1930's a move was made towards bringing the two sections
together, by the formation by young men from both sections of a
Kru football team which became the crack team of the republic's
Football League and a source of great pride to the Kru as a whole.
In the 1940's, its members came to be associated by the general
public with the political campaign of Didhwo Twe, the Kru can-
didate for the presidency of the republic, and it was disbanded.
In any case, the old geographical division of Krutown was finally
broken up in that decade by the evacuation of the entire community.

It seems that the Governor of Krutown was in the early days chosen by Krutown residents alternately from the Jloh and Gbeta sections. Since 1916, however, the governors have been nominated by the President of the republic, and have changed with each presidential régime. They are also said to be elected by the officials of the Kru Corporation. Unfortunately I had no opportunity to observe how this works in practice, but apparently the choice is made by the President after discussion with tribal officials and pressure groups within the tribal population. Governor Davies, appointed in 1916, was from the Five Tribes *dako*, and his position as one outside the two main sections of the community permitted him to form one administrative unit linking all Monrovia Kru, which obtained recognition under Liberian law as a property-owning body known as the Kru Corporation. I was unable to trace a copy of the ordinance which created the Corporation and the Borough of Krutown, but it seems that originally it was the residents of the borough who became thus incorporated. With the evacuation of Krutown and the dispersal of its residents, and with the subsequent growth of the Kru population by further immigration, the Corporation has come to be considered as uniting, in theory at least, all Kru in Monrovia, since all Kru are liable to be called upon to give it financial and moral support. That is, although many of its functions parallel those of the multiplicity of voluntary associations which exist in Monrovia, it is not itself a 'voluntary' form of association, since one does not join the Corporation or opt out of it—although one may of course opt out of obligations to support it. In practice, however, its primary concern is, as we shall see, with the organization of the stevedores.

The structure of the Corporation has changed with internal changes in the Monrovia Kru population. Originally, its Council was made up of the Governor, the Vice-Governor, and ten councillors, of whom five represented the Jloh, five the Gbeta. Later, councillors representing two other tribes, the Bassa and Grebo, as well as other Kru *dako*, were added. The Bassa left the Corporation in 1922, when the Bassa Community was founded. Today, there are seven councillors, of whom one represents the Grebo tribe in Monrovia, the remaining six, six sections of the Kru population: the Jloh, Gbeta, Pahn, Kio, 'Five Tribes' and Matro. These 'sections' as they are called (the English term being used again) do not correspond entirely with traditional *dako*, but allow for some regrouping, on the basis of contemporary characteristics, of those originating from the various Kru home towns. The Pahn 'section', for example, includes both Sasstown and Grand Cess, which on historical, linguistic and cultural grounds are certainly separate *dako*: but they were the first Kru towns to have schools and missions and to form 'civilized' townships, and they have provided the bulk of the educated Kru in the Monrovia population. I show in Figure II (p. 80) the distribution of the various Kru home towns, under the seven sections of the Corporation, as it was explained to me in 1958 by the Governor and councillors.

The main duty of the seven councillors is to act as assessors in the court of the Kru Governor, in his capacity as an urban tribal head. They are expected to take a special interest in members of their own sections who come before the court, but they make their assessments as a body. The Jloh councillor in 1958 was a woman—a new and unusual feature in Kru social organization. The remainder were elderly men, most of them illiterate, and most ex-stevedores, one or two, like the Governor himself, being retired ships' headmen. Not all live in New Krutown, where the Governor's court is situated: several live in Logantown or Claratown, and one travels each day from the Town Centre to attend court sessions. They receive allowances of $20 a month from the Corporation Treasury, while the Governor and Vice-Governor are paid by the Liberian Government. Other officers of the Corporation are the Secretary to the Governor, who is also paid from the Corporation Treasury, and the Treasurer. The latter is responsible for collecting dues from the stevedores: 75 cents from each man at the end of each trip. These dues are quite easily collected, because in 1958 at least the Treasurer of the Corporation was also the Paymaster appointed by the President to disburse their wage-packets to the stevedore gangs at the Bureau of Labour; as Paymaster, he personally is entitled to a fee of 25 cents from each stevedore.

Each of the seven sections has, in addition to a councillor, a 'chairman', and further, the various home towns and villages which are well represented in the Monrovia population have their own chairmen. The Jloh section, for example, has one section chairman and Nifu, Betu, Wissepo and several other towns which fall into the Jloh section (see Fig. II) also have their own chairmen. Some of the chairmen are members of the civilized community: the 'Five Tribes' section, for example, has had as chairman a lawyer and a

FIGURE II. *The Kru Corporation*

Governor

Vice-Governor

Pahn section	Kio section	Gheta section	Matro section	Five Tribes section	Jloh section	Grebo section
Grand Cess (Siklio)	Butaw	Nyifa	Blubale (Du)	Nana Kru (Maola)	Nifu (Talo)	Takpo
Sasstown (Gilau)	Kabor?	Nuangpoint	Wulie	Settra Kru (Wetu)	Betu (Gilepo)	Bwa?
Barclayville (Blepo)	Rosse	Klepo	Tatue	Nyigbi	Kau	Wea?
Bolo?	Tasu	Gbeta	Wau	Lettikru (Dufa)	Shogbo	Trempo
Bwa?	Sarpo	Wluke	Nyenau	King Williamtown	Buliu	Webbo
	Plahn		Drepo	(Wea)	Kabor?	Bepo
	Nyau		Nanke		Wissepo	Barrobo
	Trau				Wapi (Diu)	Tumpo
	Sikon				Tuelu	Buipo
					Botrau	Jelepo
					Bolo?	Palipo
						Kelipo
						Tienpo
						Klarapahng
						Kuanpo

Names in parentheses are the original names, the alternatives are those normally used today. 'Nana Kru', for example, is said to be a corruption of 'London Kru', arising out of an association between the Maola and the London 'colony'.

Question marks are placed against towns concerning whose placing there was disagreement.

dentist. Other chairmen in 1958 were carpenters, masons, a tax collector—mostly elderly men who in their youth had had some experience as stevedores. Their role is more varied than that of the councillors. Chairmen on both levels are responsible for calling their people together for meetings and generally acting as liaison officers between them and the Governor, and they may also act unofficially in a judicial capacity, attempting to settle disputes which arise within their populations before they reach the Governor's court. In addition they act as welfare officers, and for this purpose they control separate treasuries, whose ordinary use is the provision of assistance—normally amounting to $30 or $40—towards funerals. Some of these treasuries also support students, often on the understanding that on completion of their studies they will return to the home area to teach. Some treasuries have contributed towards the cost of schools in the home towns, others have given direct financial help in times of need: for example, to make up local deficits in hut tax, to pay fines incurred by the home town as a result of land disputes with neighbouring towns, or old 'war fines' dating back to the insurrections of the 1930's. Some are prepared to help their Monrovia members by paying fines or standing 'bond' (bail) for them when they get into what is locally known as 'government trouble'. The size of the treasury, the uses to which it is put, and the manner in which dues are collected, differs from one group to another. Some chairmen collect from men in all occupations and also from women, others rely primarily on the stevedores. Educated members are more usually expected to contribute, according to their means, towards funds being raised for specific purposes. Collection from the stevedores is the simplest operation, because they are paid in gangs at the Bureau of Labour at the end of each trip, and the sections and towns which contain many stevedores have the best-organized treasuries. This means that a stevedore from a well-organized section will be paying dues separately to the Corporation (75 cents) to his section chairman (usually 25 cents), and to his town chairman (50 cents to $1), and, as we shall see later, he may also be paying regular dues to his *panton* or patriclan, if it has a chairman in Monrovia. How this works out in terms of individual budgets, I discuss in a later chapter, and in Appendix B. The Corporation also plays a part in the actual distribution of 'tickets' for work on the ships. The shipping companies hand over to the ship's headman tickets whose number corresponds with the number of men they require. The headman gives a quarter of these tickets to the Corporation, and they are shared out among the councillors and chairmen. Thus, if sixty men are required for a ship's gang, fifteen will be regarded as working for the Corporation. This system was originally introduced, I was told, during the depression in the 1930's, to ensure that, since jobs were scarce, persons other than Jloh and Gbeta should get tickets. Today, the Corporation 'employees' are often young men on their first trip, undergoing a type of apprenticeship, who retain about 50 per cent. of their earnings, the rest going to the Corporation, or to the official concerned.

It is apparent that the participation of large numbers of Kru in this one occupation provides the basis on which the organization and financing of the Corporation rests.[2] The Corporation, in turn, takes on some of the functions elsewhere carried out by trade unions: in 1958, for example, it hired a lawyer—himself a well-known Kru—to put the men's case in a dispute with the shipping companies over wages and conditions. But this is not its only function. It concerns itself, as we have seen, with welfare activities both in the Monrovia population and in the home areas. Its Governor and councillors form a judicial body recognized by the Government. It is also responsible for the purchase and administration of the land on which New Krutown is being built. And finally, it has a peculiar significance in that it can draw on the loyalty of the local members of all the Kru *dako*, which makes it a new phenomenon in Kru social organization, and an important one, since the Monrovia Kru are today the largest cluster of Kru in the republic. The unique role of the Governor of the Corporation was apparent when in 1959 he organized a demonstration of the tribe's loyalty to President Tubman, in which representatives of the various Kru settlements abroad—in Ghana, Nigeria and Freetown—as well as of the towns and villages of the Kru coast, took part. Like the first Governor of the Corporation, the present Governor has the advantage of being outside the main factions in the urban Kru community, for he comes from the Matro section—the 'Bush Kru'—which includes few 'big men' and civilized members, and has not so far been involved in political rivalries.

The system of internal administration which I have described

---

[2] Banton, 1957, pp. 24–25, describes the operation of a similar system in the large Kru community in Freetown.

appears to be paralleled in Kru communities in other West African ports: in Freetown, for example, where the Kru have settled with their wives and families since the 1860's, and now form one of the major tribal groups. The functions and history of the Freetown Kru 'Committee', as Banton has described them, resemble the Corporation in Monrovia.[3] In Freetown, the Kru are isolated from the rest of the population as an immigrant tribe and as the only sizeable tribal group which is strongly Christian, and not Muslim; few, according to Banton, have become educated or taken up occupations other than stevedoring (although quite a few of the educated Kru in Monrovia had their schooling in Freetown). In Monrovia, the Kru are not isolated in this way: on the one hand, they have set the pattern for the development of tribal administration by other tribes, and on the other, they have provided a large proportion of the 'civilized' population, and there are indeed signs that they are beginning to predominate in the Civil Service. But the stevedoring tradition remains: many of the civilized Kru have in their youth worked on ships, and almost all had fathers who did so. Participation in this common occupation appears to be the basis of the strength of Kru urban organization. The degree of tribal solidarity which it implies is particularly interesting since traditional Kru social organization involved a very high degree of local autonomy, and there was no mechanism for co-operation between the various *dako*. Indeed, the history of the Kru coast is marked by bitter rivalries, amounting to frequent warfare, between the several *dako* and sometimes within them.

OTHER TRIBAL COMMUNITIES AND THEIR ADMINISTRATION

The Kru are the largest tribal group in Monrovia and have developed the most complex form of urban organization. I have therefore discussed them in some detail: the characteristics of the other main tribal groups I summarize more briefly.

(a) *The Vai*

Vaitown, which faces Cape Mesurado from across the lagoon, is an Islamic community. Educated Vai, who are probably in the majority among *educated* tribespeople, normally adopt Christianity. This gives Vaitown a quite different significance from

[3] Banton, op. cit., pp. 24 and 157.

New Krutown, *vis à vis* the total urban tribal population, although, of course, not all Vai Muslims live in Vaitown. The settlement is at least a century old. Büttikofer described it in 1879 as a 'poverty-stricken hole' with a few small, circular huts, whose inhabitants were working as domestics for Americo-Liberians and foreign traders.[4] Today, with a population of about 2,000 on a total area of about 25 acres, it is probably the most congested area in Monrovia. The traditional circular huts remain, but more solidly built square houses with zinc roofs and shuttered windows are at least as common; they follow no street plan, and are so closely built that it is often difficult to walk two abreast on the paths which wind between them (see Plate p. 69). The deed for the land was granted in the 1930's, by the Liberian Government, to the Vai people of Vaitown and their chief, on the basis of their long occupation of it, and, theoretically, anyone of Vai descent may claim, without payment, a plot on which to build. Actually, the area is already very heavily built up. Some plots near the road have been leased to Lebanese storekeepers, and many Vai houseowners lease their houses or let rooms. As a result, the Vaitown population today includes many members of other tribes, of which the most numerous are carpenters and fishermen from Ghana. Socially, these strangers remain quite distinct from the Islamic Vai-Gola-Mende-Mandingo majority, especially since they eat different foods. But the fact that they share one cultural feature—the retention of tribal dress by men as well as by women—makes Vaitown the most colourful community in Monrovia. It is also one of the busiest, since today over half the adult men are carpenters, tailors, goldsmiths, blacksmiths or weavers, or apprentices to these craftsmen, many of whom have their workshops in or attached to their houses. Of the Vaitown women, about two-thirds are traders, most of them selling their goods at the main Monrovia market across the bridge, i.e. about ten minutes' walk from Vaitown.

Despite its age as a settlement, Vaitown's population is much less urbanized than those of the Kru communities, in the sense that it includes relatively few who have passed all or much of their lives in an urban area—Monrovia or any other. Among the adults in my sample, more than two-thirds had arrived within the previous ten years, and there were few elderly people. These figures reflect a situation in which people move fairly freely between the

---

[4] Büttikofer, loc. cit.

city and the tribal territories in Cape Mount County, whose borders are only fifty miles from Monrovia. Women often return home when they are about to give birth, or when there are family crises at home, and many children are sent home for initiation into the Poro or Sande societies—although a few of the Vaitown girls attend the Sande 'schools' which still operate in the Sinkor area on the other side of Monrovia. Again, the occupations of the Vai tie them less closely with life in the capital, for while the Kru stevedores must work from a major port, the Vai craftsmen can make some sort of living in their home towns or in Robertsport, the capital of Cape Mount County.

The centre of social activities in Vaitown is the mosque situated near the centre of the community. This is one of the few areas in Monrovia with no Christian church. Those Vaitowners who are Christians—mostly persons from the stranger tribes—attend churches elsewhere, and children are sent to schools outside the community. Of the adults in my sample, 80 per cent. were illiterate (Table 9), although these did include a few who knew a little Arabic, usually not more than one or two prayers. A peculiar feature of Vai culture is the Vai script, a syllabic form of writing invented by a tribesman in the nineteenth century. This is one of only two forms of indigenous writing in the whole of black Africa, and is a source of great pride to the Vai. Although I personally met very few persons who could reproduce more than a few of the characters, my informants claimed that a great many people—75 per cent. of the men and 25 per cent. of the women of Vaitown on one estimate—know, and use, the script. For the Vai, Muslim culture and the Vai script offer an alternative way of acquiring a reputation for 'learning' and 'civilization'. Those who choose the more general road to 'civilization', and graduate from government or (Christian) mission schools to enter government service, live outside Vaitown and frequently know very little of life within it. Its occupational structure—as a community of independent craftsmen—also places Vaitown outside the main stream of Monrovian life.

There are, of course, large numbers of illiterate Vai, including some who are Muslims, scattered all over Monrovia: apart from other considerations, there is simply no room for the Vaitown population to expand. In addition there are several smaller Vai villages on Bushrod Island, at some distance from Vaitown, and in

G

Sinkor there are eighteen Vai villages of some age which form an administrative unit. Some of these are little more than extended family compounds, while others have fifty houses, possibly more. Their economy is part subsistence, part market, farming, and the young men take labouring jobs, especially with road construction firms.

The nucleus of the Vaitown population seems to have been originally one kin group, whose head was also head of the settlement. Büttikofer in 1880 described the then 'chief' of Vaitown as an autocrat who was sending out his 'sons, slaves and subjects' to work as domestics and labourers, retaining a commission on their wages. Today there is no Vai dignitary with a role as comprehensive as that of the Kru Governor. Instead, there are three separate and independent Vai heads: one for Vaitown, one for the Sinkor villages, and one for Vai residents elsewhere in Monrovia. The Sinkor and Vaitown chiefs have the title of Paramount Chief, and theoretically, at least, a status similar to that of Paramount Chiefs in the 'interior' as the tribal territories are called. (The system of interior administration is outlined in Appendix C.) In Sinkor the rural hierarchy is reproduced in an attenuated form: under the Paramount is one 'Clan Chief' who is more or less his assistant and deputy—the term 'Clan' as used in Liberia has roughly the meaning of 'District' elsewhere and has no kinship connotation. Under the Clan Chief are the 'Town Chiefs' of the eighteen villages. The Vaitown Paramount, on the other hand, has under his jurisdiction only Vaitown itself and one smaller village, Famina, on Bushrod Island. The third Vai chief resides in the Town Centre, has the official status of 'Tribal Chief' and functions similar to those of other Tribal Chiefs whose posts have been created in the last two decades by the Government. The Vaitown chief is appointed by the President after discussion with the elders, and after his appointment he chooses councillors to assist and advise him. He and his council form a judicial authority and have general administrative charge of Vaitown and its land. Social welfare activities— including assistance with burials—are, however, largely carried out by voluntary associations connected with the mosque. Leadership of the community is thus divided between the Chief, the local heads of several big and long-established 'families' (which may be clans in the anthropological sense), and the Imam of the Mosque.

(b) *The Bassa*

Bassa tribesmen have been coming to Monrovia to work since the beginning of the century and, as we have seen, many of them originally settled in (Old) Krutown. In the 1920's, a separate *Bassa Community* was founded by the initiative of an American Negro Baptist pastor (now a naturalized Liberian), who wished to provide a place where his predominantly Bassa congregation could live together. The settlement was established on ten acres of land which is now a part of the continuously built-up area between the Town Centre and the Capitol Building (the seat of the House of Representatives: see p. 46). The original ten acres are held by the Bassa Brotherhood and Benefit Society, and a contiguous seventeen acres, owned by the pastor of the contemporary-style Baptist church which stands within the community, is also thought of as part of the community although its exact status was in dispute at the time of my stay. Anyone of Bassa descent, on either side, may join the Brotherhood and Benefit Society by payment of $12, and this entitles him to a plot of land. The house he builds on it may not be sold, but it can be bequeathed to his descendants. In 1959 there were about 150 occupied houses in the community proper—i.e. on the original ten acres, containing a total population of about a thousand, although the *de facto* community was larger since considerable numbers of Bassa people live on the adjacent, privately owned land. House types are very varied: there are many of flimsy pole-and-mat construction, but the community, unlike New Krutown and Vaitown, includes a number of solidly built two-storey houses. Apart from the Baptist church, public buildings within the community include a government elementary school and the court-room of the Bassa Governor, who is resident in the community and also owns a rubber farm outside Monrovia. The maternity hospital, operated jointly by an American Baptist mission and the Liberian Government, stands at the edge of the community.

The population is much more mixed than those of the other tribal communities I have described. In large part, this is because of the site of the community: it is within fairly easy walking distance of the university, many of the government departments in the Town Centre, two high schools, and the maternity hospital. This makes it a popular area for students, clerks and nurses renting rooms, and a considerable proportion of the population are tenants.

There is no restriction on the tribe of tenants (Table 9). Tribal heterogeneity is emphasized by what appears to be a high proportion of mixed marriages among the Bassa: of the married Bassa women in our sample, one in five, a considerably higher proportion than in any other tribal group, had married outside the tribe. The general educational level was considerably higher than in other tribal communities, partly because of the presence of a large number of students. Nearly half of the adults (over 15 years of age), in my sample, including a relatively high proportion of the women, had attended school and 17 per cent. had gone beyond the elementary grades: these, of course, included many still studying. And there was a much greater variety of occupations than in the other areas; the men were artisans, drivers, professional and clerical workers, and domestics, while the women included shop-keepers, pastry-cooks, nurses, seamstresses, teachers, clerks and beauticians as well as market-sellers. This does not necessarily imply that the Bassa in Monrovia are, as a whole, more educated and skilled than the Vai or Kru, since large numbers of all three tribes live outside the tribal communities. The occupation usually said to be typical of the Bassa is in fact domestic service, which in Monrovia as in much of Africa is a male occupation. Only 11 per cent. of the men in our sample, however, were domestics—partly, or no doubt, because domestics often live on the plots or in the houses of their employers in other parts of the town. On the other hand, with the increasing availability of jobs with better pay and better status, the Bassa do seem to be taking up other types of employment—notably as drivers and motor-mechanics. But while the Bassa Community has some of the characteristics of the residential areas I have categorized as 'middle class' (p. 54), the Bassa do in fact appear to be more rare in 'civilized' society, and certainly in senior government posts, than either the Kru or the Vai.

The community is the only sizeable Bassa settlement in Monrovia, although there are several Bassa villages in Sinkor and the Bassa form a large part of the population of Logantown on Bushrod Island. Bassa administration in Monrovia is modelled on the Kru Corporation, from which the Bassa seceded in 1922: that is, there is a Bassa Governor, a Vice-Governor, and six councillors representing the several sub-tribes, forming a judicial body whose authority extends beyond the community to Bassa in other parts of Monrovia. The eponymous Bassa/De head of Logantown has been

given by Government the status of 'Clan Chief', but he is responsible not to the Bassa Governor, but directly to the Department
of the Interior. His position is a peculiar one, since he claims
descent from the King Peter who made the original sale of the land
on Cape Mesurado to the American immigrants. I had no opportunity to investigate his role or that of the Bassa Governor and
councillors, but in both cases they seemed to be much more
limited than that of the Kru Governor and Corporation. 'The Kru',
said several Bassa informants with some envy, 'know how to look
after their people better than we do.'

(c) *The Kpelle and Loma*

The Kpelle and Loma, who form the fourth and last of the main
tribal groups in Monrovia, are mainly newcomers to the capital and
have no officially established community there. The area known as
Loma Quarters has, however, some of the characteristics of the
tribal communities, although it is not administered as one. It is
situated near the Bassa Community and adjacent to the barracks of
the Liberian Frontier Force (the republic's army). Its association
with the Loma, or, as it is often known, the Buzi,[5] tribe, arises
from the predominance of that tribe in the army. Soldiers may if
they wish apply for permission to build in this area rather than
live in huts within the barracks proper. Here, however, they must
pay rent for the land on which they build, since the entire area is
privately owned—mostly by one individual. It is not occupied
exclusively by Loma tribespeople, although of the population in
my sample, seven out of ten were from the Loma tribe or the
linguistically related Kpelle. Houses are congested and of conspicuously poor construction. The most frequent occupations
were labourers, artisans, soldiers and police, and 55 per cent., a
higher proportion than in any other area surveyed, were earning
less than $30 a month (Table 9). Although Loma have been living
in this vicinity for several decades, they have not established a
permanent community, since, as soldiers, they tend to spend only
short terms of service in Monrovia. Eight out of ten of the adult
men in the sample had in fact arrived within the previous *five* years;
there were hardly any old people, and relatively few women and
children. Over half of the adults, a much larger proportion than in

---

[5] The tribal name is Loma, but other tribespeople refer to the Loma as
Buzi, after a famous Loma warrior chief.

any other area, had adopted neither Islam nor Christianity. Of those who have become Christians, however, the majority are Lutherans. Here we may note, in passing, that the correspondence between tribal membership and religious denominations in Monrovia (the Bassa and the Baptist church, the Kru and the Methodists and Roman Catholics, the Loma-Kpelle and the Lutherans), arises from the location of missions in the rural tribal territories. Similarly, the educated and Christian Vai are most frequently members of the Protestant Episcopal church, which operates a mission and schools in Cape Mount. The Pentecostal, Apostolic, and Prophets' churches, on the other hand, are primarily urban phenomena.

Loma Quarters contains one two-storey house, which is the residence of the Loma Tribal Chief in Monrovia, whose jurisdiction is, however, over Loma in general and not specifically over those living in this area. The Kpelle Tribal Chief lives in Bishop's Brook, an area where there is a sizeable enclave of persons drawn from that tribe. Both form a part of a system of administration which has been introduced by the Government, and to whose nature and development we now turn.

THE GOVERNMENT SYSTEM OF URBAN TRIBAL CHIEFS

Administration of the tribal population of Monrovia by the Government was not introduced according to any clearly formulated plan, but rather grew up *ad hoc* to meet the needs of the changing situation. For this reason the system is not uniform; each of the tribes represented in large numbers in Monrovia today has one or more official tribal heads, but these men differ one from another in title, status and role. There is, in the first place, a broad twofold distinction between the heads of the newcomer tribes, who have today the title of 'Tribal Chief' and whose posts have been created by Government since 1939, and the heads of the long-established Kru, Vai and Bassa populations whose internal forms of organization have now been partially integrated with the Government system of administration. And, in the second place, the statuses of the Kru and Bassa Governors on the one hand and the two Vai Paramount Chiefs on the other differ not only because they are the heads of differing types of internal organization, but because special, but not uniform, authorities have been vested in them by the Government.

Documentary records on the relationship between the Government and the urban tribespeople are almost non-existent. In the past, rulings have not been printed, or if printed not circulated, or if circulated not filed. They seem to have been based on informal discussion between officials concerned rather than on detailed inquiries into the situation actually obtaining. The lack of documentation has had the advantage of preventing rigidity in practice, and of allowing for fairly easy adaptation to new situations. It means, however, that to trace the history of the system of urban tribal heads, one must rely on the recollections of those most closely concerned: Interior Department officials (past and present), the tribal heads themselves, and lawyers who have taken a special interest in tribal affairs. The account which follows is based mainly on these three sources.

In the period up to the First World War, the Kru and Vai communities were left to their own devices, providing that they made no trouble. The Kru Governor was apparently held responsible by Government for settling disputes and maintaining law and order in Krutown, although a Supreme Court decision of 1912 suggests that he had no official means of enforcing his rulings.[6] The same decision stated, *inter alia*, that:

The Act of 1905, entitled 'an Act providing for the government of districts in the Republic inhabited wholly by Aborigines' applies in no way to the Kru town situate within the corporate limits of the City of Monrovia.

It appears, then, that neither Krutown nor Vaitown across the lagoon was assimilated into the general system of tribal government being introduced at the time, nor had any separate system been devised to contain them. They seem to have received more attention, however, during the régime of President Howard (1912–20). In 1914 the Vaitown Chief was for the first time commissioned by the President, and in 1916 the Borough of Krutown, under the administration of the Governor, who from that time has been a presidential nominee, was created by government ordinance. One may speculate that attention was drawn to the urban tribal settlements at this time, because the Kru were staging rebellions down the coast, and because the blockade of German ships and the

---

[6] *Liberian Law Reports*, 1908–26, vol. ii, pp. 63–65.

departurè of the German traders must have created considerable unemployment and its attendant problems in Monrovia. The manner in which the official commissioning of the two heads affected their powers and duties *vis à vis* the Government is, however, not at all clear: presumably the ordinance creating the Borough of Krutown would throw some light on this, but a copy was not filed, nor could I locate one in private possession. One effect of the commissioning was, however, to make the two heads officially responsible to the President of the republic.

Towards the end of the 1930's, the Interior Department took charge of urban as well as rural tribal affairs. The residential pattern of Monrovia was becoming more complex. The population was no longer clearly divided into 'Americo-Liberian' and 'tribal' communities, and the increase in commercial activities following Firestones' expansion had resulted in a certain amount of movement of members of new tribes into the capital. Also, at this period the whole question of tribal administration was under review, following the League of Nations inquiry. The factors which led immediately to the creation by the Government of urban tribal leaders are recalled, by various officials, as: the weight of petty litigation, especially concerning marriage and divorce, which swamped the magisterial court; the need for persons who would be responsible for the welfare of the immigrants, and for representing them *vis à vis* the Government, and finally the necessity of organizing the recruitment of labourers, especially porters. This last factor was apparently the precipitating one, since the haphazard method of recruiting porters, which I have mentioned previously, was creating chaos and causing considerable resentment.

A system of 'Tribal Foremen' was therefore introduced in 1939, under the auspices of the Interior Department. The duties of the 'Foremen' were: (*a*) to assist in the recruitment of porters and also of labourers for work in Monrovia, (*b*) to look after newcomers and visitors from the tribal areas, and (*c*) to hear and adjust disputes, especially those of a 'domestic and matrimonial nature', among their tribespeople, under the general supervision of the Department. The tribal heads have long dropped their role—if indeed they ever exercised it—as labour recruiters; porters are in any case no longer recruited in Monrovia, since road communications have been established. In 1945 their title was changed to that of 'Tribal

Chief'. Similar posts have since been introduced in other industrial areas—for example, at Firestone plantation and at Bomi Hills iron mine. The dates of appointment of the various foremen, or chiefs, are not recorded, but by 1958 the Kpelle, Krahn, Loma, Belle, Sarpo, Gio-Mano, Gissi, Gbande, De and Mandingo tribes each had an urban Tribal Chief. The Mende and Fanti each had two, one for the Liberian section of their population, the other for the immigrant and un-naturalized section. The Vai, as I have mentioned above, have a Tribal Chief resident in the Town Centre in addition to their Paramounts in Vaitown and Sinkor. Finally, there is a recognized 'Muslim' Chief, with the title of Paramount, who is responsible mainly for religious affairs and concerned particularly with the Alhajis—the Muslims of various tribes, but mainly Mandingoes, who have been to Mecca and form the upper class within the Muslim community. In a sense, the installation of their own Tribal Chief is taken by the smaller tribal groups as a sign that their existence is being recognized and treated with respect, and applications are still being received for the creation of Chiefs of small tribes or, more usually, sections of tribes. The Department's policy is, however, against the creation of further titles, since all major tribal groupings in the republic are now represented.

The tribal Chiefs are elected by the relevant tribespeople in Monrovia, and commissioned, if the President approves, by the Department of the Interior. However, there is no mechanism whereby the tribespeople—the majority of whom are illiterate and who are scattered all over the city—can be called together to elect a head; neither is it made explicit *which* tribespeople are to choose the Chief, e.g., whether educated persons are to have a say. What usually happens is that different factions among the Monrovia residents of the tribe concerned canvass support from the Department or, if they can get to see him, directly from the President. Sometimes the Department may be able to consult tribal organizations already formed: when the first Kpelle Tribal Chief was appointed, for example, the nomination was made by the Kpelle Association, which had been founded, previously by a group of young, mostly educated, Kpelle men to provide welfare and mutual aid among tribespeople in Monrovia. The official authority of the Tribal Chiefs rests, then, on their commissions from the Department of the Interior, but the extent to which they are in fact able to exercise leadership depends on their personal qualities and reputations, and the nature of their support from within the tribe. So far as the Department is concerned, the task of the Chiefs is limited to the settling of disputes, according to customary law, among their tribespeople in Monrovia. One who has a reputation for being a wise man and a fair judge may have considerable authority, and may even be asked to settle disputes between members of tribes other than his own. He has a material interest in establishing such a reputation, since Tribal Chiefs receive no salary, but are entitled to charge fees for settling litigation.

DEFINITION OF THE JUDICIAL AUTHORITY OF TRIBAL CHIEFS

Originally, the Tribal Chiefs were given jurisdiction only over 'domestic disputes, especially matrimonial cases', arising out of tribal customary law. Many of them, however, were asked to settle other types of dispute in addition, and unofficially they came to assume a wider authority. The situation was described in a Departmental Order made in 1958,[7] which also redefined their authority:

Here, of late, especially within the Commonwealth District of Monrovia, Tribal Chiefs have assumed the jurisdiction of a stipendiary magistrate, trying debt and damage cases and also matters in which civilized people are party-litigants. To cure the evils caused by Tribal Chiefs acting without the scope of their authority, the following regulations are hereby promulgated:

1. Tribal Chiefs within Municipal limits are prohibited from trying matters involving debt and damages under the debt and damage act.
2. Tribal Chiefs are authorized to hear and decide matters between their respective tribesmen, involving domestic relations, such as marriage and divorce, under tribal law.
3. Tribal Chiefs are authorized to hear and decide misdemeanours only among their tribesmen, subject to punishment by a fine not exceeding $5, and also petty matters of debt which had originated in the Interior.
4. Appeals . . . lie in the Appellate Court of the Interior Department.

That is, the Chief's authority is limited in effect to cases arising from tribal customary law, and it is also limited by the status of the litigants. This second stipulation is important, as it is one of the few instances where the ubiquitous dichotomy between 'civilized' and 'tribespeople' is written into law. 'Civilized status' has today no

[7] From files in the Interior Department.

legal definition, nor does it rest on any universally accepted criteria. The legal use of the concept is presumably a survival from the period when native Africans were not automatically regarded as citizens. In fact, the *Code of Laws* published in 1956 suggests that the distinction is still made on the basis of ethnic origin, for in defining the jurisdiction of the Paramount Chief in the interior, it states that he may decide:

... All cases between members of the tribe and persons who are aborigines but not members of the tribe.[8]

This phrasing was probably adopted by the compilers of the Code to avoid the use of the undefined adjective 'civilized', but it is misleading. The equivalent ruling in the *Revised Laws for Governing the Hinterland* (1949) is:

... All cases arising between strangers and members of the tribe, except they be civilized people.[9]

and this is the ruling which is generally followed in practice. In the interior, the exemption of civilized persons from the jurisdiction of tribal authorities seems to have raised few problems, at least until recently. In Monrovia, social pressure from family and community is much less, and persons with a year or two of schooling are therefore more likely to claim exemption from the authority of the Tribal Chiefs, when it suits them to do so. One Tribal Chief summed up the problem thus:

If we Tribal Chiefs are not permitted to try cases against or in favour of anybody who can read and write, how can we manage to handle cases against anybody in Monrovia... since the majority of the populace within our jurisdiction are going to school, although some might only stop in the third or fourth Grade, and are always considering themselves 'book people'. If this is permitted I believe that our own tribesmen will, after hearing this, refuse to appear before us in cases brought against them because they will contend that they are 'book people'.

Paradoxically, it is the Tribal Chiefs of the interior tribes, which are newcomers to Monrovia's population, who have the most difficulties with this ruling. Their populations are relatively young,

---

[8] *Code of Laws*, RL, 1956, 1:26.
[9] *Revised Laws and Administrative Regulations for Governing the Hinterland, 1949*. Interior Department, RL.

and therefore contain a large proportion of persons who have had some schooling. Further, these young people are usually living scattered all over the town, and not in communities where social pressure from elders may be brought to bear on them. In the long-established Kru and Bassa communities, the problem is in any case less acute because the Governors are empowered, as we shall see, to act *both* as Tribal Chiefs *and* as magistrates, so that—in theory at any rate—an illiterate with a grievance against a 'civilized' person may bring him before the Governor acting as a Justice of the Peace. But in general, the limitation on the authority of the Tribal Chiefs is very much to the disadvantage of the illiterate and non-English speaking litigant, as the following instance illustrates:

An illiterate man brought a case against a literate man, concerning illegal detention of property, in the court of one of the urban Tribal Chiefs. The defendant refused to attend the court. The Chief appealed for assistance to the Judge of the Appellate Court in the Department of the Interior, who referred the case to his senior officer with the following comment:

'Neither the Chief's Court nor my Court has jurisdiction over the Defendant, hence I should let the matter go to the Magisterial Court. This the Plaintiff is reluctant to do, and I am also reluctant to drop the matter in that way. The Plaintiff hardly understands the English language, and the amount in question is not even sufficient to buy cigarettes for a Lawyer whose services Plaintiff will be construed to employ if he has to go to the Magisterial Court.'

The senior officer replied—as he was obliged to—that the case could not be heard in a tribal court.

In practice, matters seldom reach this point because the illiterate, convinced that the odds are against him, will not normally attempt to get legal redress from one of accepted civilized status.

The Kru and Bassa Governors—and also the Clan Chief of Logantown—have been drawn into the system of Tribal Chiefs in so far as they, like the Tribal Chiefs established since 1939, are authorized by the Interior Department to hear cases arising out of tribal customary law. But they are, in addition, commissioned by the President as justices of the peace, which means that they can also try certain cases arising out of civil law, and that they can try 'civilized' litigants. In practice, their authority as justices of the peace is assumed to be over members of their own tribes only: any

FIGURE III. *Courts of law*

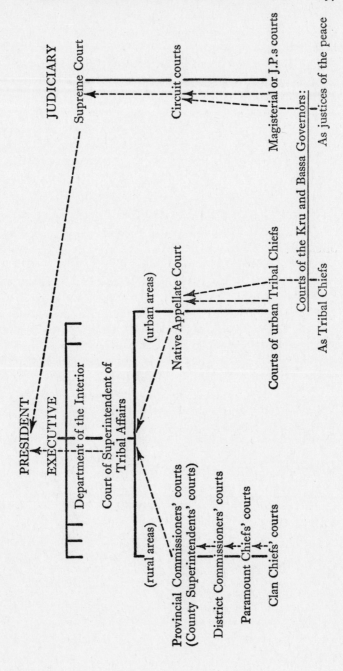

Kru man is liable to be brought before the Kru Governor as defendant in a minor case, although one of accepted civilized status would be more likely to take such a case, as plaintiff, to the Magisterial Court in the Town Centre. That is, the judicial powers of the Kru Governor, and of the other two officials I have mentioned, derive from the two separate lines of authority in the republic's legal system: from them, as Tribal Chiefs, appeal goes to the Department of the Interior, which is a part of the Executive, while from them as justices of the peace appeal goes to the courts of the judiciary. The mechanics of this rather complex situation are illustrated in Figure III.

THE COMPOSITION AND OPERATION OF THE TRIBAL COURTS

The Tribal Chiefs and Governors have their own court-rooms, often attached to their dwelling-houses, and recognizable by the flag of the republic which they are permitted to fly—a privilege otherwise reserved for government departments and the residences of 'Honorables'. The composition of the courts is not laid down by regulations: those of the Kru and Bassa Governors, when they are acting as Tribal Chiefs, include councillors representing the various sub-tribes, while other Chiefs may or may not seek the advice of elders. Cases are heard in public, and litigants may speak for themselves or through a representative. Normally, proceedings are conducted in the vernacular, but especially if the litigants engage 'legal agents' a mixture of the vernacular and 'lawyers' English' is used. These 'legal agents' are sometimes independent, but more often they are student attorneys attached to ordinary private law firms. They have, however, as a special qualification, knowledge of tribal customary law, although in practice this means that they are familiar with the so-called 'customary law' laid down in the *Revised Laws for Governing the Hinterland,* rather than with traditional custom of the particular tribe concerned. Officially, when they operate in Tribal Chiefs' courts they may speak only for their relatives or for persons for whom they act as guardians, and without receiving payment—a ruling which is, however, very frequently ignored. A peculiar feature of the tribal courts is that they are permitted to use trial by ordeal:

Ordeals . . . of a minor nature and which do not endanger the life of the individual shall be allowed and is hereby authorized.

Ordeal Doctors shall be required to procure a Certificate from the Interior Department which will be issued to them after such tests have been given and their competency and skill established to the full satisfaction of the Secretary of the Interior.[10]

All ordeal trials are commonly referred to as 'trial by sasswood', but the actual use of the poisonous bark of the sasswood tree is in fact prohibited, and I heard of no instance of its use today at least in the urban area. Minor ordeals are used, but in fact the threat of an ordeal trial is much more frequent than its actual performance.

I now turn to examples of actual cases brought to the urban tribal courts and describe the way they are dealt with. My examples are drawn from the court of the Kru Governor, and are based on cases recorded by my assistant. The great majority of disputes brought to the court are concerned with some aspect of marital problems. I have chosen as examples a series of cases involving the same *dramatis personae*, and arising from a marriage that was breaking up. The names here given are fictitious ones. The main people involved were:

Blamo, a ship's headman, 56 years old.

Gbaunyeno, 23 years old, his head wife. She was in fact his youngest wife, but she was officially his head wife because she was the first woman to whom he had become betrothed: that is, the arrangement had been made with her father during her childhood.

Wiah, Gbaunyeno's father, an illiterate stevedore, now retired.

Cooper, Wiah's brother and Gbaunyeno's uncle, who was a legal agent. Being a 'lettered' man, Cooper had in fact received the marriage payment for Gbaunyeno, and he is therefore sometimes referred to as her 'father'.

Tekwa, Blamo's legal agent.

The Case of the Chorister's Dress

This first case was brought before the Governor and Council, that is, in the tribal court. Gbaunyeno alleged that her husband Blamo had destroyed her chorister's dress, and she claimed damages. As is customary, the accusation had been submitted in writing by the Governor's Secretary when the case was notified, and was now read out to the court.

Tekwa, for Blamo, opened the discussion by pleading that the Governor and Council could not judge the case because it was a case for damages, and therefore triable before the Governor alone, as Justice of

[10] *Code of Laws*, RL, 1956, 1:422.

the Peace, and not before the Governor and Council; and further, that a civil suit could not be brought by Gbaunyeno, because she was Blamo's wife, and in any case her husband had paid for the dress. The case could not therefore be brought at all.

Cooper, acting as Gbaunyeno's agent, replied that the matter was a formality: the court of the Governor and Council was in any case simply an enlargement of the court of the Justice of the Peace. He proceeded to make a long speech in a rhetorical style much admired by Kru on the general theme of the improvement of women's rights during the régime of President Tubman, including the introduction of female suffrage, leading up to support of Gbaunyeno's right to bring her case.

The Governor then ruled that the case should be tried on its merits, that is, without spending time on technicalities.

This preliminary skirmishing on the part of legal agents is a feature of a great many court hearings; their speeches are usually made with considerable drama and oratory, and are often applauded by the onlookers, for whom this is an important part of the proceedings. In fact, as we shall see, their pleading has little effect on the final judgements made, although they often succeed in getting cases temporarily closed or postponed, to be reopened in another form. The Governor (who is illiterate and untrained in legal technicalities) frequently interrupts with the request that the case should be heard 'on the facts'. This brings the hearing, despite the participation of the agents and the introduction of Western legal concepts, into the more familiar pattern of procedure according to African customary law. In this instance, the case should probably, strictly speaking, have been tried before the Governor as J.P.

The Governor then called on Blamo to make his statement.

Blamo said, very briefly, that he did not deny destroying his wife's dress, and that he agreed to accept the judgement of the court.

Cooper arose at this point to say that the case was more complex than had so far been described. Because Blamo had destroyed the dress (and here Gbaunyeno whispered to him that her husband had also destroyed her menstrual napkin), he was suspected of having evil intentions (*wolo kulu*, implying witchcraft intent) towards her. He should therefore be asked to sign a 'life insurance bond' (using the English phrase), to the effect that if anything happened to her, he would take the blame. If he refused to sign such a bond, Blamo should be asked to bring to the court the pieces of the dress he had destroyed (so that he could not use them to make witchcraft).

The term 'life insurance bond' refers to a traditional Kru custom of requiring one suspected of witchcraft to swear an oath that no harm will come to the suspected victim. He is then held responsible if anything does happen. The English phrase was probably introduced by Kru returning from abroad, since life insurance companies and policies are unknown in Liberia.

The councillors retired to discuss the case, and returned to give their decision: that the case before the court was damages and must be dealt with as such, that is, since the other matter had not been mentioned in the initial 'writ', i.e. the written statement made when the case was notified.

The Governor ruled that since the husband had admitted destroying the dress and 'confessed judgement', he should pay the full cost of the dress ($25) as well as the costs of the court: 'leading fee' (to the Governor) $1.50; Government tax ($1.00); 'court costs' (to the Councillors) $6.00; and Record fee (to the Secretary) $0.60. Blamo paid $12.50 immediately, and asked for time to complete.

In this instance, the Councillors retired to discuss the matter and returned to give their decision as a body. But the procedure varies from case to case: sometimes the Governor discusses the case with them, without their retiring, and sometimes they themselves interrogate the litigant or witnesses. In this case there was little to discuss, since the defendant had pleaded guilty to the original charge, and had made no attempt to vindicate himself. And, in fact, after the hearing had been officially concluded, the Governor asked Blamo informally why he had destroyed the dress.

Blamo, who was not a frequent churchgoer and who was generally considered to be jealous of his wife because of her prominence in church affairs, said he had forbidden his wife to go to church, but she had disobeyed him. He therefore lost his temper and tore up her chorister's robe, an act which he now regretted. He said, further, that he did not like his wife to attend the church because the (male) choir leader was always 'making signs' before his wife.

Blamo could not give his defence earlier, because admitting his jealousy would have meant loss of face, especially since it was generally known in the community that his young wife had taken several lovers. The tension in the marriage had clearly not been resolved by his paying Gbaunyeno the cost of the dress, especially since she had accused him of intending to bewitch her. So it was

H

not surprising that the same protagonists came before the Governor a few weeks later.

The Case of the Deprived Wife

In this hearing, no official writ was made out and no costs were involved. The matter was, instead, put informally to the Governor —a not infrequent procedure.

Gbaunyeno complained that her husband was depriving her of her privileges as head wife, and in particular, that when he had last returned from his ship he did not give her all the gifts he had brought with him. Further, he refused to have intercourse with her. Gbaunyeno therefore suspected that he 'did not have a clean heart' towards her. This, she said, was even worse than the matter of witchcraft. She had therefore brought her uncle and her husband to the Governor to discuss the matter.

Stevedores usually bring back from their trips, in addition to their wages, cloth and household articles bought down the coast, and also food-stuffs from the ship. At the end of the trip the European mess steward often shares out gifts of food among them, especially if the stocks of food bought to provide for them have not been used up. Customarily such gifts, particularly the food-stuffs, should be given to the head wife to distribute appropriately.

The Governor then asked Gbaunyeno's uncle what he had to say.
Cooper suggested that since the husband, Blamo, had in the meantime refused to sign the 'life insurance bond', Gbaunyeno, 'the woman who is my daughter', should be given to him to look after whenever Blamo was abroad.

That is, he suggested again that Blamo intended to harm Gbaunyeno by means of witchcraft. Here I should mention that the two spouses were from different Kru *dako*: Gbaunyeno from the 'Five Tribes' and Blamo from the Kabor people. The Kabor are considered by other *dako* to have the most powerful witchcraft, and are said to be the only *dako* to have secret 'witchcraft societies'. Blamo was, in fact, suspected of being a member of one of these societies. It is noteworthy that the allegations of witchcraft were repeatedly made by Cooper, who was the only 'lettered' man in the case.

Blamo was then asked for his statement. He claimed that he had not brought very much from the ship, and that he had therefore kept the key to his box himself, instead of giving his to his wife. In any case, he said, when in the past he had given the key to Gbaunyeno, she had distributed goods to everybody, 'even outside friends'; that is, she had not distributed them among kin in the correct manner.

At this point, Freeman, a 'big man' from the Kru community in Lagos, who had been staying in New Krutown as a visitor for some weeks, broke in to relate a parable:

Once a man was carrying the trunk of wisdom. In the course of his journey he met a huge log across the road. He did not know how to get across it, without leaving the trunk behind him. A passer-by advised him to put the trunk on the log and crawl under the log. After he had done this, he refused to take up the trunk again saying ' I thought that I was the only man who has wisdom, but since it is not for one man, let it stay there.'

This was an oblique reference to the current gossip that Blamo, on his way from the port, had taken food to a girl friend in Claratown, but unknowingly had carried it on the lorry of one of his wife's relatives. In other words, he must not think himself the only smart operator. He had not fooled his wife.

Blamo then said he was willing to send his wife back to her parents whenever he went on a trip down the coast.

This would, in effect, have been the first step towards dissolution of the marriage, implying that Blamo did not want his wife any longer. This was probably what Gbaunyeno's relatives wanted, because if Blamo could be made to say that he did not want her any more, they would not be liable for refund of marriage payments. The Governor, however, attempted to bring about a reconciliation:

The Governor advised Blamo that he must do the right thing by his wife in 'sleeping palaver' (*ti beng blidi*), otherwise she would be bound to give him trouble, because he was treating her like an old woman when she was only 23 years of age. 'Now,' he said, 'take your wife, satisfy her, and let her have her choice of your goods, as it used to be.'

The Case of the Disobedient Daughter

Two weeks later Gbaunyeno again brought a case before the tribal court of the Kru Governor. By now she was living with her parents, and had left her husband. But this time she was suing her father, Wiah, for refund to her husband of the marriage payment:

that is, she was *de facto* bringing a divorce suit. On this occasion she spoke for herself while Cooper, her uncle, spoke for Wiah.

Cooper opened the discussion by pleading that technically Gbaunyeno was not entitled to sue her father, on the grounds of the Interior Regulations, Articles 55, section (h). Since her family had instructed her to return to her husband she must do so.

The regulation in question states: 'If a woman declares her resolve not to continue to live with her husband, the husband may appeal to her parents for a refund of the dowry. In case the family refuses or is not in a position to refund the said dowry, she is compelled to live with him until the family is willing or able to make the refund.' However, divorce suits of this type—where the woman sues her family to make them refund marriage payment to her husband—are frequently brought in the urban area, and apparently in the hinterland also.[11] In several such cases which I came across in Monrovia, the family eventually agreed to the refund. In some, however, the woman herself cut proceedings short by making the refund on her own account. The legal 'dowry', i.e. marriage payment, is laid down by the same Interior Regulations at a maximum of $40. In effect, this is the maximum amount legally recoverable at divorce.

Gbaunyeno then spoke: 'Governor, since I am the one that wears the shoe, and since it is I who feel the pain of the nail in my shoe, I should be the one to take it off my foot. The law says if you do not want the husband you must sue the father. That is why I sue my father. Do not consider what my uncle has told you. He is a book man. I do not know book.'

Gbaunyeno, that is, was referring to the locally established precedent, rather than the technicalities of the law.

The Governor, after consultation with the councillors, ruled that the case should be dismissed and the costs ruled against Gbaunyeno on the grounds that she had refused to obey her parents and return to live with her husband. He also pointed out that the husband was entitled to sue for refund of dowry.

The costs totalled $7.40, made up as follows: government tax $1.00, court fees $6.00, record fee $0.40. Gbaunyeno, however, already disobedient to her parents, proceeded to show her rejection of the court's decision.

[11] Gibbs, 1960.

Gbaunyeno said: 'Governor, since my people have said I have no right to sue my father I cannot do anything. But my father must pay the amount, because I will not stay married to the man.'

When a woman is determined on divorce, there is little to be done about it. Further, two legal agents who arrived at this point in connexion with another case, informed the Governor that Gbaunyeno *was* entitled to sue.

Wiah, the father, at this point spoke for himself: he was willing, personally, to refund the marriage payment. It was his brother, the legal agent, who had advised him not to do so.

The Governor ruled that, since the present court session was officially completed, the refund would have to take place at another session of the court.

A week later the same couple came before the tribal court again. This time Gbaunyeno was the defendant. Her husband Blamo brought her for trial by ordeal for adultery. Gbaunyeno, called on by the Governor to plead her case, said she had no men's names to confess, and refused to submit to ordeal.

Unfortunately—from my point of view—the proceedings were interrupted at this point, the case was adjourned, and it was not resumed before I left Monrovia a few weeks later. Things were, however, falling into an accustomed pattern: Blamo was trying to collect adultery damages before the divorce from his wife could be effected. Adultery is probably the most frequent theme of cases which appear before the urban tribal courts. The 'customary law' on which the proceedings are based has long been written into the Interior Regulations. The original (1923) ruling[12] reads:

The amount to be paid for cohabiting with one's wife [*sic*] is fixed at $3. If a man is enticed by a woman, however great a flirt she may be known to be, he is nevertheless to be held responsible for the payment of $3 to her husband or her parents.

But the present regulation[13] has a more sophisticated form:

A husband may bring suit against a man who has engaged in illicit intercourse with his head wife or any of his secondary wives. The

---

[12] Quoted by Huberich, vol. ii.
[13] *Revised Laws for Governing the Hinterland*, 1949.

damage awarded in such acquit shall not exceed $100 if the head wife was involved, or $10 if a secondary wife was involved. The payment of damages shall not entitle the defendant to the possession of the wife.

Unlike 'dowry refund' adultery damages do not have to be collected in court, and in many cases the matter is settled privately. The woman either voluntarily, or under threat of 'sasswood' tells her husband the names of her lovers; the husband then demands damages from them. Should an alleged lover refuse to pay, the husband may take him to court. In cases of this type which I came across, the lover's defence was usually that the woman had told him that she was unmarried: if he can produce witnesses that this was the case, he is not required to pay damages. Actual intercourse is rarely denied, and if women 'confess the names' of lovers it is usually assumed that they are telling the truth. In a close knit community like New Krutown, love affairs are in any case difficult to conceal. Sometimes, however—as happened in the case of Gbaun-yeno—women refuse to admit adultery, and are brought to the tribal court to stand trial by ordeal. Should matters reach this stage, however, the tension between the spouses is probably so great that the marriage is in any case about to break up. But the court may still try to bring about a reconciliation, as it did, successfully, in the following case:

The Case of the Cuckolded Husband

Jah brought an action in the tribal court, accusing his wife Doe of adultery and demanding that she stand trial by ordeal.

Doe, called to the stand, said that she had been justified in taking a lover because her husband had not been maintaining her adequately.

Jah pointed out that he had brought his wife to confess men's names, and, if she still refused to do so, to stand trial by ordeal.

The Governor asked: 'But you want to keep your wife. And, woman, do you want your husband.'

Doe replied that if her husband would maintain her, she was willing to stay with him.

Jah then stated: 'Father, she is my wife: I will carry her home.'

The Governor made his decision: 'You cannot finish cutting a farm in one day' [a well-known proverb meaning that it takes a long time to get to know a woman]. 'The mothers of old were altogether different from this generation. Therefore, my son, since you love your wife, take her home and care for her.'

In other cases, the wife who refuses to admit adultery is administered 'trial by ordeal'. I have the impression that the actual performance of an ordeal trial is rare, despite the frequency with which
it is threatened, and during my stay in New Krutown, I did not in
fact witness such a trial, although one or two, which I did not
attend, did take place. From the accounts of informants (and
from the one ordeal trial—not for adultery—which I witnessed),
the ordeals used are of a very minor nature, involving the manip-
ulation of sticks, drums, medicines and so forth, by the ordeal
doctor, while in a state of trance, and inflicting little if any bodily
damage on the accused. In the case of wives charged with adultery,
the effectiveness of the threat of 'Sasswood' was said by my informants to lie not in fear of the actual ordeal, but in the shame involved
in the subsequent procedure. For a woman whom the ordeal finds
guilty is taken around the town and required to point out all her
lovers.

The series of cases quoted illustrates the manner in which the
urban tribal courts operate and the types of problem brought before
them. Basically, the procedure is that of traditional African courts
elsewhere, that is, by way of statements by the litigants.[14] Super-
imposed on this procedure, and often appearing quite extraneous
to it, are the pleadings by the legal agents on technical points of
law. These pleadings—which are in any case usually unintelligible
to the court members—seldom affect the final decisions reached
by the court—and indeed their actual effect may run counter to
the court's function of resolving conflicts between the litigants.
For the technical pleadings often simply draw out the case by
leading to postponements and re-trials, and thus exacerbate the
grievances being aired. In the first of the series of cases quoted,
Gbaunyeno was not at all sure what she wanted; certainly not just
payment for her ruined dress, although this was the complaint
notified in the 'writ' so that the case had to be decided on this basis.
The crux of the matter came out, in fact, in an informal hearing,
quite uncircumscribed by 'writ', when she complained that her
husband would not have sexual intercourse with her: this, she
said, was the worst thing, even worse than the 'witchcraft intent'.
As the case dragged on, she became increasingly bent on divorce.

A second peculiar feature of the Monrovia urban tribal courts
is that, while they are in principle authorized to hear cases under

[14] See Epstein, 1954.

the customary law of the tribes concerned, provided that these do not conflict with the rulings laid down in the *Revised Laws and Administrative Regulations for Governing the Hinterland*, in practice cases are almost always decided on the basis of these written regulations. In the cases cited, the only instance where traditional custom peculiar to the Kru entered the argument was in the (tangential) suggestion that Blamo should sign a 'life insurance bond'. In Monrovia at least the 'customary laws' written in to the *Regulations*, on matters of dowry refund, adultery damages, and the custody of children, have become accepted, are acted on, and are to that extent 'customary', although they may by no means conform with traditional custom of specific tribes. For example, the Kru elders say that adultery damages as laid down by the *Regulations* and outlined above are quite foreign to traditional Kru custom, but Kru in Monrovia certainly claim, and receive, damages from their wives' lovers today. And a third set of norms—in addition to those of traditional tribal custom and written 'customary law'—is operated by the courts: namely, those arising out of accepted urban usage: for example, the duty of the stevedore to hand his 'box' to his head wife, her duty to distribute it among family and relatives, and the *de facto* right of a woman to obtain divorce irrespective of her father's co-operation, if she has managed, as she very often has through her trading activities, to accumulate enough money to refund, personally, the marriage payment made by her husband to her father.

In summary, the administration of the tribal population of Monrovia, that is, of the vast mass of people with little or no education —is through the heads of individual tribes represented. In the long-established Kru, Vai and Bassa communities, these heads are also part of a system of internal administration developed independently of Government by the tribe or community concerned. In the case of the Kru, this system involves a complex hierarchy the success of whose operation derives from the long association of the tribe with the occupation of stevedoring. So far as the Government is concerned, however, the main duty of all tribal heads is a judicial one. In settling cases, the courts of the urban tribal heads use three separate sets of norms: traditional tribal custom, which may or may not be specific to the tribe concerned; written 'customary law' as laid down in the government *Regulations*, and accepted urban precedent. The great majority of cases brought before such courts in Monrovia—as in other African towns—involve domestic conflicts arising out of changes taking place in family structure and relationships, and, in particular, out of changes in the status and role of the women.

CHAPTER IV

KINSHIP AND THE HOUSEHOLD

I N his introduction to *Social Change in Modern Africa*, Southall relates the strength of family ties in African urban populations to types of urban administration and housing policy, and to economic structure:

> Where movement into town is unrestricted, housing built by African private enterprise and independent employment frequent, the situation is altogether more favourable to family life and even extended families and larger groups of kin may be found.[1]

Monrovia is a rather extreme example of this situation. The absence of a formal administrative network, the inadequacy of social services, especially medical services, the casual nature of a great deal of employment available, and the low levels of wages, are additional factors which contribute to the degree to which kinsfolk rely one on another for mutual aid and security. Large households whose members are related by actual or fictitious kinship are common in all strata of the population, although the size, composition, and functions of the household differ from one community to another, reflecting both social class divisions and tribal characteristics. Here I shall be discussing particularly households in New Krutown, but I also attempt to show the extent to which these households resemble and differ from those in other sections of Monrovia's population.

CONTRACTING A MARRIAGE

Two types of marriage are legally recognized in Liberia: marriage under tribal customary law, and marriage according to the general law of the republic. Contracts of the latter type are usually referred to as 'marriage according to Christian rites' or 'legal marriage'. Any man may contract either type of marriage, i.e.

---

[1] Southall (ed.), 1961, p. 33.

tribal or legal marriage. Which type of marriage he chooses is one index of his identification of himself as a member of civilized or of tribal society.

'Legal' marriage can be carried out either by a minister of the church or by a justice of the peace, but even in the latter case is normally by Christian ritual. The decision between marriage by a justice of the peace in a private house, or by a minister in church, is largely a matter of income, since church marriages are usually much more elaborate and expensive affairs, involving an enormous amount of display. Certificates of such 'Christian' or 'legal' marriages are issued by the Registrar of Marriages for the Commonwealth District of Monrovia, but since statistics are not compiled —or records filed—I can give no figure for the number of such marriages contracted. Our sample survey showed, as one would expect, that they were much more frequent in communities dominantly 'civilized' and middle class (Table 10). In Kwi Street, which

TABLE 10. *Incidence of legal or church marriage*

Residential area	Percentage of married men who were married in this manner
Kwi Street	60
Bishop's Brook	25
Old Krutown	8
New Krutown	6
Vaitown	5
Claratown	5
Loma Quarters	None
Total these seven areas	13

Bassa Community: inadequately recorded, but proportion seemed relatively high.

it will be remembered was the most clearly 'civilized' area in my survey, two out of three of the married men had contracted 'legal' marriages, and all but one of the professional and clerical workers (the dominant occupational category in the street) had done so. The one exception had in fact been married in church previously, was divorced, and now, as an elderly man, had remarried—this

time in customary law. On the other hand, in the tribal communities, even where there are many Christians and active church-
goers, the contracting of Christian marriage is unusual. Nor, in these
communities, was there any particular correlation between type of
marriage and occupation: most professional and clerical workers
were, like other members of the communities, married in customary
law. Among the few cases of legal marriage we did encounter in
these areas, several had been contracted by men who had positions
of leadership in church, several by persons who had since 'come
down in the world'. In these communities the contracting of
Christian marriage does not in itself confer status.

Marriages according to tribal customary law are arranged privately between the individuals concerned and their families, the
formal completion of the contract being signified by the final payment of bridewealth by the man to the woman's relatives. The
maximum legal 'dowry' as it is locally called, is $40, but actual
amounts paid vary a great deal, and sometimes payment is waived
altogether. Among the Kru, the traditional marriage payment is
relatively low. The first marriage gifts may be made when the girl
is still a child. Later, she may come to live with the man's family
for a trial period; if they get on well together, she returns home
and arrangements are made for the final marriage payment. (If
they do *not* get on well, I was told that the girl's parents may be
asked to return the first gifts, although I came upon no example of
this actually happening.) When the bride finally comes to the man's
household, she is expected to bring a trunk of clothes, food and
other goods. For about three months she does no work and is confined to the house with her face painted with white chalk. She eats
well, takes a bath twice daily, and may sleep with her husband. At
the end of this period, which is intended to 'nourish' the new wife,
she washes the chalk off her face, dresses in fine clothes, and if she
is a Christian, attends church. A similar procedure is followed at
the birth of her first child, except that she is likely to return to her
mother, or go to some other female relative living in Monrovia, for
the three months' seclusion. Such a procedure is normally carried
out only in the case of a girl's first marriage, not in the case of a
woman already divorced or widowed who may have already borne
a child. And further, in the Kru urban communities, the couple
often start living together before the marriage payment is completed, and where this situation continues long enough, they often

come to be regarded as man and wife. On the other hand, a number of cases occur where, although the man has made the final marriage payment, he delays the procedure of going officially with his relatives to the girl's house to claim his wife—because he has no home to take her to, because he feels unable to support her, or because of domestic complications with other wives or girl friends. The actual status of many marriage contracts is therefore difficult to determine—and this is one reason for the frequency of adultery charges mentioned in the last chapter.

A clear distinction is made, however, between unions in which the formal customary procedure has at least commenced, and the individually arranged extra-marital unions with *megi* or lovers. A man may bring his *megi* to live with him, but this is relatively unusual: more often, he pays her an allowance for food and clothing, and sometimes she cooks for him. Most men, and a large number of women, have several such unions before contracting marriage; they may lead to marriage, but there is no special expectation that they will do so. According to some Kru informants. it was traditionally acceptable for either a married or a single man to keep such a *megi*, and many married men in New Krutown have such arrangements today—usually, but by no means always, despite their wives' disapproval. Some women prefer the *megi* arrangement to marriage, since it can more easily be broken off. Where much employment is of a casual kind, a man's income is subject to many vicissitudes: when he is unemployed, his wife may be expected to provide for the household out of the proceeds of her trading. A *megi* on the other hand can simply look for a wealthier man to attach herself to. However, such women usually marry eventually. Of all the women in our sample, only a tiny proportion were still single at 25 years of age, although some had already been divorced once or several times. Outright prostitution exists on a small scale in Monrovia, and is said to be increasing—but was very rare within the residential areas covered by our survey.

Marriage according to customary law, of course, permits polygyny, and polygyny occurs in Monrovia especially in the longer-established tribal communities with older populations. For the purposes of the survey, we counted as polygynous only those marriages where two or more wives were resident in Monrovia, since it was often difficult to determine the precise status of marriages with women living elsewhere. On this rather rigorous definition, fifty-eight of the men in our sample (13 per cent. that is, of all the married men) were polygynists, and forty-eight of these were living in Vaitown, New Krutown or Old Krutown. Forty of the men had two wives in Monrovia, fifteen had three, and three had four wives. Sometimes the wives were sharing the same house, sometimes the husband had housed them in different houses in the same community or in different parts of Monrovia. Managing a polygynous household in the urban situation is a complicated affair. Often, a girl is betrothed during childhood in the home area, and is brought to town when she grows up; but in the meantime, the man may have contracted marriage with a townswoman. The marriage of Gbaunyeno and Blamo, discussed in the last chapter, was of this kind: Blamo, a ship's headman, introduced into his household, which already contained two wives and their adult children, a young girl who claimed the position of head wife because she had been the first person for whom he made a marriage payment. Again, many young men, who are not at all in a position to establish a polygynous household, nor enthusiastic about doing so, commence making marriage payments for girls in their home villages, before coming to Monrovia, and have subsequent problems with town girls whom they take as *megi* and who—especially if they bear children—may want to be taken on as wives.

Where a man whose *megi* bears children continues to provide for her but does not marry her, the arrangement may gradually slide over into the type of union known as 'outside marriage'. More usually, however, the (English) term 'outside wife' refers to the long-term extra-marital unions of civilized men living in Christian marriage. Usually, the outside wife is a tribal woman from a lower social stratum than the man. Sometimes, however, she may be an educated woman, for, apart from questions of affection and sentiment, an educated woman may be able to do better for herself and her children by remaining the outside wife of a rich and influential man than by marrying lower in the social scale. She has a recognized social status, and although she is rarely, if ever, admitted to the man's home, her children are often taken over by the man when they reach school-going age, to be reared by him and his official wife. Such unions are widespread, and contracting them often adds to, rather than detracts from, a man's prestige.

CHILDREN

Households containing simple nuclear families, consisting of the man, his wife, and their children, are unusual in all communities and social strata. In the first place, the great majority of households contain other children as well: these may be outside children of the husband, relatives of the husband or the wife, wards and foster-children, or servants.

Legally, a man can be held responsible for maintaining all his illegitimate children—whether by outside wives or resulting from more fleeting unions—during their minority, and he is entitled to claim them when they reach the age of 7 years. There is a certain amount of social pressure on the official wife to take such children into her household, especially if she herself is childless: this is true in both civilized and illiterate communities:

A woman of American origin but long naturalized and married to an Americo-Liberian, was the object of much criticism because, although she had no children, she refused to take into her household any of her husband's outside children, and in particular, a son of whom he was especially fond, whom he had legitimized, and whom he was educating at some expense. Her uncharitable behaviour was usually ascribed to the fact that she had been born a foreigner, and had never learned Liberian ways.

In any case, it has long been the custom for civilized households to accept children who will help in the household in return for their keep and, these days, for their school fees, and the husband's own children are likely to get priority over those of relatives or strangers. We did not, in the course of the social survey, inquire in detail about the presence of 'outside children', who were recorded simply as the husbands' offspring, or occasionally the wife's, along with children of previous marriages. Sometimes such information was volunteered—one informant told me that her daughter had had 'two children by her first husband, two by her second, and the last one all by herself'. However, to make specific inquiries would have aroused resentment. To have many children—outside as well as inside—increases a man's prestige, but although he may boast about outside children in private, official Christian morality prohibits their public discussion. Nevertheless, this is a favourite topic for gossip, and the presence in the household of illegitimate children is usually an open secret.

In addition, many households contain children of relatives who have been taken in for a variety of reasons: because the parents have died, or cannot support them, because the parents live elsewhere and want children to attend schools in Monrovia, and so on. Often such obligations fall most heavily on educated families, who take in and help children of their less fortunate kin. Households in New Krutown and Claratown contained two particular types of relationship arising from tribal custom: the *nanaju*, or 'walking son' (the child who walks behind you), who is a boy given to one, usually by a relative or *panton* member, but occasionally by a close friend, and the *negbajlo*, usually translated 'servant'. Traditionally, a *negbajlo* was a young unmarried man who had not yet built his own house and was regarded as the 'servant' of the head of the house—the *sla bi* or 'house father', of the house in which he was brought up, usually that of his own father but sometimes that of some other relative. Today, in the home areas as well as in Monrovia, many young men have insufficient resources to build their own houses when they marry, and they therefore bring their wives into the household where they have lived as bachelors and remain in the position of *negbajlo* to their original *sla bi*. But Kru households, compared with those of other tribes, contained few children who were not related by kinship to the household head. In fact, the Kru criticize other tribes, notably the Vai, for their practice of sending children away to be brought up by strangers, and many consider this a greater disgrace than having an illegitimate child. On the other hand, some of the educated Kru claim that this prejudice has retarded the process of 'civilization' among the Kru and accounts in part for their late entry, compared with the Vai, into 'civilized society' and positions in government. For this practice has long been of major importance in enabling children of illiterates to get an education, and most persons of tribal origin who now have prominent positions in government were in fact taken into 'civilized' households in this way. In their generation, this normally meant Americo-Liberian or missionary households, but the process is a cumulative one so that today many households taking such children are themselves made up of tribespeople.

Some idea of the extent to which the custom persists is given in Table 11, which gives, for the eight residential areas of my survey, the distribution of wards and other children who were *unrelated* by kinship to the households in which they were living. We entered the child's relationship to the household head as it was categorized by the informants concerned, but since the terms 'ward', 'foster-child', 'servant' and 'small boy' are used vaguely and inconsistently, I have not attempted to differentiate these categories one from another in the table. In any case, variations in the child's actual relationship with the household are often as great within as between categories.

TABLE 11. *Wards, foster-children, servants and small boys*

Residential area	Houses in sample	Houses with wards, etc.	Number of wards		Wards as percentage of total population
			M	F	
Vaitown	50	34	47	41	20
Kwi Street	50	20	27	6	12
Bassa Community	50	13	10	6	5
Bishop's Brook	50	11	11	2	5
New Krutown	50	6	7	1	2
Loma Quarters	50	5	7	—	3
Old Krutown	50	2	3	—	1
Claratown	50	1	—	1	—
Total	400	92	111	58	6

Among the 400 households in the sample, one in four contained such unrelated children, and the children accounted for 6 per cent. of the total population. Two-thirds of them were boys, and most were under 15 years of age. They were markedly more numerous in some areas than in others, the variation reflecting differences in both social class and tribal custom. The Kru tribal areas contained few such unrelated children, for reasons I have already mentioned. In Loma Quarters and Bishop's Brook there were several instances where a bachelor had taken on a 'small boy' to fetch and carry for him. The large number of such children in Vaitown was interesting, for Vaitown is, as we have seen, a Muslim community outside the main stream of urban life. A number of boys come from Cape Mount to stay with families in Vaitown and attend schools in Monrovia, but in Vaitown (as in no other area) almost as many of the wards were girls. In Kwi Street, on the other hand, almost all the wards were children of illiterate families who had been sent to educated ones to attend school and learn 'civilization'.

But whether the child is categorized as 'outside child', child of relatives, ward, servant and so on, his actual relationship with the

I

nuclear household varies enormously. At one extreme, he may be treated in exactly the same manner as the 'inside' children, if any. At the other, he may be regarded as truly a servant, and although he must by law be sent to elementary school, clothed and fed, he may be summarily ordered about and seldom seen outside the kitchen unless he is waiting on the adults or inside children. The older literature on Liberia is full of stories of 'small boys' who run after children of the élite carrying their school satchels, and this situation does persist: one of my university students used to sit outside in her chauffeur-driven car, while her 'small boy'—who was probably older than she—delivered her essays to me. Between these two extremes there lies a whole gamut of human relationships arising from individual attachments and dislikes, whose detailed study would throw a great deal of light on the social processes at work on the civilized population. I was not able to make such a study, but I give a few examples which illustrate the range of relationships involved:

Mr. and Mrs. A. were both of illiterate tribal parents, were brought up in civilized households—she in that of an Americo-Liberian, he in a missionary's—and are now well-established members of civilized society. They have three inside children, who are being educated abroad. Mr. A. has in addition two adolescent children by an outside wife who is also an educated woman: the girl lives in the A household and attends high school locally, the boy lives with his mother but is provided for and sent to school by Mr. A. Mr. and Mrs. A are also paying for the schooling of Mr. A's niece, who lives in her school hostel and spends her holidays in the A household. Both girls who live in the household are well-dressed and treated like daughters, except that unlike Mrs. A's own daughter they have not been sent to school abroad. Mr. A has several other small children by an illiterate tribeswoman who lives on his rubber farm, and one of these lives in his Monrovia household and helps in the kitchen. The household contains, in addition, several smaller children who are relatives of Mrs. A and who attend elementary schools and help around the house.

The practice of sending inside children abroad to school, while outside children attend schools in Liberia, is fairly common in the upper strata of society. It is more or less expected that what money is available will be spent primarily on the inside children:

Mr. B, an Americo-Liberian, gave his daughter a big church wedding and an elaborate reception, which was attended by many of the élite.

Gossip claimed that, although the girl lived in Mr. B's household, she was not the child of Mrs. B—who had however produced three children herself. It was said that Mr. B's rubber farm must be thriving, if he could afford to marry even an *outside* daughter in church.

The acceptance of tribal children as wards has long been considered a Christian duty by Americo-Liberians. Where the children are well fed and clothed, this demands considerable generosity from the guardian family. In return, the guardian gets not only household assistance but also emotional satisfaction and, in some cases, increased security of status:

Mrs. C is an elderly Americo-Liberian widow who had no children of her own. Through her household, however, have passed more children than she can remember—perhaps fifty, she told me. At the time when I met her, she had four Kpelle and Bassa wards, all boys whose ages ranged from six to fourteen. These boys did the cooking and cleaning, were summarily ordered about and kept in the background. On the other hand, they were very well dressed and sent regularly to school—in fact Mrs. C. had engaged a private tutor for two who were backward in reading. She was very upset when the father of one took him back in order to send him to Poro bush school, since she had hoped to rear him to enter civilized society. She has a large 'family' of ex-wards and foster-children, who frequently visit her, and she 'spoils' their children and grandchildren. Some of them have become important government officials, and she derives considerable status, as well as security, from her relationship with them. She told me that she had willed her property to the children and grandchildren of her deceased brother, but she has also made bequests to two former foster-daughters who have remained especially attached to her and often visit her.

The motivation behind the taking in of wards is sometimes similar to that of the 'patron', the influential and/or rich man who helps young men with their school fees or in their search for subsequent employment. The patron thus binds to him young men who may be useful political supporters, and apart from this, he becomes one in whose house people congregrate, and obtains status from this fact.

Apparent variations in the treatment of outside children, the treatment of wards, and so on, have to be seen against a situation where older children in general are expected to help in household tasks and to care for the younger ones. Often, there is an abrupt alteration in a child's treatment and status when he reaches three or four years old—or when another child is born—and again when he reaches puberty. This applies more especially to children of tribal origin.

Mr. D is a wealthy and educated man of tribal origin, who had been twice married in church. His first wife had no children, and his second wife has given him one child aged eighteen months. His household also contains: his outside son of three years, two six-year-old outside children of different mothers but born (as he told me with no little pride) in the same month, and finally a five-year-old nephew of Mrs. D. None of the children are attending school yet, but two other outside children are supported by Mr. D at schools outside Monrovia. The one inside child—the eighteen-month-old—is made a great fuss of and is generally the centre of attention in the living-room, even when guests are present. The three-year-old outside child is usually with him, and is equally well dressed, but receives much less affection. The three older children, on the other hand, are poorly dressed and are seldom seen in the living-room. They do much of the household chores, including the removal of sanitary buckets and waiting on the two infants.

Mrs. E is an educated woman of tribal origin, who has been twice married but has no children of her own. Her household contains: two infants who are relatives of her present husband, one six-year old who is his outside child, and a boy of fourteen who is known as her foster-son. One of the two infants is conspicuously well dressed, because she is the outside child of a relatively wealthy man, Mr. E's uncle. The six-year-old, Mr. E's own outside child, is expected to look after the two infants; but all three small children are treated with considerable affection. The fourteen-year-old, on the other hand, is from a stranger tribe and can communicate with the family only in English. He had been sent down from the interior by his parents to live with a family who, he claims, were unkind to him. He left this family and moved about begging until Mrs. E took pity on him and accepted him into her household. He is, however, poorly dressed, has difficulty in getting his school fees from Mr. and Mrs. E (who are not very well off), and although he is fed and housed, is otherwise expected to fend for himself.

THE INCIDENCE AND EFFECTS OF INFERTILITY

The frequent incidence of childlessness among the 'inside wives' in the examples of households I have given is no coincidence: that a very large proportion of women in all strata have no children is apparent to anyone who lives in Monrovia, and it is also a topic very often mentioned in conversation and gossip. In my (effective) sample of 790 adult women from the eight residential areas, no less than 49 per cent. had no living children, and only 24 per cent. had more than one living child. If single women were excluded— although some of these had children—the proportions were 43 per cent. childless and 29 per cent. with no living child. I took as 'adult' all women aged 15 years or more, but dividing the women into age groups made little difference to the phenomenon: of those aged 25 years or more, the proportions were 41 per cent. childless and 25 per cent. with only one living child. The conventional fertility ratio (the numbers of living children under 5 years of age, per 1,000 married women) is shown in Table 12, for the eight areas separately and for the total population.

TABLE 12. *Fertility ratio*

Residential area	Number of children still alive and under 5 years of age per 1,000 married women
Kwi Street	714
New Krutown	543
Vaitown	500
Old Krutown	481
Bassa Community	327
Bishop's Brook	321
Loma Quarters	313
Claratown	315
Total sample	448

I had previously carried out a sample survey of the population of Livingstone, in Northern Rhodesia, a town considered to have a very low fertility ratio and a high rate of infantile mortality.[2] There I found that the fertility ratio was 673 children under 5 years of age per 1,000 married women, a figure considerably higher than that of 448 obtained from the Monrovia survey. The latter, how- ever, did not cover very adequately the areas predominantly occupied by the educated, civilized section of the population, and that there is a clear correlation between socio-economic status and fertility is apparent from Table 12: in middle-class Kwi Street,

[2] McCulloch, 1956, p. 79.

the fertility ratio was markedly higher than in any other area. This may arise from the higher educational level of its inhabitants and/ or their better financial position, either of which may lead them to make better use of the very limited medical facilities available. Relatively high ratios in New Krutown, Vaitown and Old Kru- town suggest that residence in long-established communities with established *mores* may also be a contributing factor. Tribal custom may also be relevant: in the case of Vaitown, for example, the fer- tility ratio is probably affected by the fact that many women are sent back to Cape Mount for their confinements and may remain there while suckling. A great deal more analysis would, however, be required before any authoritative statement could be made on the extent, nature and causes of the low fertility ratio: most importantly, we did not make inquiries concerning children who had been born alive and since died—because this would have en- cumbered the schedule too much and—as I had learned from the Livingstone study—was likely to meet with resistance. But what- ever its causes, one of the *results* of the high incidence of childless- ness is the situation where 'outside' children, and children of relatives and strangers, are welcomed into the household. Barren- ness is also partly responsible for the instability of marriage and the frequency of divorce in all sections of the population—civilized and tribal. And these three factors are often interrelated, since the childless woman may attempt to make her marriage more stable by establishing a large household: in particular, by taking in her husband's illegitimate children, she decreases the risk that her husband may leave her for his fertile outside wife. She also pro- vides in this way for her own security in old age.

HOUSEHOLDS: DEFINITION AND SIZE

The household, for the purposes of our survey, consisted of all persons living in each of the fifty houses selected from each of the eight residential areas. In these particular areas, while 'houses' varied in size and manner of construction, they were quite recog- nizable and comparable units. The situation would have been different if we had tried to cover, for example, certain areas in Monrovia where there are blocks of flats or very large houses divided up into apartments. The average size of the total house- holds, on this definition, is shown in Table 13: it varied between five persons per house in Loma Quarters to nine persons per house in New Krutown and Vaitown, men, women and children included. This, however, included persons renting rooms in the houses, who accounted for one in five of the total population and were especially numerous, for reasons which I have mentioned earlier, in the Bassa Community and Vaitown. Therefore, to give a more accurate picture of the size of the nuclear household units in the various areas—that is, of the units which live and eat together—I have also shown in Table 13 the average size of households excluding 'roomers'. Households defined in this way were noticeably larger in New Krutown where the households still contained an average of nine persons per house, because here there are very few roomers. The overall average household size—six persons per house—was identical with that reported from the 1956 census of the total population of Monrovia.

TABLE 13. *Size of households*

	Average number of persons per house	
Area	*Total household including roomers*	*Nuclear household excluding roomers*
Loma Quarters	5	4
Bishop's Brook	5	4
Bassa Community	7	4
Kwi Street	6	5
Old Krutown	6	5
Claratown	6	6
Vaitown	9	8
New Krutown	9	9
Total sample (400 houses)	7	6

I have used the word 'roomers' rather than 'tenants' because in some cases the whole house was occupied by one family renting it from an absentee landlord. Although such families were technically tenants, I counted them among the nuclear households, because I was interested in extracting from the 400 houses, 400 nuclear families whose composition could be compared, and not, in this context, in the extent of landlordism. In any case such instances were not numerous: the great majority of tenants were what I have called 'roomers'—individuals or couples renting one or two rooms from owner-occupants or from occupants who were relatives of the owner. (It is most unusual for relatives to be charged rent.) Where the entire house was rented out piecemeal but one tenant was recognized as being in charge, he and his family, if any, were counted as the nuclear household: this applied in only six or seven cases. In a further seven houses, the rooms were rented out to separate individuals or couples, none of whom were in charge: in these instances I quite arbitrarily chose the largest unit of people who lived and ate together and called it the nuclear household.

By excluding 'roomers' from the discussion of household composition which follows, I am of course selecting in favour of the more permanently established section of the population.

COMPOSITION OF THE NUCLEAR HOUSEHOLDS

Of the 400 nuclear households, only five contained adults unrelated by kinship to the household head or his wife. Two of these —the households of craftsmen in Vaitown—contained apprentices, one a housekeeper, and two (in New Krutown) contained persons whose relationship to the household head was explained as 'church people', i.e. fellow churchmen.

The composition of the kin groups making up the 400 nuclear households is shown in Table 14: I have excluded the unrelated wards, foster-children and so on, whose distribution has been indicated in Table 11. I have divided the houses into those with male heads, on the one hand, and those with female heads on the other, and subdivided those with male heads into 'elementary families' and 'extended families'.

1. *Households with female heads.* Normally, a man is regarded as the head of the household. Of the sixty-two houses which had female heads, four of the heads were married women, who were living with their husbands, but who were regarded as the heads of their households because they owned the house: three had inherited their houses from former, deceased, husbands, the fourth had built her own house out of the proceeds of trading. Thirty-six of the households with female heads contained no adult males, except, in a few instances, the son of the head. (The more usual pattern in such houses is for the son to be regarded as the head, unless he is very young.) The remaining twenty-two houses contained adult men who were neither the sons nor husbands of the female heads—either more distant male relatives, or lovers. By no

means all of the sixty-two female heads were financially independent: they included outside wives, forming part of a polygynous family (whose husband normally lived elsewhere), and women whose husbands were separated from them but were still maintaining them.

2. *Households with male heads* accounted for 85 per cent. of the houses in the sample, and they are subdivided in Table 14 into

(a) *Elementary families*, that is, families made up of a man, his wife or wives (where several wives were living in the same house with him), their minor and adult unmarried children (if any) and other related minor children (if any). That is, since the presence

TABLE 14. *Composition of nuclear households*

Area	Households in sample	Households with female heads	Households with male heads		
			Elementary families	Extended families	Other
New Krutown	50	11	3	32	4
Claratown	50	6	14	26	4
Vaitown	50	11	15	16	8
Loma Quarters	50	1	21	16	12
Bishop's Brook	50	2	23	16	9
Old Krutown	50	10	25	14	1
Bassa Community	50	11	22	12	4
Kwi Street	50	9	24	10	7
Totals	400 (100%)	62 (15%)	147 (37%)	142 (36%)	49 (12%)

of 'outside' children and relatives' children is such a frequent occurrence, I have included such children as part of the elementary family. Polygynous households should really have been excluded from this category, but in any case the majority of such households contained adult relatives also and were therefore listed as extended families.

(b) *Extended families*, that is, families made up of an elementary family as defined above, *plus* adult married children and their spouses, and/or other adult relatives, male or female. The largest of these households contained six interrelated elementary families.

(c) *Other types of household*. Of the forty-nine houses with male heads, which fell under neither (*a*) nor (*b*) above, twenty-five contained no adult women. The rest included households whose heads were living with daughters or mothers or lovers, with or without other relatives. The five households which included unrelated adults were also included under this heading.

With the process of 'civilization', the elementary family becomes increasingly isolated from the wider group of kin and economically independent of them. While in the total sample, households consisting of elementary families and of extended families occurred in almost equal proportions, there was a marked variation in their distribution within the several residential areas. In those areas made up largely of recent immigrants to Monrovia—Loma Quarters, Bishop's Brook, and, in spite of its age as a settlement, Vaitown—extended families have had less time to establish themselves. But both New Krutown and Kwi Street, at opposite extremes of the distribution scale, contain high proportions of old Monrovians. In New Krutown, households consisting only of one elementary family numbered only three of the fifty in the sample, and there were eleven times as many extended families. In Kwi Street, on the other hand, elementary families accounted for nearly half of the households in the sample and were twice as frequent as extended ones. That is, in the civilized, middle-class communities, individual families become the most frequent residential and economic unit. Such families, however, do not necessarily lose contact with their kin today: indeed, because their kinsfolk are often poorer than they, particularly frequent demands are made upon their generosity. Often, this makes it difficult for them to keep up the material standards of civilized life, and the conflicts of economic obligations thus involved are a very frequent topic of conversation. The situation is especially difficult where only one spouse has relatives in Monrovia. Further, in nearly half of the marriages in Kwi Street, the husband and wife were from different tribal groups and this presented many problems in the field of social interaction, especially if the relatives spoke no English and could not therefore converse with their in-laws. Children in areas like Kwi Street usually grow up speaking nothing but English, so that with each generation the social gap between the two sections of kin—the civilized and the uneducated sections—increases, and the strength of social contact and of economic obligations is diluted. Thus, although the educated tribespeople no longer attempt to 'pass' for Americo-Liberian, the very process of education and Westernization, while it unites them with other 'civilized people' of different

origins, divides them from the main body of their kin and tribespeople.

EXTENDED FAMILIES IN THE URBAN AREA

Extended families occurred in all areas, but they were the norm
in Claratown and New Krutown, where they also took their largest
and most complex form. In the remainder of this chapter I con-
centrate on the New Krutown households. First, however, I want
to make it clear that the composition and functions of the New
Krutown households are urban phenomena, and do not represent
a survival of the traditional kinship system or its transference to
the urban area. In the first place, the household itself does not in
the urban area form a part of a localized group of kin. Sometimes
there may be kinship ties, affinal or conjugal, linking neighbouring
households one with another, but there is no evidence of localized
lineages similar to those which exist among the Yoruba at Lagos,
for example.[3] There is, however, a form of dispersed clan or *panton*
organization among those clans which have many members long
established in Monrovia. Traditionally, Kru towns in the home
area were divided spatially into *pantons* (usually translated 'quarters'
by the Kru themselves), in which resided the members of one
patriclan and their wives, the word *panton* being used for both the
geographical section of the town and for the kin group concerned.
The same *panton* names usually appear in several different Kru
towns, often widely separated one from another, and whether the
panton localized in each town was itself a sub-clan or some form of
lineage is difficult to ascertain. In the Kru coast town which I
visited, Grand Cess, the original composition of the *panton* is
obscured by the absence, temporary or permanent, of a large
number of its members, because they are living in Monrovia or
other cities in Liberia or abroad, or because they have moved over
to the adjacent 'civilized' Municipality of Grand Cess.[4] But such
absentees—even when they settle abroad or are children of those
who have settled abroad, and seldom, if ever, return to the home
town—retain their *panton* rights and obligations and may be
called on for assistance by fellow *panton* members. Some *pantons*
with many members in Monrovia have local, Monrovia, 'chairmen'
(the English term again being used), who are responsible for collecting cash for the assistance of needy *panton* members both in

[3] Izzett, 1961, p. 305.   [4] Fraenkel, Merran, article in *Africa* (forthcoming).

Monrovia and in the home town. That is, they have a role which, within their more limited authority, is similar to that of the town chairmen and *dako* chairmen which I have described in the previous chapter. *Panton* claims fall alike on the civilized and uncivilized members of the *panton*, and sometimes fall more heavily on the former because of their relative wealth and influence. The *panton* chairmen themselves are sometimes chosen from the civilized population. But members of the *panton* are scattered in the urban population. I was told that in the first Krutown there was a type of localized *panton* organization but if so, it has not reappeared in New Krutown where, it will be remembered, plots of land are individually purchased. Next-door neighbours may of course be '*panton* people', but are more likely to come from different towns or *dako* (sub-tribes). However, as an illustration of the way in which, in the urban situation, wider bonds may come to be expressed in (fictitious) kinship terms, I may mention that the word *panton* is often used loosely in conversation to refer to one or two small areas within New Krutown where there are clusters of persons originating from the same town or the same *dako*.

In the second place, while the household itself is made up of a group of people related by kinship of some kind or another, the actual constellation of kinship ties involved is haphazard and fortuitous, and quite different from that of the traditional household. For one thing, it may include paternal or maternal relatives of either the household head or his wife, or of some other member of the household, and in such cases individual members of the household are drawn from a number of different *pantons*. As Southall writes of kinship in urban Africa in general:

... the range of kin provided for any town dweller is essentially incomplete. Many of the key positions in the kinship system to which he was reared remain vacant in town. The collection of relatives with whom he is able to establish and maintain kinship in the urban context is haphazard. This leads to improvising ... Because the range of kin presented in the urban population is incomplete, the individual is left to cast about and pin obligations of kinship on to whom he can, while himself endeavouring to evade them when it seems worthwhile.[5]

This occurs in most industrial societies where there has been a great deal of geographical mobility, and not only in Africa, although elsewhere kinsfolk form only one of a number of categories of

[5] Southall, op. cit., p. 32.

people to whom a newcomer may turn for help. In African towns, kinsfolk—or, failing that, people from the same home town or village—provide the newcomer's main, and sometimes only, possible contact in the urban population, and traditional laws of hospitality and generosity are strong. The *range* of kinsfolk between whom obligations are accepted may in fact be larger in the urban community than in the traditional one.[6] Most men coming to Monrovia from towns on the Kru coast, or returning from abroad, manage to locate kin of some kind in Monrovia with whom they can live at least for a short period. But their relationship with the head of the household in which they settle—the *sla bi* or house father—may be quite distant. The household often includes relatives of the wife of the *sla bi*. It may include members of only one generation, or of three or four, and where there are several generations they may not be linked by direct lineal descent. It may, and very often does, include several elementary families—for example, where a young man of the household marries but, being unable to build his own house, brings his wife to live with him and remains in the position of *negbajlo* to the household head. Examples of households of five different types of composition are given later in this chapter.

Thirdly, the economic significance of kinship is completely changed in the urban area. As Southall puts it: 'the solidarity which obtains where relatives must rely on one another for the production of their food is absent'.[7] Kin do not work together, or if they do, they work as fellow-employees of a third party. The majority of New Krutown households draw their corporate income from a number of different sources. Of the fifty households in our sample, thirty contained more than two income-earning adults, and the number of such earners per household was greater in this community than in any other surveyed (Table 15). One large house, with ten rooms, containing in all thirty-four interrelated members, had no less then twenty income earners, including stevedores, a carpenter, women market-sellers and fish-sellers—all eating together and making their budget as one unit.

The community's occupational structure means that households do often contain members whose livelihood depends on a measure of co-operation. Those whose head is a ship's headman, for example, are likely to include one or two men who work in his gang

---

[6] Epstein, 1961, p. 45.   [7] Southall, loc. cit.

and to that extent depend on him for a living. For in choosing his gang, he will sometimes take kinship obligations into account. A not dissimilar situation exists where the household head is a mason or carpenter employing apprentices and helpers, or a fisherman employing a young relative as assistant. Again, the fisherman usually does not sell his own fish directly, but through a woman fish-seller, who may be his own wife or some other female member of the household. But, interestingly enough, some fishermen choose to sell their fish through stranger women, even where they have kinswomen available. Often, the fishermen makes a verbal

TABLE 15. *Number of income-earners per household*
Tenants and minors excluded; women traders included

Area	None	1	2	3	4	5 or more	Total houses	Total earners
New Krutown	—	9	11	11	5	14	50	187
Claratown	1	20	11	8	7	3	50	113
Vaitown	3	21	6	6	6	8	50	125
Loma Quarters	2	20	17	7	3	1	50	92
Bishop's Brook	—	15	27	8	—	—	50	93
Old Krutown	2	17	18	9	4	—	50	96
Bassa Community	1	33	11	2	3	—	50	73
Kwi Street	3	26	16	4	—	1	50	76
Total houses	12	161	117	55	28	27	400	
Total earners		161	234	165	112	183		855

contract with some woman fish-seller, whereby she takes over his whole catch (apart from fish which he keeps for consumption or gifts), at a price agreed daily as a result of mutual bargaining. She then takes over the risks of sale: if she sells the fish at a price above the amount she has paid, the profit is hers: so is the risk of loss. A business arrangement of this kind has obvious problems where kinship obligations are involved. 'You cannot make business like that with relatives—they humbug too much,' said one fisherman. Therefore, where one household contains both fisherman and fish-seller, they do not *necessarily* work together: in some cases each works in partnership with some person outside. The conflict between 'business' interest and family obligations, here explicitly expressed, underlies also the complaints ships' headmen sometimes make about the problems they have with relatives who are members of their gangs.

The members of a household normally eat together and contribute to a corporate budget. Cooking may be done in turn by the women, or one woman who is not engaged in market-selling may be assigned this task. Wages and trading profits are, theoretically at least, handed to the household head, and reallocated by him among the various members of the household. The man who brings in cash normally gets part of it back, the *sla bi* retains a part to cover household maintenance and repairs, purchase of land, and so on, and sometimes for his personal use; the remainder he hands to his wife, or his head wife if he has two. She in turn subdivides the amount into cash to be spent on food and cash used for the purchase of trade goods (i.e. goods for sale), and divides the latter sum between herself (if she is a trader) and other woman traders in the household. Profits from the women's trading return to the *sla bi* through the head wife, a fairly clear distinction being made between capital and profits, the individual traders retaining the capital. This income is then reallocated by the *sla bi* in the same manner as the wages of the men in the household. But this is a somewhat idealized picture, since individual members do often retain some of their earnings for personal use or for their own wives, or to cover personal obligations within or outside the household. Again, there is considerable variation in the balance of authority between the household head and the head wife, and the latter sometimes has virtually sole charge of household finance, members handing their contribution to the household budget directly to her. Or again, where there are several married couples within the household, each couple may be given a certain amount of autonomy in the management of its earnings. To discover the actual manner in which household economics were organized, and the extent to which the ideal system I have described is in fact followed, I compiled, with the help of a woman assistant, budgets of five New Krutown households over a period of one month each. The complexities of the system of budgeting made this a lengthy procedure and precluded the making of a larger sample, but the five households were chosen as representing five different types of household composition in terms of both kinship and occupations. The budgets were *not* intended to provide a basis for conclusions regarding standards of living. For this purpose, they would have had to be compiled over a much longer period of time, both because of the seasonal variation in employment, especially of fishermen and stevedores, and in order to cover the stevedores' intermittent absences from home.

The households were visited by my assistant every other day, or every day where the complexities of the budget made it necessary, for a period of one calendar month each during the period February–April 1959. This was during the dry season, which for fishermen and fish-sellers especially is a relatively prosperous period. On each visit, details of *cash* income and expenditure were entered in the form of individual budgets for each productive adult member of the household, 'productive' members being defined as those who were bringing in income from outside, whatever its source. Special attention was paid to the manner in which cash changed hands within the household, and to the specific financial responsibilities allocated to its various members. Food expenditure was listed under the budget of the person who actually spent the cash, usually the head wife, except that where she had sent other members out to shop for specific items and had given them the money for these items, the expenditure was listed under her budget rather than theirs. We did not attempt to assess the value of fish brought into the household by fishermen and fish-sellers, for consumption, or of capital in the form of either food or trade goods on hand at the beginning or the end of the month, except in the relatively simple case of Mrs. Togba's household. A fish-seller may bring home for consumption any fish which she has left over at the end of the day, but in other cases the women traders make a fairly clear distinction between consumption and trade goods. Mrs. Togba, for example, had on hand at the end of the month a whole sack of rice for trading, in addition to about half a sack which was being used by the household. For this reason, in the summarized budgets which follow, the difference between 'proceeds of trade' and 'expenditure on purchase of trade goods' does not accurately indicate the actual profits (or losses) the women were making, since some of them were selling trade goods which they had had on hand at the beginning of the month, and some retained trade goods at the end of the month. The names used in the budgets which follow are fictitious.

Budget A. Wiah household
The house was markedly superior to the four others, being built

of concrete blocks, with corrugated iron roof; electricity had been laid on and the house was well furnished. It had five rooms. The household was a relatively simple one consisting of two elementary families. The household head was a navigator employed in the Coast Guard Service, and his wife was earning a little money by sewing. They had a baby son, an older foster-son, and a girl who was Mr. Wiah's cousin also lived with them. The second couple were Mr. Wiah's uncle and the uncle's wife, who were working in partnership as fisherman and fish-seller, but not under the contractual agreement I have described above, so that it was impossible to separate their budgets. They had a baby daughter living with them. The fisherman (No. 3) did well during the month and gave unusual help towards the household budget. He also brought in a certain amount of fish for consumption. For the total household, however, it was a bad financial month, because Mr. Wiah's salary had dropped: previously, he had been employed at a salary of $65 by a shipping company, but he had changed employment because he wanted to work in Government service, and was now getting $45 a month.

The household budget was managed primarily by Mrs. Wiah, to whom her husband paid over half of his wages. The fisherman and his wife paid $25 directly to her, from their fishing profits, for the purchase of their food, and out of this she gave $5 back to No. 4 for the purchase of dried fish for trading. In this household, the manner in which income was redistributed among the members was affected by the fact that the two couples were approximately the same age—in fact the head was somewhat younger than his uncle.

Summary of Wiah household composition

Relationship to head	Age	Occupation
1. Head (M)	30	Navigator
2. Wife to 1	26	Seamstress
3. Uncle to 1	37	Fisherman
4. Wife to 3	25	Fish-seller
5. Son to 1 and 2	2	
6. Foster-son to 1 and 2	9	
7. Cousin to 1	9	
8. Daughter to 3 and 4	2	

K

CASH BUDGET IN DOLLARS

| | Individual members of household | | | Total |
	1	2	3 and 4	household
Income				
Cash in hand beginning month	5.00	30.00	15.00	50.00
Wages	45.00	—	—	45.00
Income from sewing	—	4.30	—	4.30
Proceeds of fish trade	—	—	42.25	42.25
Total income	50.00	34.30	57.25	141.55
Redistribution of income				
Paid over to head	+4.00	—	−4.00	—
Paid over to head wife	−25.00	+50.00	−25.00	—
Paid to 4 for purchase of trade fish	—	−5.00	+5.00	—
Redistributed income	29.00	79.30	33.25	141.55
Expenditure				
Purchase of food	—	50.54	3.00	53.54
Purchase of clothes	5.50	4.00	13.00	22.50
Purchase of wood, kerosene, light bulb	—	0.60	—	0.60
Payment of electricity bill	3.50	—	—	3.50
Purchase of trade fish	—	—	5.00	5.00
Medicine	—	0.82	—	0.82
Fish hooks, twine, etc.	—	—	3.20	3.20
Church collections	2.00	1.70	—	3.70
Contribution to savings club	—	9.00	—	9.00
Personal expenditure	0.10	—	—	0.10
Total expenditure	11.10	66.66	24.20	101.96
Excess income over expenditure	17.90	12.64	9.05	39.59

This influenced the respect due to the household head: theoretically, No. 3 and 4 should have paid over *all* their fish profits to No. 1, who would have returned part of the amount to them. In fact they gave $25 directly to Mrs. Wiah to cover the cost of their food and keep, and made a token payment of $4 to Mr. Wiah. The remaining $13.25 they kept for themselves. Mr. and Mrs. Wiah may have known about this, or they may not: our individual budgets were, of course, made privately.

Budget B. Nimely household

The house was of the more usual New Krutown type, with walls made of plaited mats and the roof of a type of tarred paper. The household contained one polygynous family, together with three adult relatives and two tenants. Its head was a mason employed at the time by a private individual. The two wives were both fish-sellers: both bought fish from the Mesurado Fishing Company for resale, and one also worked in partnership with an (unrelated) fisherman who lived in another part of New Krutown. The senior wife also sold goods, especially rice and sugar cane, on the general market, and her co-wife had supplementary income from her practice as a herbalist. The household also contained three temporary members at the time: the senior wife's brother, up from the Kru coast on a visit to Monrovia, and earning cash by fishing during his stay; the second wife's cousin, a stevedore, who, however, made no trip during the month—he was seeking a separate place to live and left the household at the end of the budget period; and the second wife's niece, a married woman of 19 years, from another part of Monrovia, staying with her aunt for the birth of her first child. Apart from this girl, the members of the household were all aged between 45 and 60, and there were no children. Of the two tenants, one was a married woman from Freetown who had come to visit her father, quarrelled with him, left his house and came to rent a room in this one. She had established a friendship with the two wives and, although she was paying rent (at $2.50 a month), sometimes ate with them. The other tenant was a man of 58 who lived in the house but ate with a female relative in a house near by.

The 'Jagba' mentioned in the budget was the head of the house next door, which also belonged to Mr. Nimely. He is a stevedore, and brother's son to the senior wife. Mr. Nimely built this second house for his present head wife because his first wife, now divorced, refused to share the main house with her. When he married for the third time, the first wife left him for good, and the second wife (now promoted to head wife) moved back into the main household to share with her new co-wife, leaving her nephew Jagba in charge of the second house. Jagba had living with him his own wife, her brother and the latter's child, as well as his own mother's brother and father's sister. Jagba paid no rent, but he 'paid respect' to Mr. Nimely by handing his wages over to him: in the month concerned, two-thirds of the wages were handed back. The food budgets for the two households were, however, managed quite separately.

The family considered that the month had been a relatively good one, financially, mainly because the dry weather permitted the fishermen to go out more regularly, and they had had especially good catches. The household depended very largely on the proceeds of fish sales during the month, and in addition both wives were bringing in fish for consumption. The head wife retained all the profits she had from trading, using them for food and also for the purchase of further trade goods—she bought a barrel of fish ($18) and a bag of rice ($7.50) during the month. The transfer of the second wife's profits from hand to hand illustrates the working out in practice of the ideal pattern. On the first day of the budget, the head wife gave her $7.50 for the purchase of trade fish. The second wife already had some capital on hand, in the form of both cash (included in the $12) and dried fish. In the subsequent week, she went out trading on four days and at the end of each day she handed to the head wife her day's profit, which varied between $2 and $3.50. During the whole month, she gave the head wife $29, being her entire profit from her fish sales, although she retained for herself her herbalist's income. The head wife handed the cash on to the household head, as the second wife brought it in. The household head paid over $13 to the senior wife to help with the household budget, and he also made a gift of $6.50 to his second wife. He paid a larger sum— $22—to a *megi* living elsewhere. Mr. Nimely and his two wives were all contributing to savings clubs of

Summary of Nimely household composition

Relation to head	Age	Occupation
1. Head (M)	50	Mason
2. Wife to 1	53	Fish- and general market-seller
3. Wife to 1	50	Fish-seller and herbalist
4. Brother to 2	58	Fisherman
5. Cousin to 3	45	Stevedore
6. Niece to 3	19	Nil
7. Tenant-visitor (F)	35	Nil
8. Tenant (M)	58	Petty trader

CASH BUDGET IN DOLLARS

	Individual members of household			Total household
	1	2	3	
Income				
Cash on hand beginning month	12.00	11.00	12.00	35.00
Wages	12.00	—	—	12.00
Proceeds of fish and other trade	—	48.25	29.00	77.25
Payment from patient	—	—	7.00	7.00
Payment of rent by 7 and 8	5.00	—	—	5.00
Received from Jagba from wages	23.38	—	—	23.38
Received from 5 and 6, from sale of fish	12.00	—	—	12.00
Received from 7, as repayment of debt	—	—	9.00	9.00
Payment from savings club	—	—	12.00	12.00
Total income	69.38	59.25	69.00	197.63
Redistribution of income				
Paid over to head	+29.00	−29.00	—	—
Paid over to head wife	−13.00	+42.00	−29.00	—
From 2 for purchase of trade goods	—	−7.50	+7.50	—
Gift from household head	−6.50	—	+6.50	—
Redistributed income	78.88	64.75	54.00	197.63
Expenditure				
Purchase of food	—	19.07	4.55	23.62
Purchase of clothes and trunk	—	5.50	10.00	15.50
Purchase of wood and kerosene	2.15	2.00	—	4.15
Repairs to roof	2.50	—	—	2.50
Purchase of trade goods	—	28.50	7.50	36.00
To *megi* for clothes, etc.	22.00	—	—	22.00
Returned to Jagba	19.00	—	—	19.00
Paid to savings club	7.50	1.00	3.00	11.50
To friend for saving	—	—	20.00	20.00
Farewell gift to 5	5.00	—	—	5.00
Gift to 6	—	—	3.00	3.00
Gifts to relatives outside	—	5.00	5.50	10.50
Transport	—	2.00	—	2.00
Total expenditure	58.15	63.17	53.55	174.87
Excess income over expenditure	20.73	1.58	0.45	22.76

various types: the second wife, for example, belonged to a group of twelve fish-sellers each of whom contributed $1 each Sunday and took it in turns to receive the lump sum of $12.

Budget C. Brown household

Mr. Brown's house was a seven-roomed one made of plaited mats with a corrugated iron roof. His household also was a polygynous one, and it was the most complex of the five in the variety of occupations followed by its members. Eight separate adults were normally bringing in cash. Mr. Brown was a self-employed carpenter, who worked on the premises and employed an apprentice —who lived elsewhere. His two wives were both market-sellers, but the senior wife was sick during the month so that the second wife had control of the food budget. Also living in the household were the head wife's three brothers—one single, one divorced, and one with a *megi* living in the house with him. One of the brothers, a stevedore, sailed during the month and had not returned by the time the budget was completed; the other two were a fisherman who also worked as a house painter, and a labourer employed by a private rubber company on Bushrod Island. There were four other adults: the household head's sister and niece, both divorced, both market-sellers, and the former's daughter, who was married but had not yet been collected by her husband, and finally the *megi* of the stevedore mentioned above. This girl, it was expected, would soon return to her family, and her lover was already paying dowry for another girl whom he hoped to marry.

The month when the budget was taken was considered to be quite a good one for the household, in spite of the expenses incurred over the senior wife's sickness and the fact that the second wife, who normally sells at the market, was too busy with household affairs to do any trading. Mr. Brown received, in addition to his income of $44.50 from his carpentry and painting, an instalment on the sale of a house which he had built. No payments were made over to him by any member of the household, even by the one wage-earner, the labourer. But all members of the household made some contribution to the budget of the head wife, or, when she fell sick at the end of the first week, of the second wife. The two market-sellers, Nos. 7 and 8, paid over almost all their profits to her, their own expenditure being limited to clothes and trade goods. The tribal association to which Mr. Brown contributed was

Summary of Brown household composition

Relationship to head	Age	Occupation
1. Head (M)	45	Carpenter
2. Head wife to 1	30	Market-seller
3. Wife to 1	32	Market-seller
4. Brother to 3	46	Fisherman and painter
5. Brother to 3	35	Stevedore
6. Brother to 3	24	Labourer
7. Sister to 1	38	Market-seller
8. Brother's child to 1 (F)	26	Market-seller
9. *Megi* to 5	25	Nil
10. Daughter to 7	15	Nil
11. Daughter to 7	13	
12. Sister's child to 1	5	
13. Daughter to 8	2	

CASH BUDGET IN DOLLARS

	Individual members of household								Total household
	1	2	3	4	5	6	7	8	
Income									
Cash on hand beginning month	40.00	3.00	8.00	2.00	—	0.50	12.00	2.50	68.00
Wages	—	—	—	—	8.00	16.00	—	—	24.00
Income, carpentry and painting	44.50	—	—	15.00	—	—	—	—	59.50
Proceeds trading and fish sales	—	4.25	—	6.25	—	—	6.45	13.75	30.70
Instalment on sale house	13.50	—	—	—	—	—	—	—	13.50
Allowance from divorced husband	—	—	—	—	—	—	—	8.00	8.00
Allowance from *megi* (outside)	—	—	—	—	—	—	—	5.00	5.00
Gift from relative (outside)	—	—	4.00	—	—	—	—	—	4.00
Total income	98.00	7.75	12.00	23.25	8.00	16.50	18.45	29.25	212.70
Redistribution of income									
Paid over to head wife	−15.00	+23.00	—	−3.00	—	−5.00	—	—	—
Paid over to 3, acting for 2	−25.00	−5.00	+58.25	−6.50	—	—	−5.00	−16.75	—
From 3 for purchase of trade goods	—	—	−12.50	—	—	—	—	+12.50	—
Gifts from household head	−3.50	—	—	—	—	—	+2.00	+1.50	—
Other gifts within household	—	—	—	—	−0.75	+0.75	—	—	—
Redistributed income	54.50	25.25	57.75	13.75	7.25	12.25	15.45	26.50	212.70
Expenditure									
Purchase of food	—	—	43.76	—	0.30	0.21	—	—	44.27
Purchase of clothes	14.50	2.50	4.35	5.75	—	—	3.75	5.20	36.05
Purchase of wood, kerosene, soap	—	—	5.00	—	0.40	1.90	—	—	7.30
Purchase of goods for trading	—	6.50	—	—	—	—	3.70	14.00	24.20
Payment, medicine and doctor	4.50	14.00	—	—	—	—	—	—	18.50
Payment to apprentice	7.50	—	—	—	—	—	—	—	7.50
Allowance to *megi* 9	—	—	—	—	2.00	—	—	—	2.00
Instalment on dowry payment	—	—	—	—	4.00	—	—	—	4.00
Transport	—	1.80	—	—	0.05	—	—	—	1.85
Contribution, tribal association	2.25	—	—	—	—	—	2.00	—	4.25
Gin, tobacco and other personal costs	7.00	—	—	0.30	—	—	—	—	7.30
Total expenditure	35.75	24.80	53.11	6.05	6.75	2.11	9.45	19.20	157.22
Excess of income over expenditure	18.75	0.45	4.64	7.70	0.50	10.14	6.00	7.30	55.48

a Bassa association, for both he and his second wife were Bassa, although they had long lived in the Kru community, being former residents of (Old) Krutown. The senior wife, on the other hand, was Kru. This was, in fact, one of only two or three mixed marriages in New Krutown, and the absence of the usual 'respect' payments to the household head may have been connected with this.

Budget D. Twe household
Mr. Twe's house was a solidly built one of pole and daub, painted white, with wooden shutters and a corrugated iron roof. It had seven rooms. At the time of the budget the household contained no one in full-time employment, and it was in fact chosen to show how interrelations within the household are affected by hard times. Its head was an elderly man who had worked in his youth as a stevedore, later as a missionary, and now held a more or less honorary appointment as a preacher at a local church. His wife, who baked and sold *fufu* (cassava cakes) virtually supported the household during the month, although even she did less well than usual because she had no help with the cooking and shopping and therefore less time for trading. The household also contained a second married couple: a man aged 31, Mr. Twe's cousin's grandson, and his wife. The former is usually employed as a checker on ships, and travels down the coast with them in this capacity. However, in the previous month, following the dispute between the shipping companies and the stevedores already mentioned, wage rates were increased and the company for whom he was working decided to cease carrying checkers on board, and rely rather on finding them at the several ports; he had therefore lost his job and was having difficulty in finding another. Previously, he had been the household's main bread-winner. His actual relationship with Mr. Twe fell into a special category, for his mother, having been childless for many years, prayed for a son and promised that if she bore one, she would 'give him to the church': when the child arrived, she gave him to Mr. Twe, who was her husband's father's cousin, to rear as his own son. However, the man (No. 3) retains contact with his real parents, for whom he was at the time of the budget building a house on the outskirts of New Krutown. His wife, who normally works as a fish-seller, was absent at Bomi Hills for two weeks during the month, and her brother (No. 5), a steve-

dore, returned from his ship only in the last week of the budget period. The household also contained three other adults: an old woman, nearly blind, who was Mr. Twe's sister; Mr. Twe's son by a former marriage, a 17 year-old boy still at school; and the great-grandson of another cousin of Mr. Twe, a young man who had worked as a driver but was out of work, not for the first time. The latter normally had his *megi* living with him, but she had returned to her own family for the birth of a baby. Finally, the tenant, who normally pays $3 a month for her room, paid no rent during the month. She is the daughter of Mr. Twe's next-door neighbour, and is supported jointly by her father and her *megi*; her own mother died and she could not get on with her stepmother, and therefore moved out of her father's house, although a child whom she had by an earlier *megi* remains there.

With three unproductive adults to support—as well as four children—the household had been badly off for some time, but in this particular month its members nearly starved: a total of $21 was spent on food, and no one was bringing in fish or other consumption goods. Of the total income of $149, $75 came in only in the last few days of the budget and did not go into the corporate budget at all. The stevedore returned with $20: this did not represent his total wage, since a large number of deductions are made

Summary of Twe household composition

Relationship to head	Age	Occupation
1. Head (M)	59	Retired preacher
2. Wife to 1	41	*Fufu* seller
3. Grandson to cousin of 1	31	Checker (unemployed)
4. Wife to 3	26	Fish-seller
5. Brother to 4	22	Stevedore
6. Sister to 1	70	Petty trader
7. Great-grandson to cousin of 1	22	Driver
8. Son to 1	17	Student
9. Son to 3 and 4	4	
10. Daughter to 3 and 4	7 months	
11. Niece to 2	8	
12. Nephew to 2	6	
13. Tenant (F)	23	Nil

CASH BUDGET IN DOLLARS

	1	2	3	4	5	6	Total household
Income							
Cash on hand beginning month	—	5.50	—	7.00	—	—	12.50
Wages	—	—	10.00	—	20.00	—	30.00
Proceeds of fish and *fufu* sale	—	40.25	—	10.00	—	0.76	51.01
Proceeds from sale of contraband goods	—	—	—	55.00	—	—	55.00
Gift from niece (outside)	—	—	—	—	—	0.50	0.50
Total income	—	45.75	10.00	72.00	20.00	1.26	149.01
Redistribution of income							
Paid over to head	+36.00	−20.00	—	—	−16.00	—	—
Paid over to head wife	−12.50	+28.50	−8.00	−8.00	—	—	—
Gift from head (1)	−3.00	—	—	—	—	+3.00	—
Wages 5 paid to sister	−16.00	—	—	+16.00	—	—	—
Contraband profit paid to 3	—	—	+55.00	−55.00	—	—	—
Redistributed income	4.50	54.25	57.00	25.00	4.00	4.26	149.01
Expenditure							
Purchase of food	—	20.47	—	—	—	0.93	21.40
Purchase of clothes	—	5.75	—	—	—	—	5.75
Purchase of wood and kerosene	—	1.50	—	—	—	0.10	1.60
Purchase of trade goods	—	4.10	—	—	—	2.51	6.61
Transport for wife	—	—	2.50	—	—	—	2.50
Building materials for parents' house	—	—	38.50	—	—	—	38.50
Gifts to relatives (outside)	2.75	—	—	—	1.00	1.50	5.25
Gifts to friends	—	—	—	—	1.50	—	1.50
Contribution to *panton*	—	—	—	—	1.00	—	1.00
Contribution to mother's *panton*	—	—	—	—	0.50	—	0.50
Church collection	—	0.10	—	—	—	—	0.10
Total expenditure	2.75	31.92	41.00	—	4.00	5.04	84.71
Excess of income over expenditure	1.75	22.33	16.00	25.00	—	—	54.30

from stevedore's wages before they reach home (Appendix B). Of the $20, he gave $16 to Mr. Twe, the remaining $4 being used for gifts and *panton* contributions, so that he retained nothing for himself. Mr. Twe, however, handed back the entire $16, not to the stevedore, but to the latter's older sister (No. 4). That is, the formalities were observed, respect was paid to the household head, but at the same time recognition was given to the existence of a second family unit within the household, even though the corporate household budget badly needed reinforcing. In fact, No. 4 subsequently handed some of the $16 over to Mrs. Twe, but this was after the end of the budget period. The second last minute addition to the total income of the household—though not to its corporate budget—was the sum of $55 brought back by No. 4 from Bomi

Hills as a result of her sale of contraband goods, which had previously been acquired by her husband. She handed the total profit to her husband, who used most of it for materials for the house he was building for his parents who, it will be recalled, were not part of the household. Normally, No. 4, who was a fish-seller, would have handed her profits to Mr. or Mrs. Twe, but in this instance Mr. Twe could not be told about the transaction because as a pastor and No. 3's 'father in god' he would certainly have disapproved. At the end of the month, therefore, no part of this $55 had gone into the corporate budget: the $8 which No. 4 had previously paid being profit from fish sales in the first week of the month, and the $8 which No. 3 had paid Mrs. Twe being part of a payment he had received for a short-term clerical job.

Budget E. Togba household

The last household was chosen because it had a female head. Mrs. Togba was a woman of 60 who had been married four times: once she had been divorced, and the remaining three husbands had died, the last one having left the house to her. She had two adult daughters, one married and living at Firestone plantation, the other living with a *megi* in Sinkor. Her household was a small one, as were most of those with female heads: she had two young women living with her. One, her sister's daughter, was a woman of 25 who had once been divorced and who had since had three *megi*, the last of whom was still paying her an allowance. Three of her children were also living in the household, the oldest being a girl of 10 years for whom she was still receiving an allowance from her divorced husband. The other two were the children of an earlier *megi*. The other young woman in Mrs. Togba's household was the daughter of another sister of Mrs. Togba, a girl of 19 who had for four years been the *megi* of a married 'civilized' man, from whom she was getting a liberal allowance; she was seven months pregnant at the time of the budget, and the relationship was probably sliding over into the more permanent one of 'outside wife'.

The only person actually earning money in the household was Mrs. Togba herself, a general market-seller, who had a roadside stand on the main road at which she sold such articles as rice, ground-nuts, soap and biscuits. The niece usually stays home to care for her three children, and she does the cooking. The grand-niece normally helps Mrs. Togba with trading, but at the time

Summary of Togba household composition

Relationship to head	Age	Occupation
1. Head (F)	60	Market-seller
2. Sister's daughter to 1	25	Nil
3. Sister's daughter's child to 1	19	Nil
4. Daughter to 2	10	
5. Son to 2	5	
6. Daughter to 2	2	

CASH BUDGET IN DOLLARS

	Individual members of household			Total household
	1	2	3	
Income				
Cash on hand beginning of month	6.00	8.00	2.50	16.50
Proceeds of trading	19.34	—	—	19.34
Allowance from divorced husband	—	12.00	—	12.00
Allowance from *megi*	—	20.00	44.00	64.00
Gift from own mother	—	4.00	—	4.00
Total income	25.34	44.00	46.50	115.84
Redistribution of income				
Paid over to head	+21.00	−15.00	−6.00	—
Redistributed income	46.34	29.00	40.50	115.84
Expenditure				
Purchase of food	26.96	—	3.50	30.46
Purchase of clothes	—	8.75	29.35	38.10
Purchase of wood	0.70	—	—	0.70
Purchase of trade goods	13.10	—	—	13.10
Payment to doctor	—	7.00	—	7.00
Transport	0.30	2.00	1.00	3.30
Church collection	1.85	—	—	1.85
Total expenditure	42.91	17.75	33.85	94.51
Excess income over expenditure	3.43	11.25	6.65	21.33

could not work because of her pregnancy. Nevertheless, the month
was a good one financially because the two girls received generous
allowances from their lovers and one from her ex-husband also.
The younger girl spent most of her allowance on clothes for herself and for the new baby, but both made payments for their food
and keep to Mrs. Togba, who managed the household budget.
Because the household was a simple one, in this budget we assessed
the value of goods which were on hand, in addition to cash, at the
end of the month. Mrs. Togba had about half a sack of rice for
food (value about $3.75), and, in addition, the following goods for
trading: ground peas (50 cents), rice ($7.50), soap (60 cents),
biscuits (43 cents), and flour ($2), totalling $11.03.

THE ROLE OF WOMEN IN HOUSEHOLD ECONOMY

Market-women buy fish for trade either from individual fishermen or from the Mesurado Fishing Company, whose headquarters
are about two miles from New Krutown. They buy imported trade
goods such as kerosene, cigarettes, flour and rice at ordinary retail
prices from the stores, and sell them in small quantities—cigarette
by cigarette—with a few cents profit on each. Palm-nuts, sugar
cane and cassava they buy from villagers who come to sell at the
market at the St. Paul bridge, and a certain amount of produce is
also grown by the women themselves—a very little in New Krutown, whose sandy soil makes cultivation difficult, the rest in villages in the vicinity. They sell their goods either at the main
Monrovia market, a distance of some four or five miles which they
normally have to walk, or at the roadside *en route*.

The importance of the women's trading activities to the household economy is apparent from all five budgets, and especially
from that of the Nimely household, where the proceeds of women's
trading amounted to 47 per cent. of the total income of the household (excluding cash on hand), and the Twe household, where the
equivalent figure was 78 per cent., and which was in fact almost
entirely dependent during the month on Mrs. Twe's *fufu* sales.
In all cases where the household contained women traders other
than the head, the women worked as a group, the head wife sharing
out cash for the purchase of trade goods, and the other women, in
return, handing their profits to her. This does not mean, of course,
that the latter make nothing for themselves, for they retain the

capital to use as they wish—for spending, for saving, or for the purchase of more trade goods. The woman who is a successful trader is, of course, likely to be given more capital for trading than is the one who makes poor profits. In the Nimely household, the head wife gave the second wife $7.50 during the month for buying trade goods; the latter spent this money on the purchase of fish, and she also sold other trade goods which she had on hand at the beginning of the month, making a total profit of $29, which she handed to the head wife as it came in. The capital of $7.50 she retained. This woman was considered a very good trader, and was investing money in a *neklondi* or savings club. In addition, she was paying some of her savings over to a friend for safe keeping. But by no means all of the women traders are so successful. One man complained to me:

My wife, she lose everything, even most of the capital. Everything she have, she spend, spend, spend—just like an American [i.e. a civilized] woman.

He compared her unfavourably with a former wife—who had left him:

I give her [the former wife] a packet of cigarettes, she twist small-small, and come back in the evening with 5 cents profit. I give her a carton, and she bring me back two cartons. I love that woman, she is like my ma, my heart was broken when she left me. Some time man has no work, woman must provide.

The seasonal and intermittent nature of much male employment emphasizes the household's underlying dependence on the women. Men out of work sometimes go fishing or painting houses—but only during the dry season; women on the other hand can go out trading all the year round, although it is sometimes difficult for them to get to the market during heavy rains. Now, women traders are a relatively new phenomenon among the Kru and there are very few in the home towns on the Kru coast, where indeed, a cash economy hardly exists. The new authority and independence which women therefore have in financial matters has profoundly altered relationships between the sexes, and this, plus the periodic absence of many of the men on trips down the coast, is the situation underlying the frequency of marital disharmony discussed in the last chapter.

THE KIN GROUP AND SOCIAL SECURITY

The Nimely, Brown and Twe households all contained adult men who were unemployed or only partially employed during the period when the budgets were made. These men were being supported by their respective households, the financial drain being hardest on the Twe household, which was also the one household whose head had no regular source of income. Members of the household are prepared to surrender a part, sometimes the major part, of their individual incomes because they can be fairly sure of support by the household in times of need. This is the basis on which the urban extended family rests. The occupational structure of the community is such that times of need recur frequently: fishermen may need support during the rainy season when storms prevent their going out to sea, and stevedores always need it in the periods—which at the shortest last a month—while they await the return of their ships. Indeed, without the support of the extended families, it is difficult to see how the stevedore system could operate, and this is presumably one reason why extended families are more common in the Kru communities, which also provide the majority of the stevedores. The Bassa, who also work in small numbers as stevedores, say that the Kru are more successful because they 'know how to look after one another'.

'Looking after one another' is not, however, limited to members of a household. Gifts frequently pass, as the budgets showed, between members of the household and relatives living elsewhere. Few are hesitant in asking kinsfolk for help, and such help would seldom be refused unless the requests are repeated too often and without justification. In the same way, a man who makes little real effort to find employment is likely to earn the disapproval of his household—as, in fact, was happening to No. 7 in the Twe household—and may eventually lose its support, although I never came across a case of such a man being actually turned out. On the other hand, the extended family system militates against the emergence of individualism, and this is one reason why the community remains an 'uncivilized' one in its standard and way of life. Ambitious young men tend to move out of the community and set up house elsewhere, where kinship obligations are less strong or at least more easily avoidable. This does not mean that New Krutown families discourage their children from getting educated: on the contrary, they usually want their sons, more particularly, to 'learn book' and find better-paid employment; even the impoverished Twe household was supporting such a student. But such young men are expected to conform to community norms in their attitudes and their behaviour. Thus, a young high school student who was being supported by his household, at considerable sacrifice on their part, complained that he could not do his homework because of the continuous household noise, and asked for a room of his own. 'We want none of your *kwi* ways here,' replied his aunt crossly.

Financial obligations also go beyond the household and the relatives, to the *panton*, the dako, and the tribe. The extent of these obligations was not fully apparent from the five budgets, because in many cases customary deductions are made before the wage comes into the household. Contributions of this kind seem to fall most heavily on the stevedores, or at least to be most regularly collected from them. The manner in which they receive their payment makes this a simple procedure: for each gang is paid at a set time, usually a few days after the end of the trip, at the Bureau of Labour. The various officials and chairmen therefore attend, or send representatives, on pay-days, to collect their dues. In our five sample families, only two stevedores were working during the month, and one had not returned by its end. The other, in the Twe household, made contributions both to his own and to his mother's *panton* chairman in Monrovia. To get a more complete picture of the stevedore's total financial obligations, we made an analysis of what happened to the *total* wages of twenty-four stevedores, and especially of that part of the wage which had gone by the time the men came back to their households after getting their pay. The analysis is given in Appendix B. All the men paid dues of 75 cents to the Kru Corporation, plus 25 cents to the Paymaster. Fifteen paid amounts varying between 25 cents and $1 to the chairman of their section within the Corporation, twenty-two had paid sums varying between 50 cents and $2 to their *dako* chairmen, and eighteen had paid similar amounts to their *panton* chairmen. Many had also made direct gifts to relatives before they reached their homes. In some cases, the total amounts deducted in this way from the wage-packet came to over a third of the total wage.

This budget analysis illustrates the manner in which members of the household form a co-operative economic unit, and the extent to which financial obligations extend beyond the household to the wider group of relatives, to people from one's 'home' town (even among second- and third-generation Monrovians), and to one's tribespeople in general. Kinship is a basic social institution in Monrovia: this applies to all tribal groups, although so far as the provision of social security is concerned, kinship rights and obligations operate more effectively among the coastal peoples who have long-established urban communities with their own internal structure and traditions, than among the scattered, and mostly young, immigrants from the interior tribes. Even for the 'civilized' tribesman, his ultimate security lies in the claims he can make on his kinsfolk for assistance, and this is one reason why such a man seldom completely disregards the financial claims made on him by his less-well-off kinsfolk, even if this means accepting a lower standard of living than his income permits. The strength of kinship ties arises in part from the lack of any formal provision by the Government for the assistance of Monrovians in need (see page 65 above), and on the other hand it disguises the necessity of making such provision. Family obligations are also regarded as important among Americo-Liberians; but the circle of relatives from whom one may expect assistance is limited and is not, as it is for the tribespeople, a part of a widening network of kinsfolk and tribespeople on whom one can hope to rely in times of need. Genevray mentions this point in his study of Grand Bassa County: among the Americo-Liberians,

l'économiquement faible ... tombera inéluctablement dans une misère profonde et se retrouvera, socialement, dans un standard de misère beaucoup plus bas que celui d'un indigène, car il ne profite même plus de la charité primitive qui est un solidarité beaucoup plus forte que le système civilisé du débrouillage individuel.[8]

This relative isolation of the Americo-Liberians was mentioned to me by several officials, themselves Americo-Liberians, in the course of discussions on the problems of administering the capital, and one asserted that this was why government practice was to provide grants and annuities to those in need (usually long-standing government employees or their widows) by special Acts of the Legislature passed in each individual case, rather than to attempt the formal provision of security benefits. But of course, Monrovia is not unique in this respect. In many African towns with a recent influx of immigrants, the administration relies upon the general acceptance of the duty of kinsfolk to help each other.

[8] Genevray, 1952, pp. 66–67.

L

People belong to kin groups and to tribes by the circumstances of their birth: they do not opt for membership of either, though they may choose to recognize or disregard the rights and obligations entailed. A different type of obligation—towards associations which individual members of the households had chosen to join —also showed up in the budgets, notably in church collections and contributions to savings groups. To these and the multitude of other types of association of people of similar interests, we now turn.

CHAPTER V

CHURCHES AND SOCIETIES

A GREAT deal of Monrovia's social life centres round voluntary associations. The adults in my sample included members of over one hundred and fifty such organizations, and there were at least another fifty which were established in Monrovia at the time but did not happen to be represented in the sample. A number of reasons can be advanced for this plethora of associations. In the first place, it is another reflection of the general insecurity of life in the capital: membership of associations is used, as tribal and kinship bonds are, to provide a measure of social security. A great number and variety of associations include mutual aid—especially burial insurance—among their aims. Secondly, Monrovia lacks a formal social structure through which its citizens might participate in the management of their affairs, and through which they can exercise leadership. Many of the associations provide such opportunities, and some have, indeed, almost as many office-holders as members. The same individuals often hold offices in a number of different associations. Thirdly, the multiplicity of associations arises from the correspondence of their membership not only with class, but also with tribal, cleavages in the overall population. Certain types of association are formed among the civilized, and membership of them is a mark of civilized status. Membership of organizations of this kind usually, but not invariably, cuts across tribal groupings. On the other hand, associations formed among the less-educated section of the population are almost always tribally homogeneous in their membership, aligning people of like interests within each of the urban tribal populations. In all social strata, the most frequent basis of association is community of religious interest. Church congregations may, in this context, be regarded as a special kind of voluntary association, not only because a great many people are first-generation church-goers, but also because of the frequency with which children of Christian families choose to join churches other than those to which their parents belong. All that I have said about voluntary associations in general applies also to churches. Because of the siting of missions, there is a strong correlation between denomination and tribe. Membership of specific churches is an index of civilized status. Churches provide a wide range of opportunities for people to exercise leadership roles. And they provide mutual aid: obligations of 'church people' to help one another are very strong. This was expressed very simply, if negatively, by one New Krutown woman: 'Why should I join the church?' she asked. 'My *panton* will bury me.'

TABLE 16. *Membership of associations*

1959 Sample Survey

Type of association	The five tribal communities	Mixed areas (Bishop's Brook and Old Krutown)	Kwi Street	Total
	Percentage of adults who were members			
(a) Churches and mosques	65	74	83	70
Attached clubs	6	3	5	6
YMCA and YWCA	3	6	14	4
(b) Traditional tribal societies	26	23	5	24
(c) Urban tribal societies	14	15	11	13
(d) Masonic-type lodges	2	6	7	3
(e) Football clubs	3	2	2	3
(f) Occupational associations	1	1	2	1
(g) Other	1	1	6	2

Total adult population   100% = 1,246   100% = 360   100% = 171   100% = 1,777

In Table 16, I have grouped voluntary associations in Monrovia under six main headings:

(a) Those arising from the sharing of religious interest, mainly church congregations but also clubs attached to them.

(b) Traditional tribal societies—especially Poro and Sande—to which many urban dwellers belong.

(c) Associations which have been formed within the urban tribal populations, grouping, for example, the women, or the young educated people, in each tribe.

(*d*) Masonic lodges and organizations with similar aims and ritual, whose members are primarily drawn from the civilized population.

(*e*) Football clubs and teams, which are the only form of sports association in Monrovia.

(*f*) Associations of people sharing a common occupation, mainly professional.

(*g*) 'Other' associations listed in the table are primarily of the types formed among the civilized: crowds, fraternities and sororities, glee clubs, philanthropic associations, and so on.

In terms of the numbers of members, the six types of association fell into the order in which I have listed them. The importance of religion as a basis of association is very obvious: two-thirds of the adults in the predominantly uneducated communities belonged to churches or mosques, and in the one predominantly 'civilized' area the proportion was over 80 per cent. In the first part of this chapter, therefore, I discuss the nature and role of religious organizations, especially the Christian churches, and in the second part I discuss certain other types of voluntary association.

Liberia was envisaged by her founders as a Christian state with an evangelical mission, and indeed it is said that one name which was considered for its capital city was 'Christopolis'. The close interconnexion of church and state is implicit in the political ideology of the republic, and few public speeches omit some reference to this fact. I quote from one of President Tubman's speeches:

> When I state that the history of the Church is coeval with that of the founding of the state I do not intend only to imply that that is a thing or fact apart; but to give the impression that their respective fabrics are indissolubly interwoven . . . You may be assured that Liberia, having always been, shall continue to be a Christian state. . . .[1]

The exact nature of the connexion has, however, never been made very clear, and there is no single established church. In a sense, one might say that Christianity itself is 'established', since officers of Government are expected to be Christians and usually are, in fact, members of certain specific congregations—a point to which I return later. However, the Muslim faith has long been followed

---

[1] Speech made by the President at a luncheon given by the National Baptist Convention, Cleveland, Ohio, 1954.

by sections of the Vai and neighbouring tribes. Until recently, Islam has been largely a rural phenomenon, but the appearance, in recent years, of wealthy Muslim merchants in Monrovia, together with the incorporation into political life of larger numbers of tribespeople of Muslim origin, have led to some querying of the precise interconnexion between church and state. This has not yet seriously affected the social order. In the absence of a reliable population figure for the republic—variously given as three-quarters of a million and two and a half millions—estimates of the proportion who are Christians and who are Muslims can be little more than guesswork. Nor was the topic covered in the 1956 census of Monrovia. Of the adults in my own sample survey, 59 per cent. were Christians and 13 per cent. were Muslims, and I believe this may also provide a rough indication of the proportions in the overall urban population.

THE MOSQUES

Monrovia has today two mosques: one small one, hardly distinguishable from the surrounding houses, in Vaitown, and the main and more imposing edifice in the Town Centre, largely supported by Mandingo merchants. Those Lebanese who are Muslims are Shia's and do not normally worship at the mosque, nor do they have a separate one of their own. There is, in addition, an Ahmaddiyya Muslim mission which holds prayers in the missionary's house, but its following is small. That the mosques are well attended is apparent to anyone who passes by at prayer time. Of the adults in our sample survey, twice as many Muslims as Christians were regularly attending their place of worship, and three-quarters of the Muslims claimed that they had, in fact, attended prayers at least once a day during the four weeks preceding the interview.

The relationship of the mosque with the state is a peculiar one. The main mosque, which was built in 1953, was dedicated by President Tubman, at a ceremony also attended by ex-President King and the Vice-President. The Imam is commonly referred to, both in conversation and in the press, as 'the Muslim Bishop'. In 1958, the officiating Imam, a naturalized Liberian originating from Guinea, died, and was buried with full military honours. As is the custom with leading dignitaries in Liberia, his cortège was escorted by a battalion of the Liberian Frontier Force, and the mourners included many senior government officials. In the same year, the marriage took place, in the mosque, of a Mandingo diamond merchant and a woman from an influential Christian family, of Americo-Liberian-Vai origin, and this most unusual event was attended by members of the élite. But Muslims, however rich they may be, are not accepted into middle- or upper-class society, and they do not hold government positions—which sometimes creates an awkward situation *vis à vis* diplomats and visiting dignitaries from other African states. Among the 188 entries in the Who's Who section of the 1956 *Yearbook*,[2] there was only one professing Muslim, and he was a tribal representative from Cape Mount. Persons originally Muslim who enter government service profess no religion or become, nominally at least, members of one or other of the Christian churches. In fact, most conversions take place at school: of 500 school children who filled in a questionnaire for me, thirty had Mohammedan fathers, but only four were themselves Muslims, and fourteen had already joined one or other of the Christian churches. For this reason, some Muslims prefer not to send their children to school or, if they are wealthy enough, they send them to schools in neighbouring countries—especially in Freetown—or abroad. By and large, however, Monrovia's Muslim population is an uneducated one. Of the adult Muslims in my sample, 86 per cent. were illiterate and only 4 per cent. had got as far as first-year high school—and of the latter, three had been educated in Freetown. Among the illiterate majority were some who claimed knowledge of Arabic, but real knowledge of either spoken or written Arabic is rare. There are no organized Islamic schools in Monrovia, nor, so far as I am aware, anywhere else in the republic.

Islam is, then, continuously losing that section of its younger population which opts for a Western-style education and for careers in government. There is no question, as yet, of the Muslim faith offering the educated an acceptable alternative to Christianity—as it does in Freetown, for example.[3] Islam is commonly said to be gaining adherents in the *rural* areas, and spreading to new tribes. There was, however, no evidence of this in my sample survey of Monrovia: apart from one or two cases where Vai or Mandingo men had married women from other tribes and the women had become Muslims, there were no instances of persons other than

[2] Cole (ed.), *The Liberian Yearbook, 1956*, RL, pp. 211–78.
[3] See Banton, 1957, chap. vii.

Vai, Gola, Mende and Mandingo tribespeople professing the Mohammedan faith.

THE CHURCHES

The Christian population worships in at least forty different church buildings operated by some twenty different denominations. The majority of denominations are connected, some closely, some very tenuously, with foreign, usually American, missions. The latter include both white and Negro organizations, and they also include both the long-established American denominations and the relatively new ones which are often referred to as 'sects'. Because religious bodies which are called 'sects' in America are often established and respectable churches in Liberia, I prefer to use the word 'denomination', in this context, for organizations of both kinds.

Four denominations were already operating in Monrovia in 1848 when the republic was declared: the Baptists, Methodist Episcopalians, Protestant Episcopalians, and Presbyterians. By 1900, Lutheran, African Methodist Episcopal, and African Methodist Episcopal (Zion) churches had also been founded, the second of these being the main Negro offshoot of the American Methodist Episcopal church, the third a church which separated in America on grounds of dogma and ritual from the second. After a false start in the nineteenth century, the Roman Catholic church was permanently established in the early 1900's. Some idea of the relative strength of these eight denominations in the republic today may be gained from the membership figures given in the 1956 *Yearbook*,[4] although I am not sure whether the basis of computation is strictly comparable from one denomination to another, and the figures for Baptists are incomplete because there are, in fact, four and not only two Baptist conventions operating.

Methodist Episcopal	17,351
Roman Catholic	11,000
Liberian Baptist Missionary and Educational Convention	5,200
National Baptist Mission (USA)	3,000
Protestant Episcopal	7,391
Lutheran	5,000
African Methodist Episcopal (Zion)	2,500
African Methodist Episcopal	1,700
Presbyterian	960

[4] Cole, op. cit., pp. 161–2.

Of these, the relatively small Presbyterian church has been independent since 1868, and the Liberian Baptist Missionary and Educational Convention also operates without foreign assistance. The rest are under varying degrees and types of control by the parent organizations in America. Usually, mission activities are financially supported from abroad, but the churches, in the coastal towns at least, get considerable local support. All eight denominations have at least one church building in Monrovia, but mission work in the capital is confined to the operation of schools, and, in the case of the National Baptist Mission, the maternity hospital.

A second group of churches comprises those of seven American missions which have founded churches in Monrovia since the 1930's, although some were operating in other parts of Liberia before this period. Three of them are of Pentecostal type—that is, they stress the importance of the 'pentecostal experience', the filling of the apostles with the Holy Ghost at the time of Pentecost, ecstatic participation and 'speaking in tongues' being an important part of their services. Of these three churches, one, the Assembly of God, has white missionaries, while the other two, the Pentecostal Assemblies of the World, and the Church of God in Christ, are both American Negro organizations. The Seventh Day Adventists, Jehovah's Witnesses, and the Ba'hai faith also have churches in Monrovia—the last-named being, correctly speaking, a syncretist rather than a Christian cult.

Finally, there are a number of independent local churches—the 'Pentecostal', 'Apostolic', 'Holy Ghost', and 'prophets'' churches—which have been formed in Monrovia since the Second World War, usually by separation from the churches of one or other of the Pentecostal missions, or less usually from the Baptists. Most are operated by local Monrovians, who are usually members of the community in which the church building stands. In doctrine they do not differ greatly from the mission churches: the mission's attitude to polygyny among its congregation has been a frequent cause of dissension, but few, if any, of the local separatist churches explicitly permit polygyny.[5] Rather they have arisen through a combination of the initiative of some religiously inspired individual —they are often referred to, in fact, as Mr. X's or Mrs. Y's church —and the desire of specific groups of people, often members of a local community, to have a church of their own. Their services are

[5] An exception is the local mission of the Nigerian Church of the Lord.

characterized by a high degree of participation by the congregation;
by the giving of individual testimonies; by the prominence given to
singing and dancing, drums, rattles and tambourines being used as
accompaniment, by ecstatic experience and 'speaking in tongues',
and by spirit healing. There are at least a dozen churches of this
type in Monrovia, including three in New Krutown alone. Of
similar type are two churches which are, in fact, mission churches
of separatist groups from other African territories: the Church of
the Lord from Nigeria—which has been described by Parrinder in
his study of the churches at Ibadan,[6] and the Musama Disco-
christo church from Ghana.[7] Most of these churches are of Pentecostal type, and I refer to them below as the 'Pentecostal churches.'

Church membership and social status

We have seen in the first chapter how the professing of Christianity, the wearing of Western-style dress, and the use of the English
language, were the main cultural features differentiating the
Americo-Liberian community from the surrounding tribespeople,
and became the three chief characteristics of the Americo-Liberian
way of life. Today, the professing of Christianity remains a basic
requirement of 'civilized' status, but does not in itself confer that
status, for in Monrovia the majority of the uneducated are also
Christians. Rather, it is membership of specific church congregations—which is not the same thing as specific denominations—
which indicates one's social position. Uneducated tribespeople in
tribal dress are seldom seen in the fashionable churches in the
Town Centre, and some of them say that they have in the past
been turned away from such churches; in any case, most prefer
to worship in the smaller churches which hold services in the vernacular, or at least provide interpretation into it. Therefore, the
civilized and uncivilized, even where they are members of the
same denomination, do not meet in the same congregations. The
division of the Christian population among the many congregations
thus coincides with the dichotomy of the population into 'tribal'
and 'civilized' elements, and helps to maintain this dichotomy
rather than break it down.

The great majority of the civilized population belong to churches
of the first group I have listed, that is, to those denominations
which have long been established in Liberia, and, in particular, to

[6] Parrinder, 1953, p. 123.   [7] See Baeta, 1961.

the Methodist, Baptist, Protestant Episcopal or Roman Catholic churches. Each of these denominations, except the Protestant Episcopal has, in addition to its main church or cathedral in the Town centre, small local churches in or near the tribal communities: the Methodists and Roman Catholics in the Kru communities, and the Baptists in the Bassa Community, corresponding with the rural areas in which their work is concentrated. The Protestant Episcopal church has only one congregation—at its Pro-Cathedral in the Town Centre; its lack of a following among the uneducated probably arises from the fact that its mission work has centred on Cape Mount, which is a Mohammedan area, so that such converts as it has gained have been primarily those who have passed through its high school at Robertsport or the residential college which it

TABLE 17. *Religious affiliations of the élite*

Compiled from the Who's Who section of the 1956 *Yearbook* of Liberia

	Men	Women	Total
Protestant Episcopal	69	5	74
Methodist Episcopal	35	8	43
Baptist	15	1	16
Presbyterian	7		7
African Methodist Episcopal	6		6
Roman Catholic	4	1	5
'Christian'	3		3
Muslim	1		1
Unstated*	33		33
Totals	173	15	188

* There appeared to be no special reason for omission to state religious affiliation.

operates in the Central Province. In addition, the formality of its services, compared with those of the Methodists and Baptists, affects its lack of popularity, and this is also true of the Roman Catholics. But whatever the reasons, the Protestant Episcopal church draws its members almost exclusively from the civilized population, and is the favoured church of the élite, within that population, as it is among upper-class Negroes in the United States.[8] Clear confirmation of this is provided by tabulation of the

[8] Myrdal, 1944, p. 865.

Liberian entries in the Who's Who section of the 1956 *Yearbook* of Liberia. Of those who stated their religious affiliations, no less than half belonged to the Protestant Episcopal church, one in four was a Methodist, and all (except, of course, the one Mohammedan) belonged to one or other of the long-established denominations (Table 17). Presidents have in the past normally been members of the Protestant Episcopal church, although the present President of the republic is a Methodist.

The overall class-patterning of religious affiliations was apparent from the results of the sample survey of eight residential areas (Table 18). In the predominantly civilized area, Kwi Street, the bulk of the population was Methodist, Baptist, Roman Catholic, or Protestant Episcopalian. In the tribal communities, on the other hand, while the Methodists and Baptists had large followings, the Pentecostal-type churches, taken as a whole, claimed more adherents than any other denomination.

TABLE 18. *Religion and residential area*

	The five tribal communities	The two mixed areas	Kwi Street	Total sample population
				Percentage of adults
Methodist	12	25	35	17
Pentecostal*	15	13	3	14
Baptist	12	4	6	10
Roman Catholic	5	6	16	7
Protestant Episcopal	4	8	19	6
Other churches†	4	8	1	5
Muslim	15	13	4	13
Pagan or nil	33	22	17	29
Total	100% (1,216)	99% (342)	101% (166)	101% (1,724)

* Including 'Pentecostal' 185 persons; Holy Ghost 12; Assembly of God 10; Holy Cross 10; Church of the Lord 5; other prophets' churches 4; Apostolic 6.
† Including Lutheran 55 persons; Jehovah's Witnesses 11; Seventh Day Adventist 6; Presbyterian 3; African Methodist Episcopal 2, and AME (Zion) 2.

Had the sample areas been differently chosen, the distribution of Methodists, Baptists, and Pentecostalists might have varied— for my sample included New Krutown, which has three separate Pentecostal churches and probably the greatest concentration of

Pentecostalists. But the general popularity of these new churches is certain, and this is the more remarkable since they operate relatively few schools, while other denominations make their converts primarily from the schools. With one interesting exception, the Pentecostal congregations are predominantly uneducated: of the Pentecostalists in our sample, two-thirds were illiterate and only 5 per cent. had entered high school; that is, they were in this respect the antithesis of the Protestant Episcopal congregation. They also included more women than did other congregations (Table 19).

TABLE 19. *Characteristics of the main denominations*

Percentage of total adherents of the denomination who:

	Were illiterate	Had entered high school	Were women	Were regular attenders	Were office holders
Pentecostalist	67	5	55	43	36
Methodist	49	22	47	41	25
Baptist	45	19	45	42	15
Roman Catholic	28	32	32	40	5
Protestant Episcopal	18	37	36	23	12

They had a much smaller proportion of nominal adherents—43 per cent. had attended Sunday service four times in the four weeks preceding the interview, compared with 23 per cent. of the Protestant Episcopalians. Similar contrasts would probably have appeared had it been possible to isolate figures for the several Methodist and Baptist congregations. The figures I have given only reflect a situation obvious enough in Monrovia, since the small local churches are invariably packed, while the large fashionable ones in the Town Centre are, except on special occasions, poorly attended. The decline of religious fervour among the civilized is deplored by many of the older people among them, and it seems to be related to the disappearance of the old, close-knit, Americo-Liberian community in Monrovia:

In my young days we always went to Sunday School and everyone had to go to church, sometimes twice on Sunday. Nobody would dare to stay home. People were friendly and all day long on Sunday you saw children carrying food to their family people (i.e. in other households). It's not the same any more. Now they drive in their cars, they go to their rubber farms . . . Oh, my people. Only us old ones remember the Lord.

For a great many of the civilized, church membership has become largely a question of social status, and has little more significance than membership of other types of association. For the uneducated who are Christians, on the other hand, much of their social life centres on their churches, which take on something of the aspect of community centres. In this respect certain small, local Baptist and, more especially, Methodist congregations have more in common with the separatist Pentecostal churches than with their parent church in the Town Centre.

The significance of the Pentecostal churches

For a description of the main features of the services, I have chosen one of the separatist Pentecostal churches in New Krutown.

At about 10 to 11 o'clock on Sunday morning, the church bell—which, suitably enough in this community of seafarers, is an old ship's bell—peals out. The white-surpliced, black-capped choristers (mainly women, with a male leader) form into procession and start singing hymns as they make their way towards the church. This is the sign for members of the congregation to hurry to the church, and they arrive in their best clothes—the women in lappas and head-ties, the men in Western dress. Inside the church, the men seat themselves on the right of the preacher, the women on the left; the choir enters, still singing, and takes its place on the dais in the front; their song reaches a mounting crescendo and, at a sign from the choir leader, the drummers beat the rhythm to a close.

The service is made up of hymns, prayers, scriptural readings, the lifting of the collection, the giving of individual testimonies, and the sermon or, frequently, several sermons by different preachers—and it seldom lasts less than three hours, usually much longer. Since there are no scriptural texts in Kru—or at least none available to the general public—the readings are made in—halting—English, and immediately translated by the reader into fluent and voluble Kru. Prayers are made by the preachers—with interruptions from the congregation—and there is also a period of simultaneous individual prayer, which gives a weird impression of mounting anger as voices are raised one above another, shouting requests at the Almighty. This period is brought to a close by the preacher's leading the congregation into simultaneous recitation of the Lord's Prayer. Another part of the service is allocated to the giving of individual testimonies, which most frequently relate how the Lord has helped the testifier or his family in times of sickness or trouble, but sometimes simply allow individual members the opportunity to lead the congregation into prayer or further singing. As in all parts of the service, the congregation interrupts with cries of 'Amen' or 'Praise the Lord', and the drummers and choristers urge the speaker on. At collection time, individual members of the congregation, more usually the women, make their contribution publicly; the singing continues and some of the older women dance ecstatically, while others leap up to wipe the sweat from the brow of a good dancer. The service may include 'healing' or anointing with holy oil: at one such ceremony, the daughter of a prominent member of the congregation, a girl about to sit a school examination, was thus anointed by the 'bishop' to bring her luck and ward off evil influences. The sermons are delivered in a highly dramatic manner, and often the preacher himself breaks into song. I heard one fiery young preacher deliver his entire sermon calypso fashion, to the great delight of the congregation. The themes of the sermons fall into two broad categories: that is, they tend to be concerned either with the virtues of good neighbourliness, or with inveighing against the ways of 'the world' and in particular its practice of drinking, smoking, fornication and corruption. Very often, 'the world' is explicitly identified with the *kwi klo*, the civilized town [which roughly speaking means the locality which I have called the Town Centre], and attention is often drawn to the falseness of its version of Christianity: 'In vain do they worship me, teaching for doctrine the commandments of men' was the text of one such sermon. 'Not everyone that saith unto me, Lord, Lord, shall enter into the Kingdom of Heaven' (Matt. vii).

It is the singing which holds the service together. There are no hymn books—the worshippers are in any case mostly illiterate—but since the words are simple and repetitive, the congregation easily follows the choir. In some separatist churches new hymns are composed, but this one uses the hymns of the mission churches, although these are not easily recognizable as the tempo quickens and changes to jazz rhythm. 'Abide with me' is popular; so are 'We thank you, Jesus, healer of all diseases', 'Jesus is passing this way', 'Take the world and give me Jesus', 'There is honey in the rock for you'. These phrases are repeated over and over again, with occasional antiphonal variations by individual singers, for as much as half an hour. This has a peculiarly hypnotic effect, and in the course of the singing several members of the congregation or the choir—almost always women in either case—become 'inspired' and fall to the floor making spasmodic jerky movements while muttering unintelligible sounds—'speaking in tongues'. Those standing near by look after them and gradually calm them down.

I or one of my assistants attended services at five different separatist churches, whose ritual appeared to be broadly similar to that of the church I have described. Some lay greater emphasis on the rites of baptism, others place great importance on the relation of dreams and prophecies, which most frequently have to do with the fate awaiting the rich, the corrupt, and the greedy:

. . . There I saw a man with a light skin inside the coffin groaning very uneasy. . . . When coming back, we reached the same place of this man in the coffin, I saw the whole place covered with ants. . . . Then I asked the soldier in spirit, 'What has this man done so much on earth?' It seemed the man in the coffin heard the question. He answered: 'I ate one poor boy's money the other day, whom I promised I would find some work for, whereas I knew I had no work to give him. This made God vexed and brought me here.' Then the soldier answered and said: 'Don't mind him, this man on earth had great influence, he could do anything he liked then, but here we can do anything we like unto him.' Immediately I woke up and it was a dream.

The Christian festivals are celebrated in these churches in a highly dramatic manner. In the church whose services I have described, for example, on Good Friday, at midnight, the congregation walk in black-robed silent procession to the graveyard, to 'bury the Lord', and return, white robed and singing joyfully, on Easter morning to 'bring him back to the church'. Some of the separatist congregations wear a special form of dress: worshippers at the Church of the Lord, for example, wear white robes with red sashes, and their annual candle-light procession, at the end of a period of fasting, to a feast on the 'Holy Mount Taborrah' (Lighthouse Hill) is a dramatic and exciting affair. Surprisingly enough, the one communion service I succeeded in attending—again at the Pentecostal church whose service I have detailed above—was a very quiet and decorous ceremony of conventional Nonconformist type, involving the passing around, by the elders, of trays of small individual glasses of wine and plates of neatly diced bread, with little singing and no ecstasies. At one other church the Last Supper is re-enacted, the worshippers washing one another's feet and sitting around a table after the pattern of Da Vinci's painting, a copy of which hangs on the wall.

The most obvious point about the services and religious celebrations is that people enjoy them. 'Come and enjoy yourselves spiritually', reads an advertisement for a celebration of the Church of the Lord. In many respects the rituals and practices of the churches seem to be identical with those of Negro cults in America, and

V *a*. Stevedores returning from trip

V *b*. Market sellers

VI *a*. Vaitown women at Ramadan

VI *b*. New Krutown choristers

they have similar functions. Fausset, for example, ascribes one role of cults in Philadelphia to the relieving of psychic tensions, especially among southern-born Negroes confronted for the first time with the complexities of northern, urban life,[9] and this situation is paralleled in Monrovia. The singing, dancing, and ecstatic experience, allow an outlet for pent-up conflicts and frustrations to people who have little other opportunity to let off steam. The question arises, to what extent do these cults, transplanted to Africa, combine the new Christian doctrines and practices with the traditional tribal ones? In fact, all the churches are fervently Biblical in doctrine, and the preachers inveigh against the pagan gods. But certain tribal practices have been carried over and adapted and these, although not central to the doctrine and *raison d'être* of the churches, help to knit the new institutions into the existing social fabric. I have mentioned in a previous chapter that in New Krutown a girl, after her marriage or after the birth of her first child, dresses up and shows herself to the congregation. In other Kru communities, where the church influence is less strong, a specific traditional women's society has charge of dressing such girls and conducting them around the town. Again, certain familiar rituals of protective magic have been taken over: in the anointing with holy oil, which I have mentioned in the description of a Pentecostal service, the actual aim was to ward off 'evil intent' (witchcraft), which might be expected from those jealous of the student's prowess. Similarly, an evangelist (actually a Methodist) told me that by use of the holy oil he protected himself from harm when he visited his pagan home village. Again, some churches prohibit the attendance of menstruating women, others demand sexual abstinence at certain times. One divorce suit at least was instigated by the refusal of a woman to sleep with her husband while she was preparing the sacramental bread and wine.

The Pentecostal service allows a great deal of participation by ordinary individuals who are members of the congregation. The churches also provide many formal offices: rather more than one in three of the Pentecostalists in my sample were choristers, deacons, elders, preachers, treasurers, or had some other church title. The preachers and officials of the churches are more usually men, but the women hold their own prayer meetings during the week, and at the Sunday service, although the sermon is usually

[9] Fausset, 1944, p. 87.

M

preached by a man, it is the women worshippers, especially the
older ones, who are for much of the time the centre of attention
and whose singing and dancing set the tone of the service. In addition, the women are rather more vociferous than the men in advo-
cating asceticism, particularly the prohibition of drinking and
smoking, and they often use this prohibition in an attempt to keep
their men in order. Instances of conflict between family and church
obligations are not at all unusual. I described in an earlier chapter
one quarrel which arose out of a husband's jealousy of his wife's
prominence in church affairs. On another occasion, a man sued
the church for keeping his wife too long at choir practice, so that
she could not cook his meal. For there are many households whose
members are divided among several congregations, and marriages
in which only one spouse, more usually the woman, is a church
member.

The service permits self-expression to the individuals who take
part in it. But individual prayers, testimonies and experiences of
spirit possession take place within a congregation of people, and a
congregation which is very strongly bound together by the emo-
tionally charged atmosphere induced by the drums and the repetitive singing. This community of emotional experience, which is the
basis of most rituals, has a particular attraction in the urban situation where, compared with the smaller-scale tribal communities,
people are 'out on their own'. The service permits self-expression,
and at the same time escape from one's self through identification
with the rest of the congregation. A member of one of the (Apostolic) churches, whose worshippers wear uniform white robes, explained to me that when they were wearing the robes, individual
members were not always easy to identify—'it makes us feel together . . . we are all the same, it doesn't matter whether you're a
big shot or not', and at the same time it gave them a greater feeling
of freedom to 'let themselves go'. The 'self-expression' of individuals is a question of emotional outburst rather than one of articulate statement. In the loud, angry-sounding individual prayers, the
worshippers draw attention to themselves as individuals, above
the babble of tongues, reflecting a demand for recognition of one's
identity in the chaotic, impersonal babel of the urban situation.
For a more articulate statement of the underlying attitudes and
points of view which bring these particular people together in a
congregation, one must look elsewhere.

The words of the hymns provide one clue: 'Take the world and give me Jesus' in the church whose service I have described; in another congregation, which composes its own hymns: 'Where will we be, on that morning when the Lord will come?, Where will the rich man be, on that morning when the Lord will come?', or 'Oh Father Abraham, I pray for the day when we can all eat around the same table'. For these are congregations of the under-privileged, and the sermons are, more often than not, *against* rather than for: against the wickedness of the 'world', the materialism, the corruption, the immorality, the greed and hypocrisy of the rich and the influential. Through their teaching of the virtues of asceti-cism, the churches *reject* what their members believe—rightly or wrongly—to be the characteristics of civilized society. One young Pentecostalist put this to me quite explicitly: 'Why don't we drink and smoke? Because we hate the things of the world, and love the things not of the world. The world drinks and smokes, so we don't.' Similarly, a local evangelist delivered to me a long sermon on Monrovia as the 'whore of Babylon'. The growth and popularity of the churches of this type, then, can be seen as one example of a process which has occurred in many parts of the world, at different periods of history. Nottingham, for example, describes how churches originally fundamentalist and protesting against the social order gradually become established and tend to endorse the *status quo*:

But throughout history from within established religions there have been periodic resurgences of groups dedicated to a thorough-going observance of what they believed to be a pure form of a traditional religious ethic which their society had neglected. These resurgent groups are at first quite small ... little islands of active faith and ethical strictness in a wicked world. Their emergence coincides as a rule with some degree of social, economic, and political upheaval within the larger society ... members are frequently, although not exclusively, recruited from those who have reason to feel themselves to be unjustly treated under existing systems of social arrangement.[10]

Paradoxically, a similar situation underlies the popularity of the one Pentecostal church whose membership is mainly civilized and Americo-Liberian. This church, the Lighthouse Full Gospel Church, was founded in 1936 by an American Negro immigrant, the late Sister Leila January, with the explicit aim of 'introducing

[10] Nottingham, 1954, p. 50.

the Baptism of the Holy Ghost to the Americo-Liberian element in Monrovia'.[11] Today, it is known as the church of her successor, Sister Blatch, who is in fact of Kru origin but long identified with the Americo-Liberian population. In addition to her religious duties, Mrs. Blatch runs, in a building behind her church, a small workshop where the flags of the republic are made, the lone star and white stripes being appliquéd by hand-operated sewing machines. Her husband, a former West Indian who immigrated in 1930 under the influence of the Garvey movement, assists in the running of the workshop and is also one of the few male officials in her congregation. Now apart from the fact that the service at Mrs. Blatch's is in English—many of the speakers using the local, creolized version of English—in its main aspects its ritual is identical with that of the Pentecostal service I have described. The singing, however, is accompanied by tambourines only, and the rhythms are those of Sankey and Moody choruses rather than of syncopated jazz. There is less dancing, and the dancing which does take place is much more formal: at the end of the service, the choristers, who are also the 'Band of Missionary Saints', perform a sort of ritual quadrille, shaking hands with one another to show their fellowship. The dress of the congregation is of Western type —although (unlike that of most other upper-class congregations) not particularly fashionable. Head-ties occasionally appear in the congregation, but the 'Saints' wear hats. The collection plate contains many dollar notes, while in the other Pentecostal churches it is usually filled with coins. But the ecstasies, the testimonials, the individual angry prayers remain, and the church lays great emphasis on healing by prayer and anointing with holy oil. The preachers and officials, and also the members of the congregation, are mainly women. Most are drawn from the poorer, less influential Americo-Liberian families, but they also include several women members of the social élite. Frequently, such women are also members of the more conventional upper-class churches. One, a Protestant Episcopalian who is also one of Sister Blatch's 'Band of Saints', explained to me:

Some months ago my sister was ill with what seemed to be asthma. The hospital gave her up, so we called in . . . [several foreign doctors], but they offered no hope. So I went to see Mrs. Blatch, and she called together a group of Sisters, and we all prayed all night, sanctifying the

[11] *The Liberian Woman Missionary*, Monrovia, 3, 2, March 1956.

oil. Mrs. Blatch took it to my sister in the morning, and told her to rub it on herself in faith that she would recover. She is quite well now. This is why I attend the church—because of the wonderful power of its prayer. My husband goes too, because he likes the singing so much.

Its religious fervour alone attracts people to Sister Blatch's church, where the services are certainly a great deal more lively and enjoyed than are, for example, the more formal ones of the Protestant Episcopal church. But the fervour arises also from the fact that Sister Blatch's is, like the other Pentecostal churches, a church of protest, and like them it preaches a return to a purer form of Christianity. One of the sermons I heard in this church was on the text of the Sermon on the Mount: 'Blessed are the meek.' More usually, the preachers were against rather than for: against the hypocrisy of the powerful, the rich, the corrupt, the adulterous, those with 'pockets stuffed with greenbacks' (dollars), those with rubber-farms, who let the people starve, yet consider themselves Christians. One of the most stirring of these sermons took its theme from Matt. xix: 'It is easier for a camel to go through the eye of a needle, than for a rich man to enter into the kingdom of God.' Jesus' charge of hypocrisy: 'Why callest thou me good?' was reiterated with mounting crescendo by the preacher as she listed the iniquities of the rich and politically powerful (although not mentioning them by name), drawing forth frequent cries of 'Amen' and 'Halleluiah' from the congregation, showing their appreciation of and agreement with the points being made. 'I can say these things,' the preacher explained to me later, 'Because I don't work for Government.'

If the appeal of the Pentecostal churches is primarily to the under-privileged, as it is in America and as I have suggested it is in Monrovia, the very active existence of Sister Blatch's seems an anomaly, until one examines more closely the character of its congregation. For while the general mass of the population sees *all* the Americo-Liberians as 'big shots', in fact only a section of them belong to the group of families which make up the political and social élite. For the poorer Americo-Liberians, life can be an even more chancy affair than for the tribespeople, who have a network of kinship and tribal ties behind them. Even among the élite, the exercise of political authority is limited by the large extent to which actual power remains in the hands of the President. Most of the Americo-Liberian men in Monrovia are employed in

Government, and, especially in the senior ranks of Government, there is constant manœuvring for position (which is what 'politics' usually means in conversation in Liberia), and this creates considerable tension and insecurity. This is even more true of the women, who play little direct part in 'politics' of this kind, but must perforce follow their menfolk in and out of favour—although there are now one or two senior government officials who are women. Underlying all this is a more fundamental problem arising from conflicts within the family, and, in particular, from differing sexual standards. For while the Christian ethic of marital fidelity is officially accepted, in practice fidelity on the part of the men is as little accepted among Americo-Liberians as among tribespeople. Provided that he fulfils his obligations to support them, 'outside families' enhance, rather than detract from, a man's social status. This is not at all true of the upper-class women, among whom, at least until recently, giving birth to an illegitimate child meant expulsion from 'society'. Some of the Americo-Liberian women deplore male laxity in sexual standards as one aspect of the invidious influence of tribal Africa on the immigrant culture. But the problem is a more general one, which has been summed up by Southall:

[In African towns] there is a serious conflict over the whole social position of women, their sexual, marital and legal rights, which has no counterpart in the case of the men. The movement for emancipation of women occurs at two levels. Among the élite, it is led by the most respectable and sincere women, often deeply imbued with Christian values. At this level is has not made much impact yet, because it assumes a scale of values which is implicitly rejected by the majority of men, yet at the same time inhibits the women themselves. It is quite different at the ordinary level of the masses, where women who move out of traditional contexts simply assert themselves in a practical manner, rejecting in their own lives the traditionally held male standards for women, choosing their own mates, and supporting themselves independently. . . .[12]

Seen in this light, Sister Blatch's congregation is also made up of the underprivileged, although it is, of course, not the only church which creates outlets for the religious zeal of upper-class women.

To sum up: Liberia, alone among the black republics of Africa, is a self-professed Christian state. Christianity was identified with

[12] Southall (ed.), op. cit., p. 53.

the immigrant Americo-Liberian culture from the earliest days of its history, and its formal profession at least is today a prerequisite for employment in government service and for acceptance among the 'civilized'. Religious zeal has, however, passed to some extent from the long-established mission churches to the newer denominations and especially to the small independent churches of Pentecostal type, which draw their members from the underprivileged and their inspiration from dissatisfaction with and dissociation from the established order. A 'civilized man' must be Christian, but today many illiterate are also Christians: nearly two-thirds of the adults in my sample belonged to one or other of the Christian churches, and this is probably the approximate proportion in the overall population also.

Among the Christians, not only kinship and tribal ties, but also the bonds of church fellowship, may be used in the search for security and sometimes for personal advancement also. For example, a newcomer to the town, especially if he has no relatives already living there, is likely, if he is a Christian, to turn for help to his 'church people': the local congregation of the denomination he joined at home. In certain cases, religious bonds may be regarded as more important than tribal ones: for example, a young Kpelle student, a fervent Lutheran of pagan origin, was more perturbed because the girl he wished to marry was a Baptist than because she was a Bassa. However, the fact that two-thirds of the Monrovians are Christians creates little real unity in the capital's fragmented population, firstly because of the plethora of denominations operating, secondly because of the correspondence in some of the more important denominations between social status and specific church congregations, and thirdly because the siting of missions has produced a strong correlation between denomination and tribe.

TRADITIONAL TRIBAL SOCIETIES: THE PORO AND SANDE IN THE URBAN AREA

In categorizing the voluntary associations to which Monrovians belong (Table 16) I have included traditional tribal associations, of which by far the most important are the Poro and Sande societies. Little has described the role of the Poro among the Mende of Sierra Leone,[13] and Harley the significance of the masked Poro figures among the Gio-Mano peoples of Liberia.[14]

[13] Little, 1951.   [14] Harley, 1941 and 1950.

No study has been made of the Poro—or as it is called by them, the Beli—among the Vai, who are said to have developed the institution to its most complex form. Poro and Sande form a vital and integral part in the social and political structure of all the tribes which have them—which means all the Liberian tribes except the Kru: the Bassa are said to have taken them over recently, from their Kpelle neighbours, although we found relatively few initiates among the Bassa in Monrovia. Traditionally they were certainly not voluntary associations, since initiation into Poro was obligatory for men, into Sande for women, at least in the sense that a non-initiate could not hope to be recognized as an adult and would find it difficult to marry. Initiation usually took place at or just before puberty and involved seclusion in a 'bush school' for a period which varied from one tribe to another but seems to have lasted for a minimum of three to four years. Initation into Poro involved a symbolic swallowing of the boy by the masked 'devil' or Poro spirit, circumcision, and eventual rebirth as an adult. Once initiated, he might pass through a hierarchical series of 'lodges' each of which had its secrets from those of lower ranks, or he might remain an ordinary member. The societies as a whole were 'secret' ones in the sense that Poro rituals could not be revealed, nor Poro objects seen, by females, Sande ones by males, and both sexes were forbidden to reveal them to outsiders. Traditional tribal social structures rested on the interlocking functions of the secular chiefs and the Poro leaders, in political and economic as well as religious life.

The secrecy which surrounds both Poro and Sande is still observed, and it is reinforced by the official protection given by the Liberian Government. For the Government has proclaimed them 'cultural societies' which are permitted, as distinct from outlawed secret societies such as the Human Leopards and Negee. On occasions, Government has actively stepped in to preserve the Poro rule of secrecy. In 1958, for example, there was an outbreak of violence in the Gbandi tribal area near Kolahun, when Christian converts, said to be encouraged by missionaries, desecrated the Poro bush, destroying masks and other ritual objects, and exposing them to public, including female, view. The missionaries involved were fined $600 each and imprisoned for one year. Commented the *Liberian Age*:

Experts on Liberian Customary Laws confirmed yesterday that such societies are not dangerous in their practices and do not in any way conflict with the Christian belief. The Societies in the true sense support the cause of Christian fellowship. They are supported by the Liberian Government as part of the tribal cultures of the Republic.[15]

There is evidence, however, that even in the rural areas, membership of Poro and Sande is by no means universal today. The only information on the *present* functions of the societies among the Liberian tribes comes from Gibb's recent study of legal institutions among the Kpelle:[16]

In spite of the vitality of the Poro as an institution, non-membership seems to carry no great disadvantage. A non-member can hold land and property and marry, which is said not to have been possible in the past. The long interval between initiation schools meant that in Fokwele in 1958 there were many women who were married and had children, although they were not members of Sande.

But he continues:

Although membership may no longer have tangible advantages, it is an important part of being a Kpelle, and accounts for much of the pride which people have in their culture. It is something which they have which those who bear European culture do not.

Being a member of these exclusive and secret societies, and more especially of the Poro, has become an important part of the pride—which one is now permitted to feel—in being a tribesman. And several Americo-Liberian political leaders, including the present President, have been symbolically initiated into Poro as an indication of their sympathy with tribal custom and, in the present period of official unification, as a symbol of solidarity with the tribespeople. The Sande does not have quite the same role: Banton writes that Creole women in Freetown sometimes join the Sande,[17] but I know of no instances in Monrovia of Americo-Liberian women doing so, and it is extremely unlikely that there are any. On the other hand, the Sande has taken on a special role as a showpiece of tribal culture, and of Liberian culture as a whole. Girl trainees from the Sande bush in Monrovia and from surrounding districts are brought in to dance on festive occasions—sometimes including private parties as well as official receptions and celebrations—and their performance provides a

---

[15] *The Liberian Age*, Monrovia, 16.5.58.   [16] Gibbs, 1960.
[17] Banton, op. cit., p. 185.

regular part of the programme of entertainment provided for visiting foreign dignitaries.

It is obvious that neither Poro nor Sande can fill their traditional roles in the modern urban social system. However, analysis of the backgrounds and social status of those who are initiates would give some indication of the extent to which town-dwellers continue to identify themselves with their tribal cultures. Since my study was primarily concerned with the Kru, who have neither Poro nor Sande, I can give only a general indication, on a quantitative level, of the answer to this question. In the survey sample there were more members of Poro and Sande than of any other type of association, except the churches (Table 16), and although society members were especially numerous in Vaitown and Loma Quarters, they included a number of the educated in the 'middle-class' areas. Many young people who migrate to Monrovia have already been initiated into Poro or Sande, and children are often sent home when they reach puberty in order to be initiated—sometimes creating conflicts with the urban authorities, where children are taken out of schools for this purpose. Some of the Vai girls from Monrovia are sent to the Sande bush schools in Sinkor. But they are kept in seclusion for only a brief period, and they may later be seen in the Sande dress—which has been adapted and today includes a Western-style brassière—shopping on the Waterside or visiting relatives in the town. Poro bush schools are no longer held in the Monrovia area. The important question is, to what extent do members of 'civilized' society retain their identification with traditional culture by having their children initiated. I attempted to get an answer to this from the questionnaire administered to 500 schoolchildren— all of whom were over the age of puberty. The results were not, however, very satisfactory, since some individuals, and all individuals in some situations, are diffident about admitting their Poro or Sande membership. It is one thing for a senior official of assured social status to be symbolically initiated, another for a young tribesman trying to make his way into civilized society to admit his Poro membership. In one school, the teacher—an American—insisted on explaining my questionnaire to the children. On the question 'Have you been initiated into Poro or Sande?', she commented: 'Of course, *you* will all write "no" because these are uncivilized societies.' Only the boldest of the children—the class was a girl's one, including many Vai—subsequently answered in the affirmative. For similar reasons the proportion of Poro or Sande initiates in Table 16, may be rather low.

While membership of Poro and Sande is widespread in Monrovia the societies have, of course, no existence in the urban area as corporate bodies—except in the case of the Sande schools in Sinkor. However, Gibbs, writing of the Kpelle in the home area, describes one aspect of the Poro which has been little stressed by other writers: namely, that one consequence of the existence of bush schools is the formation of named age-sets, consisting of those who live in one area and were initiated together. He writes that

The role of the age-set ties in the formation of other groups and in the selection of persons to fill secular political offices needs further investigation.[18]

This question would bear investigation in Monrovia also—as would the question of the possible significance of Poro membership in cutting across tribal divisions and providing solidarity among people of different tribes.

ASSOCIATIONS FORMED BY THE URBAN TRIBAL POPULATION

Among the mass of tribespeople who are uneducated—or who are, at least, not accepted as members of 'civilized' society—*membership* of voluntary associations is nearly always confined to members of one tribe, even where the same, or similar associations exist among different tribes. Often, homogeneity of membership has little explicit connexion with the *aims* of the associations, and is rather a result of the overall strength of tribal loyalties within the urban population. Here, I consider three of the most usual types of association: savings groups, women's societies for recreation and mutual aid, and associations formed by the younger, more educated section of the tribal populations, usually the men, with the aim of improving their status and condition.

(a) *Savings groups*

One of the most frequent bases of association is a shared interest in accumulating savings which can be used for major expenditure: a suit of clothes, a canoe, house-building, a bicycle, a bed, and so on. In its simplest form, this type of association consists of an

[18] Gibbs, op. cit.

arrangement known among many tribes as *susu*, by which two, or sometimes three or four, men agree to pool all or a part of their wages over a period of several weeks or months, each receiving the lump sum in turn. Most frequently, *susu* is made between work-mates, and is popular among the dockworkers, for example. Special forms of *susu* include the groups of women fish-sellers which I have mentioned in the previous chapter, and associations of ship's headmen described in Appendix B. On the whole, such arrangements seem to be short-term ones, and the *susu* partners rely solely on one another for the faithful keeping of their obliga-tions. Larger and more long-term savings groups have been formed in specific residential communities, and the keeping of their obliga-tions is sanctioned by community *mores*, and by the possibility of appeal to the governors or tribal chiefs. In Vaitown, for example, the women market-sellers have an institution known as *sananyek-ang* (translated 'Bank women's club') which resembles the New Krutown fish-sellers' savings groups, except that membership is larger, operation on an annual basis, and its functions rather more varied. The Vai women in Vaitown—for stranger women do not participate—actually divide into two savings groups, one for older women and one for younger. One elderly woman acts as banker for both groups, collecting each week a dollar from every member. At the end of Ramadan the total 'bank' is divided among members. In 1958-9, each member got back $48, the balance being used for payment to the banker and for the purchase of cloth with which to make 'uniforms' for the Ramadan festival. Those whose dues fall into arrears may have their contributions refunded to them if they wish.

The Kru have developed a more elaborate 'banking' institution known as *neklondi*, which is said to mean in English 'If you live you'll see it'. The name and idea were said by Kru informants to have been borrowed from the Gola, but I was unable to get con-firmation of this from Gola tribespeople. It seems more likely that persons returning from trips down the coast introduced the idea of savings banks—there are no official post office or other savings banks in Liberia. At the time of my stay, four *neklondi* groups were operating in New Krutown, and there were others in Logantown and Claratown. Members of a *neklondi* include both men and women and are not limited to any particular occupation or age-group. No joining fee is required. A member simply contracts to

pay a sum of money—the amount depends on his own wish—each
Sunday during the calendar year. At the end of the quarter, he pays
in addition a sum equalling three times the weekly amount. For
example, a man who chooses to pay 25 cents weekly, pays during the
whole calendar year, 52 times 25 cents, plus 4 times $0.75, that is,
$16 in all. If he falls behind in paying the amount for which he
has contracted, he forfeits payments already made; if he joins the
neklondi later than January, he must make back payments. From
the capital thus accumulated, the *neklondi* makes loans to members, or sometimes to outsiders if members vouch for them—or,
in Liberian terms, 'stand bond'. Interest of 15 per cent. is charged
to members, 25 per cent. to outsiders, and in either case this
interest must be paid over *before* the loan is made. A debtor who
does not repay the loan over the prescribed period, usually three
months, has the interest increased; if he still does not pay, the
case may be taken to the Kru Governor. Most loans vary between
$3 and $20, and the maximum amount of any single loan is normally $100. At the end of the year, each paid-up member gets
back the total amount he has paid in, plus a share, proportionate to
his own contribution, of the *neklondi's* total interest earned from
loans. I was fortunate in being permitted to examine the records of
one of these remarkable institutions. This particular *neklondi* had,
in 1957, 122 members. During that year, $2,073.70 was accumu-
lated from subscriptions, only three members having lapsed in
their payments. Just under $1,100 was paid out in loans to a total
of 120 people. On these loans, a total amount of $148.70 was
collected as interest, and this amount was shared out among the
119 paid-up members at the annual meeting held at the beginning
of 1958. This *neklondi* had been established in 1956 and was still
thriving. It had as officials a president and secretary, and four
treasurers with separate functions: one to collect weekly dues, one
quarterly dues, one to pay out loans, and one to collect interest:
the responsibility for handling the cash was thus carefully divided.
At least one of the treasurers was illiterate—I came across several
examples of a remarkable ability to commit figures and facts to
memory. Written records of each persons' contributions and debts
are, however, kept by the secretary. The officials were paid by the
members in proportion to their contributions: in the case I have
described above, the man paying 25 cents a week pays at the end
of each quarter 5 cents as 'bankers' money, a man paying 50 cents

a week, 10 cents, and so on—in addition to the amounts I have listed previously. For most of the officials (who include both men and women), the *neklondi* work is a sparetime occupation: only the president, a retired carpenter, depends on *neklondi* for his income.

Clearly, the success and growth of a *neklondi* depends on the reputation of its officials for honesty and reliability, and not all groups operated as efficiently as this one. It probably could not exist except in a small, closely-knit community, although there were one or two New Krutowners who belonged to a *neklondi* centred in Logantown near by. But in its operation it is impersonal, and members do not necessarily know even the identity of their fellow members, although they may, if they wish, meet one another at the quarterly and annual gatherings held to report on the *neklondi*'s financial position and to discuss applications for loans. It is, in fact, simply a privately, and often very efficiently, operated savings bank.

(b) *The Kru women's societies*

Apart from the savings groups, the most numerous voluntary associations in the Kru tribal population are the women's societies, whose functions may be summed up as the provision of entertainment and mutual aid. Similar societies exist and are popular among Bassa women. They have no counterpart among the Vai, although some of the functions of these associations—such as the expression of the unity of the members by the wearing of a special uniform dress on festive occasions—are provided by the Vaitown 'bank women's clubs' I have described, while others—notably the provision of burial insurance—are provided in Vaitown by the Mawidi and Tinjani associations attached to the mosque.

Some of the Kru societies were originally associated with particular *dako*, largely because of the correspondence which has existed as we have seen, between specific *dako* and particular ports. Thus, Shosimmy, whose name derives from one of the society's songs, 'Don't show your shimmy when you talk to me'—or, in other words, 'show me respect'—started in the Gold Coast, whence it was brought in the 1930's by a Grand Cess woman, who established it in her home town and later brought it to Monrovia. Another society, Geponyano, came to Monrovia from Freetown, where it was established in the 1930's by a group of women, mainly

from the Five Tribes, who were fellow-members of a church choir.
Its name, which is translated 'know yourself', originates in the
Greek phrase, and arose from the habit of the choirmaster, a young
Fourah Bay student, of using this phrase in admonition when his
choristers misbehaved. Other societies—Fenwong, Fancy, Liberia
are among the largest—seem to have originated in Monrovia, sometimes initially among the women of one *dako*. But none of the
societies limits membership to members of one *dako*: women join
because they are friends or neighbours of existing members, and
may come from different *dako*.

A new member pays an entrance fee of 50 cents to $1, and may
also be required to give a party for the other members. Thereafter,
regular dues are not required, but levies are made on members for
specific purposes, and in particular when a member or perhaps
one of her near relatives dies. I was told that the amount normally
collected for such a purpose is $30 to $40—the same amount which
is contributed by the deceased's *panton* and townspeople, if these
are organized in Monrovia. The women regard as at least equally
important the gathering of members in the house of the deceased
to 'play' in her honour and to 'cheer up' her family. From time to
time, members also gather in one another's houses to 'play', to
chat, and, usually, to drink. The largest societies are said to have
a membership of two or three hundred, but such informal meetings
are normally limited to residents in a particular neighbourhood,
perhaps twenty or thirty women.

The basis of the 'play' is the singing, and the basis of the song is
the recitation of sections of the genealogies of members. Usually,
one woman leads the refrain, others join in. Some songs are impro-
vised, others which have proved successful have become traditional
in the society concerned. Some of the best known songs are in
honour of leaders of the societies. The following is part of a praise
song in honour of the Wandi, literally the 'mother of the society',
usually translated the 'matron':

> I will die before Doedi's name is finished,
> Let us sing, Siklong Kai and Doedi came from the same mother,
> I will die before Twedi is finished,
> I will die before this one child's name is finished,
> I will sing of Siklong Kai's sister, I will sing of her,
> She has a lovely name, oh yes, I'll sing my Wandi's name. . . .

Here, the woman concerned is referred to as the matron of the

society, as the mother of both Doe and Twe, and as the sister of
Siklong Kai. This is the 'calling of the name', and it may continue
by reciting genealogical links one after another. Sometimes an
individual will interrupt the song to sing her own name:

> Now I want to sing about myself,
> My mother's name is Jemima, called Wuledi,
> I will sing my name. . . .

Or a member may be called upon by one of the two or three
singers who are important among the officials of each society:

> Gbaunyeno's child, come and sing, let's hear you,
> Talo's child, come and sing, Gbaunyeno's grandchild, come and
>   sing. . . .

A singer must be not only a good vocalist, but a 'historian' who is
conversant with the backgrounds of individual members. Occasionally, a woman is 'called' not by her own actual name nor by a
term describing her relationship to another, but by the name of
one of her kin. In the following song, which was performed at the
funeral of a member who had been electrocuted by a faulty water-
heater, Mimi is the name of the deceased, Wuleme that of her
grandmother.

> Wuleme, we don't come for war, but you died like a warrior
> She had the same names on her father's and her mother's side,
> Interwoven like the vine on a tree,
> Her mother's name was Mona, and the great-grandmother on her
>   father's side was Mona,
> Mimi died young, she died like a warrior.

She 'died like a warrior', that is, because the death was not a consequence of illness. Sometimes during funeral songs the names of
many different deceased members are 'called', expressing the
unity of the newly deceased with them and also with the living
members. The symbol of the 'vine on the tree', for the occurrence
of the same names on both maternal and paternal sides, appears
frequently: the coincidence is held to be auspicious.

One of the most attractive songs I have heard is another praise-
song for a Matron:

> The day our Wandi dies, we will hold up our handkerchiefs, and the
>   owls will hoot all day,
> Nyepan's grandchild, the day she dies the owls will hoot.

VII b. Sande girls and Executive Mansion guards

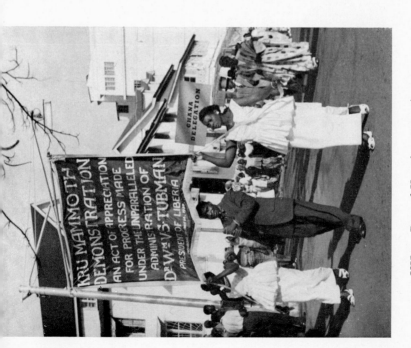

VII a. Part of Kru demonstration

VIII *a*. A Kru women's society 'playing'

VIII *b*. A Kru women's
society parading

Tapla's sister, the day she dies, the owls will hoot. . . .
The day she dies, we will play all through the night,
Just as the fishermen when they are killing the *doma*,
Just as the fishermen spend all night at sea, so we'll play all night . . .
Nyepan Wele's grandchild, when she dies, the owls will hoot. . . .

That is, there will be chaos, the owls hooting in the daytime. The *doma* is a large fish which must be speared, and takes a long time to kill. Some praise-songs call not only the names of the subject, but also recall incidents which have happened in the family: the following song is in honour of the Wambi, the 'father of the society', usually called the president, who is the only male official, although there are a few male members. 'You must have a man at the head', explained one informant, 'a man is the protector of the family':

The way our Wambi looks, if any other company's *papa* looked so,
    we would change the world.
People never get vexed enough to cross the river B.
But when his grandmother got vexed, she swam across it, and when
    she came back, she came with a basket on her back
And a child in it
What his grandmother did, changed the world. . . .

The river was a swift-flowing and dangerous stream near the home town; the grandmother was barren, and she crossed the river to consult a famous doctor, of another *dako*, who lived on the other side. But there was also a hint of scandal. A favourite type of song, which is usually more ephemeral, involves the 'calling of the names' of lovers when the society members meet for entertainment:

The boy put his tongue in my mouth to kiss me, let's sing this song
I was just sitting down, and Wuledi sent me a letter,
The boy put his tongue in my mouth, and I put my legs on top of him,
He sent me a letter, saying, always think of me,
Chiedi sent me a letter,
When he's out at sea, he paddles his canoe so gently that no one can
    hear it. . . .

Here, the boy's name was Wule: he was referred to first by his mother's name, secondly by his sister's name. The singers may then move their attention to another member: 'Penti had a *pajulu* when she was to get married, people pointed their fingers'. A *pajulu* is a lover younger than oneself. The personal allusions to members— whether to incidents in their personal lives or to events in their

N

family histories—and the habit of referring to the subject obliquely, rather than by name, means that the words of most songs are incomprehensible to outsiders. This in itself is one of their attractions for members: one must be 'in' to know what is being sung about. The very obscurity of the songs, that is, unites those who sing them and excludes non-members.

The unity of the society's members is also expressed by the spectacular, uniform dresses which they wear for special occasions: at the time of the inauguration of the President, for example, or on Independence Day, or, in 1959, during the Kru demonstration of loyalty to President Tubman. Bolts of material are purchased in bulk, and the robes prepared in an atmosphere of secrecy which has the excitement of the Paris collections. The societies attempt to out-do one another in the splendour of their appearance and the dignity of their bearing. Some of the societies have special officials in charge of preparing and organizing public parades: the Gina, a corruption of 'general', so called because 'when the societies compete, they are like armies going to war'; or the Captain, so called because when the society turns out for a 'play', it is 'like a ship setting sail'. The following song praises the deportment of a matron on such an occasion:

When you see the matrons competing, when you see ours, she's the best,
When you see Shosimmy's momma, you knock your chest,
When the mommas raced, Shosimmy's momma just sat down,
All the Kru people knocked their chests
The British momma, she sat down
She's not an Indian woman, but when they saw her, they knocked their chests
She's not a Syrian woman, but like the British momma, she just sits down. . . .

Here, the matrons are all 'racing'—that is, walking in splendour, trying to outdo one another. This matron did not need to try; she was not beautiful like an Indian woman, or light-skinned like a Lebanese woman, but 'like the British momma' she just sat down. The 'British momma' was variously identified by my informants as the Queen, and as Britannia who 'sits down' on the back of pennies. Reference to the British, with whom the Kru have long worked on ships or in other ports, are quite frequent, but not always so admiring:

Kru people, you Monrovia Kru people, they say that you are
    disrespectful,
On whom do you depend in your disrespect.
Shad is backing us, President Tubman is backing us,
Vice-President Tolbert is backing us,
So we don't respect anyone, not even the British flag.
We walk proudly, because President Tubman is behind us. . . .

and so on. Finally, some songs are calypso-like comments on
local events. During the Kru Demonstration, for example, it was
reported that the gift which President Tubman had given to the
Kru Governor to help provide food and entertainment was only
partially passed on to the organizers:

President Tubman gave a cow, but Nanklen ate the head,
Governor Nanklen, we're not angry, I'm not angry,
But we want our cow's head. . . .

One of the main attractions of the societies is that they are fun.
The women enormously enjoy the singing, and the central part it
plays in all activities gives ordinary members a chance to participate. The practical provision of mutual aid—especially burial
insurance—and moral support is also an attraction, particularly
for those women whose husbands are periodically absent for long
trips at sea. For they provide an additional source of security,
which cuts across the hierarchy of *panton-dako* organization in the
urban area. However, while kinship is irrelevant to the recruitment and organization of the societies, their songs are very largely
concerned with stating the position of members in relationship to
their respective constellations of kin. In these statements particular emphasis is laid on the maternal line of descent. Traditionally,
Kru social organization was based on paternal descent, that is, a
person was regarded as belonging to the *panton* of his or her father.
Certain rights in the mother's *panton* were however retained, and
in particular the right to claim farmland from it. Marriage into
either *panton* was forbidden. In Monrovia, *panton* organization
exists in an attenuated form, but the relationship between *panton*
members and land does not, so that loyalty to the mother's *panton*
loses its main basis, and ties with the maternal *panton* are more
likely to be forgotten. In stressing maternal descent, the societies
reassert the importance of these ties, and implicitly redefine the
circle of kin within which marriage is prohibited. In the Kru home

town which I visited, a group of older women greeted a young man who had just returned on a visit after many years' absence, with just such a recitation of genealogical links—although not, in this instance, in song. The societies I have described are formed in the urban situation and cut across traditional kinship groupings, but to this extent they are, nevertheless, concerned with the restatement of traditional kinship values.

(c) *Progressive youth associations*

A few men join the women's societies I have described, usually those to which their wives belong, but they are a small and relatively inactive minority. The societies have no real parallel among the Kru men, although there are several groups of younger men who gather together to drink and 'play'. The 'Walka Boys' is the best known of these groups among the Kru, and the 'Jolly Boys' among the Bassa seem to have a similar function. These groups are, however, smaller and more unstable in membership and comparatively ephemeral, partly no doubt because of the periodic absence of those of their members who are stevedores.

A new phenomenon of a quite different nature has been the foundation, since the war, by young, educated tribespeople—who are frequently still high school or university students—of associations whose general aim is self-improvement. Over twenty of these associations were in fairly active existence in Monrovia in 1958–9. In 1958, the senior university students carried out as a part of their course a questionnaire study of the members of six of these associations, together with a number of voluntary associations of other types. In the six progressive tribal associations, membership varied between 25 and 50, but the great majority of members were young men between 20 and 30 years old. None were illiterate, and education to high school level was quite frequent. Some were still students, others were already in employment as clerks, policemen, nurses and so on, and these included several who were continuing their studies at one or other of Monrovia's two night schools. That is, they were the socially mobile: young men who had moved out of the 'tribal' milieu but were not yet established members of civilized society.

Almost all associations of this type group men of a particular tribe or sub-tribe, and imply this in their names, although several have admitted one or two who belong to other tribes, usually because they are friends of members. They include the Bassa Youth Association, the Kpelle United Association, and the United Geh-Mah (Gio-Mano) Association. The Kru, following their usual schismatic pattern of organization, have formed a number of separate societies: the Sasstown Youth Association (grouping Monrovians from Sasstown), the Jloh Progressive Club, and the Matroe Literary Club are examples. There are one or two Kru associations—for example, Cosmos—whose membership apparently cuts across *dako* divisions, but these group mainly older men of more established civilized status. The young Grebo men had also organized along sub-tribal lines, forming separate associations of youths from Barrobo, Palipo, Jedipo and so on. In addition, there are several young people's associations with membership based on county or district of origin rather than on tribe (although these normally correspond), which have official links with the true Whig Party. There is one club, the United Friends, which was founded in Cape Mount and had predominantly Vai membership, but specifically Vai organizations were conspicuously absent. Among Monrovia Vai in general, there is a much less rich variety of associations than among the Kru and Grebo. This does not mean that tribal loyalties and consciousness of tribal membership are weaker among the Vai—who are, if anything, *more* 'nationalistic' than are the other tribes. A part of the explanation may lie in the hypothesis which Banton advanced in connexion with associations in Freetown: namely, that 'other things being equal, the more devolution of authority there is in tribal societies, the more rapidly contractual associations . . . emerge'.[19] For traditional Kru political organization was markedly decentralized, while the Vai had a more hierarchical structure. Again, the very strength of overall Kru tribal organization in Monrovia may indirectly encourage the emergence of the voluntary associations, because it provides leadership roles for the older, and less educated men, while leaving few outlets for the women and the young students—that is, for the two groups which do in fact form the most active urban associations.

I asked a group of Vai students why, in their opinion, youth associations similar to those existing among other tribes had not been formed among the Monrovia Vai. A few days later the following letter was circulated. I quote it because it illustrates the context

[19] Banton, op. cit., p. 195.

of tribal rivalries in which these associations come into at least formal existence, and also the imprecision of their aims:

Dear X. You have, no doubt, heard the expression that scattered coins do not make heap and that association brings about assimilation. You cannot dispute the truth intrinsically stored in these expressions. This has been the basis of all human society and man's unspeakable progress.

A handful of us, citizens of Grand Cape Mount, having observed the unity of other counties, have deemed it expedient to form a club or an association which, we are sure, would more or less bring us together. Let us show the people that some fruit can come out of Cape Mount. A meeting for this purpose is to be held on Sunday at . . . Please do not fail to attend. Your suggestions are needed. Remember that being together will eventually solve all our social problems and make us share the interests one of another, thus understanding one another much more closely. . . .

'Being together will solve all our social problems' expresses well enough the sentiment underlying the foundation of the associations. Their formulated aims differ little one from another, and may be summarized:

  1. To encourage members and other young tribespeople to improve their education.
  2. To provide mutual aid in times of trouble.
  3. To provide opportunities for social intercourse.
  4. To provide a training ground for future leaders of the community.

Most of the individual members who completed the questionnaires said that they had joined their association 'to get to know my fellow-men in Monrovia, to have the opportunity for social intercourse, for discussion with them'. A number had joined in the specific hope of getting financial help with their education. Among this category of mobile individuals, new interests have developed which lie outside the communities of urban tribespeople, although, in turning for support to their 'fellow-men' they still turn to those with whom they share a common tribal origin.

The extent to which the official objects of the associations are achieved differs a great deal in practice. Several students have had their education subsidized, and receptions have been held to celebrate graduations or the departure or return of students who continue their schooling abroad. One association at least has contributed financially towards the establishment of a school in the home area on the Kru coast, another acted as a pressure group in the establishment of a 'civilized' township there. Among the associations covered by our study, one had helped a member to find a job, another to find a house, and there were several instances where the association had paid court fines for members, or 'stood bond' (provided bail) for them. On the other hand, some of the associations have no practical achievements to their credit other than the holding of meetings and the election of officers, and have nevertheless had a quite active existence.

The vitality of the associations lies at least as much in their provision of formalized leadership roles as in their practical activities. Often, title-holders account for half or more of total membership, and since elections are usually held annually, a great deal of the organizations' business is taken up with election campaigns and the installation of new leaders. The most frequent titles are president, vice president, general secretary, social secretary, publicity secretary, treasurer, or financial secretary, chaplain, and critic, sentinel or marshal, with assistants in some or all cases. Meetings—at least that part of them devoted to business—are formal, with minutes and motions, and the task of the critic is to see that the correct procedure is carried out and that members deport themselves properly. Often an older man from the established civilized population acts as official adviser and sponsor. This is one aspect of the widespread custom of patronage, and in the same way, the Kru women's societies often have such a man as president, and the small separatist churches have them as board members. The associations gain respectability from this arrangement, and the patrons, for their part, expect to be able to count on the support of their members for personal and political ends.

Most of the societies have had chequered histories: bursts of activity are associated with the choice of new leaders, but later the organization becomes quiescent, or founders on conflicts of interest and opinion between its officials, to dissolve and reappear later, with a slightly different emphasis or under another name. In large part, this process takes place because the founders have been young students. As they finish their studies and take up other interests, younger men expect to be able to take over leadership. Conflicts between age-groups sometimes arise because, with the increasing general level of education, the criterion of the 'educated' man is changing. Again, some battles for leadership have mirrored general conflicts within the overall tribal population concerned: the Sasstown association, for example, split into two on the issue of the competition between the two sections of the home town for official position. In some cases, the history of the association has reflected developments within the urban tribal population. The Kpelle Association, for example, founded in 1949, had as one of its earliest activities the task of choosing the first Kpelle urban tribal chief. It subsequently broke up because of conflicts of interest between the chief, whose task is primarily concerned with the affairs of the 'uncivilized' population, and the younger men who were acquiring an education and adapting themselves to the 'civilized' way of life. A few years later the association came into being again, as a result of the initiative of members and supporters of a football team made up of Kpelle students. As the students left the university and high schools, the team became inactive but the association was still in existence in 1959.

In many respects these associations resemble the welfare societies which came into being in the Rhodesias in the 1930's and '40's and which, as Epstein has described[20] led to the development of political movements. However, the Monrovian societies do not—as the Rhodesian ones did—cut across tribal divisions, unifying the young intelligentsia from different tribes. One or two—like the *United Friends* society mentioned above—do make some attempt to do this, but they are normally identified by outsiders with the tribe of their leaders. In large part, this reflects the fragmentary nature of Monrovia's occupational structure, and its segmented residential pattern. That is, there are relatively few large labour forces in which people might meet members of other tribes and share interests with them as work-mates, and the degree of correspondence between tribe and local community in Monrovia means that many Monrovians pass their lives in a neighbourhood made up basically of their own tribesmen. Again, in Monrovia there has not been the impulse to unity which was provided in Rhodesia by opposition to a colonial and exclusive government. Nevertheless, of all sections of the urban tribal population one might expect that among the students, friendship and community of interest would cut across tribal divisions. In fact, in this section of the population tribalism is particularly strong, because in the context of the high

[20] See Epstein, 1958.

schools and the universities young people reared in their exclusive ethnic groups are often confronted with one another for the first time, and deep-rooted prejudice runs riot. Later, when they finish their studies, establish themselves in 'civilized' occupations, and become confident of their new status, they are more likely to form friendships in which tribal membership is a minor factor.

OCCUPATIONAL ASSOCIATIONS

A more direct consequence of the absence of large labour forces is the scarcity of associations of people sharing a common occupation. Those which exist among the masses of the population, tend, like other types of association, to be formed within tribal groups. The civilized population, however, forms professional associations (the National Bar Association, and organizations of teachers, nurses, beauticians and so on) and here tribal origin—or at least origin in specific tribes—ceases to be particularly relevant.

Among the large body of self-employed, there are a number of groups which have organized themselves along tribal-occupational lines. The Hausa diamond merchants, for example, have a club known as the 'Diamond Company' which receives newcomers to Monrovia, arranges accommodation for them, and shows them where to sell the diamonds they have brought; in return, it gets a commission on sales. Similar groups are said to exist among Mandingo merchants. The goldsmiths in Vaitown have a 'chief'. The Kru fishermen have a 'council' composed of a president and one representative of each of the five *dako* most concerned with fishing, their duties being to lay down rulings concerning fishing seasons and mutual aid at sea. The council has made rulings, for example, that two fishermen who leave the shore together must return together, that a fisherman who sees another in distress must go to his aid, that one must not splash at the fishing grounds or clean one's canoe except in the authorized place, and so on. Failure to observe these regulations is punishable by a fine, imposed by the council with the help, if necessary, of the Kru Governor. The Fanti fishermen have a quite separate organization, and there is sometimes conflict between the two, arising particularly from the fact that the Kru, who fish with lines, depend for bait on the small fish which the Fanti bring in in their nets.

Employed labour on the other hand is virtually unorganized. Such attempts as have been made to promote labour unions have started at the top—that is, with the formation of labour 'congresses' by government officials and with government support, rather than through the initiative of the workers. Thus a Labour Union of Liberia was founded in the 1940's, a Labour Congress of Liberia was founded in 1953, reactivated a few years later, and again for a third time, with new leaders, during the 1959 governmental election campaign. A rival organization, the Committee of Industrial Organizations, came into being in 1959 as a result of a split among the leaders of the Congress. The president of the Congress at the time was the social secretary to the President of the Republic, while the rival organization was led by a senior official of the Department of Public Instruction; later, it became associated with the son of the President of the Republic. Other prominent 'labour' leaders included the Director of Personnel in the Department of Public Works, and the Deputy Mayor of Monrovia. It is apparent that these organizations are not 'labour unions' in the usual sense. They claim to have under them workers in various industries— plantations, mines, the port, drivers and mechanics, and so on, but the congresses are privately financed, no membership dues are required, and the workers appeared, in 1959 at least, to be either unaware of their existence or to regard them as no affair of theirs. Motives behind the founding of such organizations are mixed, and include a genuine wish to assist workers to improve their lot and also a patriotic desire to give Liberia 'unions' comparable to those in other countries. Up to the first half of 1959, when I left Monrovia, their activities had been primarily in the sphere of 'palace politics', and had centred on demonstrations of loyalty to President Tubman. In February 1958, for example, a rally was held in Monrovia at which the Labour Congress of Liberia pledged the support of its '50,000 workers' to President Tubman, who was proclaimed on banners as 'The Saviour, Defender and Emancipator of Liberian Workers' and given the title of 'Most Exalted Grand Chancellor and Defender of the Knights of Liberian Labour'. The congress had, however, certainly not gained the support of the mass of the workers. The few labour disputes which have arisen—notably at Firestone plantation and at the port—have normally been settled by direct presidential intervention: the stevedores' wage dispute which I have mentioned in a previous chapter was eventually settled by discussion between President Tubman and the shipping companies concerned.

In a political system as authoritarian as Liberia's, it is indeed difficult to see how real labour organization could develop. Moreover, neither the workers themselves nor the leaders of the 'labour congresses' and 'unions' have experience of trade union activities or knowledge of their operation in other countries. In the colonial and ex-colonial territories of Africa, unions successfully established have frequently benefited by advice and/or training provided by the metropolitan unions, or by trade union experts appointed by the governments themselves. In Liberia, it is unthinkable that foreign experts should be called in for this purpose. One might expect to find the most fertile soil for the growth of labour unions in Monrovia among the dockworkers and stevedores, not only because they are the largest industrial category, but also because their work takes them to other territories where they have come into contact with trade unionism in operation. But these workers are predominantly Kru, and the Kru Corporation itself as we have seen, has taken action from time to time in an attempt to protect or improve working conditions. The weakness of labour organization in Monrovia may, then, be traced to four main causes: the general absence of large labour forces, the pervasive influence of tribal loyalties, the authoritarian nature of the Government, and the lack of a tradition of unionism which the African colonial areas borrowed from the metropolitan countries.

UPPER-CLASS ASSOCIATIONS

Associations formed within the civilized population, or within its upper strata, include clubs and societies attached to certain church congregations, philanthropic associations, glee clubs, sororities and fraternities, 'crowds' and masonic lodges. Many have prototypes among American Negro organizations, with which some—notably several sororities and fraternities—are affiliated. In most cases their stated functions fall within the general fields of social improvement, social insurance and welfare, but their latent functions often lie in the sphere of battles for personal political status. Analysis of their composition, leadership and role would involve a detailed investigation of the way in which power groups, actual or incipient, are formed and operate. Here, I give merely a brief description of the two oldest types of association, which are probably also the two which have had most influence on Monrovia's social structure: the 'crowds' and the masonic lodges.

'Crowds' is the name given to groups of men who were educated and entered public life at approximately the same time. They were already being formed at the turn of the century, within the old Americo-Liberian élite, and they continued to come into being until the late 1930's. They are no longer being established, but the old crowds remain active and some at least have considered accepting the sons of members. Most are named by numbers: Crowd 13, for example, one of the last to be formed, was established in 1938 by men born roughly within the period 1915 to 1920. In 1957, it included among its members the Secretary of the Treasury, the Attorney General, the Director of the Bureau of Budget, the Ambassador to West Germany, the Mayor of Monrovia, the Commissioner of Police, and an Assistant Secretary of Agriculture. The crowds have no club premises, but meet in private houses for discussion of social and political affairs. They are generally said to act as pressure groups whose members also provide one another with support in political affairs—which, in Monrovia, commonly means in candidature for political or governmental position.

Most members of crowds are also freemasons, and membership of the Ancient and Accepted Order of Freemasons, or at least of associated fraternities like the United Brothers of Friendship is virtually a *sine qua non* for anyone hoping for promotion to senior government offices. Of the 173 men listed in the Who's Who section of the 1956 *Yearbook*, 111 were listed freemasons and a further nineteen were members of the United Brothers of Friendship or the Oddfellows. Freemasonry has a long history in Liberia. Masonic lodges were among the American organizations which gave financial support to the Colonization Society,[21] and the craft was established in Liberia in the early days of the republic, by immigrants who had been members of (presumably Negro) lodges in America. (This, it may be noted, was before emancipation.) In 1867, a Grand Lodge was founded in Monrovia, with three subordinate lodges—two in Monrovia, the other in one of the Montserrado settlements. The craft in Liberia was independent from its foundation: the founders delegated masonic authority to one of their members (who became the first Grand Master), and then applied for recognition by other lodges throughout the world.[22] Today there are eleven lodges in various parts of the coastal region, with the Grand Temple in Monrovia. Since the earliest

[21] Staudenraus, 1961, pp. 111 f.   [22] *The Liberian Age*, Monrovia, 14.1.57.

days there has been a close association between the masonic craft
and the government—masonic and political leaders often being
the same persons: the Grand Master in 1958 was the Speaker of
the House of Representatives, and living past Grand Masters were
the President, ex-President King, and a former Attorney-General.
According to President Tubman:[23]

We know that a great many of the founders of our own country were
active members of the Craft; and I consider our Declaration of Independence to be a masonic document and that our Constitution is
Masonry put into political form and practice. . . . Masons were very
active in the formulation and putting into effect of both the Declaration
of Independence and the Constitution, as well as in the declaration of
our country as a Free, Sovereign and Independent State.

Admission to membership of the craft is by secret ballot within
the lodge concerned, and the vote must be unanimous. The entry
fee is, I was told, $500, but masons are also called upon for dona-
tions to specific causes. An affiliated lodge, the Order of the Eastern Star, which has its prototype in America, admits women as
well as men. Entry into the craft is simpler if one is already a member of the United Brothers of Friendship or Oddfellows, both of
which were also established before the end of the nineteenth
century,[24] and which have as their female equivalents the Household of Ruth and the Sisters of the Mysterious Ten. Entry into
the United Brothers of Friendship or Oddfellows is less expensive
than entry into a masonic lodge, and is easier to attain, and the
International Order of Good Templars[25] demands a still lower
entry fee and does not insist that members must be educated. Thus
it is possible to climb up the series of fraternities and lodges as
one's social and economic position improves. Of the male population in our sample survey of the eight residential areas, twenty-
five were members of the U.B.F., nineteen of the I.O.G.T., and
six of Oddfellows; only two were freemasons. Master Masons in
the entire republic number only about four hundred.[26]
     The lodges provide certain insurance benefits—notably burial
insurance and the provision of a 'dower' of $100 for 'widows and

[23] Ibid.
[24] Johnston, 1961, vol. i, p. 390.
[25] The order is frequently referred to by members and others as the 'International Order of Good *Tempers*', and the linguistic confusion is increased by
the fact that the order undertakes *temperance* work.
[26] *The Liberian Age*, 16.1.57.

orphans of any mason of good standing', payable on the death of a mason.[27] Many of the masonic celebrations are held at least partly in public. There is a close relationship between masonry and the churches, and on feast days of the 'patron saints' of the craft, special masonic services are held and masons parade through the streets in full regalia. This is one of the few occasions (other than at receptions and weddings and funerals) where men appear today in the top hats and tail coats so frequently described by writers on Liberia. Again, freemasons normally lay the foundation stone of important public buildings: the Capitol Building (the home of the House of Representatives), for example, or the new City Hall. On such occasions, masons parade through the streets bearing such objects as the Volume of Sacred Laws (the Bible), and the masonic trowel, said to have been used since the early days of the republic. Nevertheless, strict secrecy still surrounds much of the masonic ritual, and it is partly for this reason that members, and more especially leaders, of the craft are feared and suspected by the masses of the people—including some of the 'civilized'. During election campaigns, particularly, rumour quite frequently links masonic leaders with stories of 'heart men' who carry out ritual killings to enhance their power. The Liberian form of free-masonry is not, of course, unique in earning for itself a reputation for sinister practices.

The parallels between the indigenous Poro Society and the Masonic Craft, both in their organization and in their function as the mystic power behind the secular one, are obvious and striking. Their existence side by side in Liberia tempts one to speculate that the power of the Poro among the tribespeople, and the awe which surrounds it, may have been instrumental in the adoption by the immigrants of their own form of secret society. But today, while the leaders of the Masonic Craft are almost all Americo-Liberians or ('pure' Americo-Liberians being now rare) persons normally identified as Americo-Liberians, a large number of free-masons are educated tribespeople, some of whom are also Poro initiates.

The composition of church congregations and of other types of voluntary associations largely coincides, as we have seen, with the division of the population into what are locally known as the tribal

[27] Ibid., 14.1.57.

and the civilized elements. But Monrovia is no longer a caste society: on the contrary, there is today a great deal of mobility into the civilized element. One would expect to find that people change from membership of one congregation or association to another as they climb up the social scale. I came across instances of this but the extent to which it occurs is difficult to assess, primarily because large-scale mobility is a new phenomenon, coinciding with the period of rapid economic development which got under way in about 1949–50. Examination of those few instances where individuals belonged to both 'civilized' and 'tribal' forms of association indicated that their status within such associations reflected their status in the general social hierarchy. Young men still studying, or who had only recently completed their studies, belonged to the greatest number and variety of associations. One young high school graduate, for example, was adviser to a tribal recreational society, secretary of a tribal progressive youth association, a member of the YMCA, of the Methodist Youth Fellowship, and of a glee club, and was planning to join the United Brothers of Friendship. The significance of movement of people from one *church* to another is obscured by the fact that the upwardly mobile tend to move towards the Town Centre and thus geographically nearer to the churches where the 'civilized' worship.

The pervasive influence of tribal loyalties on the membership of voluntary associations has also been stressed in this chapter. These loyalties diminish in strength in the civilized population, more especially in its upper strata, where friendships often cut across tribal lines and also across the broader division between tribesman and Americo-Liberian. However, while in the composition of informal cliques and formal associations, *which* tribe a man belongs to, becomes more or less irrelevant, *whether* he is of tribal or Americo-Liberian origin does not.

To these two points—the significance of ethnic origins in the overall social hierarchy, and the extent and nature of social mobility—I return in the next chapter.

CHAPTER VI

SOCIAL STRATIFICATION AND SOCIAL MOBILITY

IN the preceding chapters I have followed local usage in distinguishing the 'civilized' from the 'tribal' element in the population. Broadly speaking, these terms may be said to refer to two social classes, differentiated by their relationship to the sources of authority, by their economic status in terms of both occupation and wealth, by their educational levels, by their style of life, and, to a limited extent, by their consciousness of a corporate class identity. But to describe social stratification in Monrovia as a two-class system would be an over-simplification, and, further, the adjectives 'civilized' and 'tribal' are themselves misleading.

'Civilized' is more or less synonymous with 'Westernized'. The civilized regard themselves, and are regarded by others, as following the Western way of life, and this, with reservations, means the white man's way of life, in contrast with an African, tribal one. Hence, for example, the use of the Kru term *kwi klo*, 'the white man's town' by the Kru in referring to the Town Centre. But by virtue of their residence in Monrovia, all sections of the population are to some degree Westernized. We have seen that 'tribe' is an important social category, and that there are in the city certain communities which have adapted some aspects of traditional tribal structure in developing their own form of urban organization. However, such communities exist in the context of an urban, industrial system.[1] The illiterate, as well as the college graduate, earns money to pay for his basic requirements. Wage-employment involves him in contractual arrangements which have no part in the 'tribal' way of life. Neighbours and workmates may belong to different tribes, and communication with them may have to be by means of English. Family life also undergoes radical changes: even in areas like New Krutown and Vaitown, where there are large households based on extended families, both the composition of the

[1] Cf. Mitchell, 1956, p. 44.

family and relations between its members are transformed by the
fact that household economy is based on the individual money-
earning capacities of its members rather than on their co-operation
in producing food. Essays written at my request by fifty-three high
school students of varying types of background, contrasting life in
the capital with life in their home towns or villages, stressed almost
unanimously that Monrovia was different not only because it had
paved streets, cinemas, dance-cafés and so on, but also because
people must pay for their food, housing, water and other basic
requirements, because neighbours and kin could not be relied on
for help, and because in Monrovia one could meet people of many
different types and backgrounds and learn from them. The
illiterate walks the same streets, has access (if he can afford it) to
the same cinemas and cafés, earns cash to pay for his needs, and
must be self-reliant. He is also a townsman, and, indeed, people
from the tribal areas may consider him a 'civilized' man simply
because he lives in Monrovia. This may seem obvious, but it needs
stating since I have chosen here to use the terminology employed
by the Monrovians themselves in describing one another.

THE SOCIAL HIERARCHY

'Civilization' is, then, a process in which all Monrovians are
involved, and theoretically a person's social position is measurable
against a scale of ranking based on varying degrees of civilization.[2]
In practice, people are seldom compared one with another in just
these terms, that is, as being more, or less, civilized. Instead, they
are categorized according to their approximate position on a social
hierarchy illustrated in Figure IV (page 199). The 'civilized'
section of the population—which can be estimated at about one-
quarter of the total—subdivides into three separate strata on the
basis of social and economic status and position in the power
structure.

The top social stratum (category A in Figure IV) is referred to
locally as 'the élite', 'society', 'high society' or 'the big shots'—
although the last of these terms may have a much wider connotation, especially if the speaker holds a position low in the social
scale. The nucleus of the élite consists of a number of Americo-
Liberian families—perhaps twenty—whose names appear again

---

[2] Cf. ibid., p. 14.

O

and again on lists of senior government officials and in leadership positions in churches, masonic lodges, and the more select voluntary associations. The same family often has members in senior positions in four or five different government departments, and the same man may hold key positions in several different spheres: for example, in 1958 the Speaker of the House of Representatives was also Leader of the True Whig Party for Montserrado County, Grand Master of the Masonic Craft, Chairman of the Board of Trustees at the University (where his wife was Dean), and owned one of the leading law firms in the republic. The élite is to some degree endogamous, so that if one carries the genealogy of any one member far enough, one sooner or later incorporates sections of the genealogies of several other of the powerful and long-established families. While, as we have seen, a great deal of political authority is vested in the President, the big families are the 'king-makers'. They are also an élite in terms of wealth, both because of the direct and indirect emoluments of their (mainly governmental) posts, and because of their income from rubber-plantations and investments in land and housing. Most of them have one house in Monrovia and another on their rubber-plantations, which are strung out along the Monrovia-Ganta highway. This means that while the male—and some female—members of the Monrovia élite are usually employed by Government, they no longer depend solely on Government for their incomes. They are freemasons and Christians—almost invariably members of the Protestant Episcopal, Methodist, Baptist or Presbyterian denominations. They are distinguishable from the rest of the population by their style of life: the grandeur of their houses, the size of their motor cars, the elegance of the dresses, often Paris-designed, of the women. They send their children to schools overseas, and they themselves periodically travel abroad on 'health trips'—sometimes for specific medical treatment, more often for a rest from Liberia's unsalubrious climate. The big families of the established élite are Americo-Liberian. Many of them include persons who have 'passed' into the Americo-Liberian group by marriage or adoption, but closer examination would probably reveal that they are ethnically 'purer' than families of lower social position. Today, there are also two or three families of known and acknowledged tribal origin, which in terms of occupation, income, and style of life may be regarded as

Senior officers of the three branches of Government, and their families.

Other government officials from head of bureau up; certain doctors, lawyers, clergymen.

Minor officials, clerks, school-teachers, nurses.

Electricians, mechanics and drivers, craftsmen.

Domestics.

Labourers.
Stevedores.
Fishermen.
Petty traders.

A
Elite

B
Honorables

C
Civilized

D
Indeterminate

E
Tribal or Uncivilized

Dress suits; Dior fashions; children schooled overseas; own rubber-plantations; own large houses and lease out others. Large motor-cars. Members of masonic lodges and crowds, Protestant, Episcopalian, Methodist or Baptist churches.

Suit and tie to work; children sent to school and usually speak English first; some starting rubber-farms. Walk or on long distances hire taxis. Members of lodges, United Brothers of Friendship, and church associations. Own their houses and may rent out others. Inter-tribal marriage frequent.

Women wear lappas, men shirt and trousers; illiterate but majority speak some English. Pay hut tax. Walk long distances. Pentecostal, Methodist and Baptist churches and associations based on membership of specific tribes. Legal redress from urban tribal courts. Inter-tribal marriage rare.

belonging to the élite, although they are not necessarily accepted as equals by conservative Americo-Liberians. By the general public, the whole élite, including those who openly maintain their tribal membership, tends to be classed as 'Americo-Liberians' To some extent, this applies also to members of category B in Figure IV, the 'Honorables', of which, strictly speaking, the élite forms a part. For these two categories, taken together, I have used the term 'upper class' in earlier chapters. The title 'Honorable' is granted to all government officials from heads of bureaux upwards: this means that 'Honorables' include persons at a wide range of levels of authority, for some of the newer bureaux have no staff other than the head. The title is also conferred upon members of the Judiciary and Legislature, and is loosely extended, in informal conversation, to cover the immediate families of the officials concerned. In terms of their social status, their style of life, the sort of parties they are invited to, and so on, members of the medical and legal professions, and some high-ranking clergymen, may also be regarded as belonging to this category. On the other hand, while the Kru and Bassa governors, and tribal representatives in the House, are given the courtesy title 'Honorable', they do not have the same social standing, neither do they mix informally with other Honorables. In general, the characteristics of the 'Honorables' may be described as the same as those of the élite, but less marked. Their houses are somewhat less grand. They may be content to rely on the cars provided for them, *ex officio* by Government, rather than, in addition, purchasing their own: like members of the élite, they are rarely to be seen walking in the streets, even where they live only a few blocks away from their offices. Their rubber-farms are likely to be newer than those of the élite families—which means a considerable difference in income, since rubber takes seven years to mature. They are usually freemasons. They include both Americo-Liberian and tribal families, the latter beng much more numerous among them than among the élite. They are distinguished from the remainder of the civilized population (category C in Figure IV) by their relatively high income, by their social standing—for example, they are frequently invited to formal dress receptions at the Executive Mansion—and by their closer association with the sources of power. Many young men complain that they cannot get jobs, or school fees, or overseas scholarships, because they do not know any

'Honorables' or 'big men' who might act as patrons. In the high school essays I have mentioned, one young man wrote:

Furthermore, I like the idea of living in Monrovia and to go to school, because it is a chief city which is the seat of Government; and as a native born I should stay in Monrovia and get acquainted with some of the Honorables of my country, in other words for me to be recognized more than a man who is not acquainted with the nobles in Monrovia. Today I find things easier with me in Monrovia than with some of my comrades who are newly coming into the city.

And one of the girls:

On the other hand, a person who associated himself or herself with an Honorable will not be in trouble, because if he or she does something and he or she is taken to the station, his or her friend will stand for his or her bond. [That is, one who is arrested and taken to the police station will probably manage to get the case settled out of court.]

The remainder of the civilized population (category C in Figure IV) is made up of white-collar workers, teachers, nurses and so on, who hold subordinate positions in the government-based hierarchy, although from the point of view of the uneducated they wield considerable authority. I have referred to this stratum as the 'middle class' in earlier chapters. They include many first-generation educated. They speak English more frequently than any other language, and English tends to be the first and often the only language of their children. The majority today are almost certainly of tribal origin, and they include a considerable number of naturalized Liberians originating from other African territories, especially Ghana and Sierra Leone. Inter-tribal marriage is frequent among them, and there are also many tribal-Americo-Liberian or Congo marriages. ('Congo', it will be remembered, is the name given locally to descendants of Africans rescued from slave ships. They are a very small minority in the Monrovia population today, although quite a number live in the peri-urban townships.) The civilized are distinguished from the 'uncivilized' less by their actual income than by what they do with it. Their houses are built and furnished in Western style, and characteristically the walls are decorated with family snapshots, religious prints, and framed certificates. The civilized eat in Western fashion, sitting around a table, although their *cuisine* is normally based on 'country' recipes. Children usually, although not invariably, eat separately. Whether or not a man and his wife sit down to eat together depends on a number of factors, including their relative levels of education and the presence or absence of visitors.[3] They quite often have guests to meals, more usually on an informal basis: a relative certainly, and frequently also a friend or even a stranger who drops in at mealtime, is offered food. They wear Western dress. For men, this means jacket and tie—compulsory wear in government offices, even in the hottest weather—but they are less likely than the Honorables to possess morning-suits or tails, since they are seldom invited to official receptions. They seldom own cars, but often hire taxis. They are all Christians —a point to which I return below. Most belong to one or other of the eight long-established denominations I have listed in Chapter V. Some are freemasons, but they are more likely to be members of the United Brothers of Friendship or some similar organization— unless they are Roman Catholics, in which case they belong to Catholic societies like the Knights of St. John. Many hope to establish rubber farms, and some have already purchased land for this purpose. A more frequent form of investment is the building of houses for renting. The following extract from an essay gives one young Kru high school student's view of the contrast between the values of the civilized man and the illiterate:

A civilized man is in all capacity superior to an illiterate man. The wealth of an illiterate man encourages him to do as he pleases. Being a rich man, he marries approximately a hundred women. He thinks, by doing so, he is utilizing his money, whereas he is mistaken. It is very difficult to reason with a wealthy illiterate man because he considers himself the superior man in his environment. He would not take any admonishment from anyone whatsoever because he feels that by admonishing him will lower his calibre. He utilizes his money buying a lot of wives for his children and relatives.

Whereas a civilized man invests his money by building houses which are being rented by his Government. He educates his children and they become his successors whenever he dies. He banks his money in order to get a commission yearly. A civilized man can become share-holder in any company. He can be sent to represent his country abroad as long as he is highly educated. An illiterate man can only become Representative. Therefore, in conclusion, a civilized man is in all capacity superior to an illiterate man.

[3] A similar situation in Sierra Leone is described by Little, 1955, p. 229.

The civilized are committed to the Western, although not necessarily the urban, way of life, and even if they are of uneducated tribal origin, do not envisage that they or their children could return to live in the tribal communities.

Category D in Figure IV represents the considerable section of the population whose status on the civilized-tribal scale of ranking is uncertain, both in their own estimation and that of others. They include a large number of the upwardly mobile—those who are, in local parlance, 'trying'—many of them young men in their twenties, still studying at school or university. Most delay marriage until their schooling ends: they would like to marry educated girls, but especially in the higher school grades, there are relatively few girls, and daughters of established 'civilized' families look down on them. Their girl friends are more usually 'lappalonians' (girls who wear lappas, i.e. girls from category E), whom they are likely to discard if and when their status becomes more assured. Some alternate periods of employment as domestics, messengers, stevedores, or lower-grade clerks, with periods of school attendance, and others work during the day and attend school in the evenings. They see education as the key to civilized life, but feel at the same time that their chances are conditioned by their contact with persons in authority—that is, with persons in the government hierarchy. The fact that the first-generation 'civilized' in category C are almost always people who have been 'helped'—by adoptive parents, guardians, or patrons—suggests that this assessment of their chances is a realistic one. Some join 'progressive' associations of young people of their own tribe, and many reach out beyond tribal bonds to join church clubs, YMCA, football clubs, glee clubs and so on. Many of their characteristics and problems are illustrated in the following autobiography, whose Grebo author was working as a steward in a private house and attending school during the afternoon. He had reached Grade 7 in the elementary school, and his level of literacy was fairly typical for those in this grade. He was, however, unusually articulate. Apart from inserting punctuation, I quote his autobiography verbatim as he wrote it, adding a few clarifications (in italics) where it seemed necessary:

I were born in the year of 1929 August 19th. I was lived in a hut the country people make by tied-tied [*plaited*] mats in the bush. About the town or village, it is Rocktown E.P.W.A. [*Eastern Province, Liberia,*

West Africa]. In that town there are about 675 huts in it. The people who lived in the town they used to make farm, I mean rice farm or palm oil, coffee, cassava, banana, plantain, by this they lived, or just what they need they lifed. [*That is, they produced enough for their daily needs.*] The family of mine they came from france side in 1862, by fighting a war in France, in native custom. [*That is, they came from the Ivory Coast.*] My mother, father, sisters, aunts and uncles they all living today in Cap Palmas, not one in Monrovia. In that time, there were not any kinds of Education in the family until 1904 April 6th, Mr. X and Mr. Y [*his father and uncle*] went to school. They got their education on 18th November 1919, before people being knowing anythings about schooling in my families. When they got their educations they went home and go on the side of a hill and make there a farm. That all they take in from schooling of theirs.

These dates were recalled from framed certificates which had hung on the walls in his father's house. His father had managed to get an education at a time when Liberia's economy was in the doldrums; with the closing down of the German trading firms, there must have been very few jobs available in Cap Palmas for an educated young tribesman, and those which existed probably offered little financial advantage over farming.

In my childhood, I was not thinking of any school until suddenly 1942 before this school question came to my mind really. I feeled that I should go to school. When I started my school, there was not any copise book or money to pay my school fees. Before I could continuing then, I had to cut palm nut and selled it, thence I paying the fee of my school. Gradually I came to Monrovia, Liberia, to get a jobs and go school more.

Here he has glossed over his reasons for leaving the mission school and his home district. According to a former school-mate from Cap Palmas, he had been expelled on a charge of theft.

When I come to Monrovia I meet high ship [*hardship*], so I get stewed [*steward*] boy jobs which give me $25 a month. It is because no big man to assist me. I do not realy like the job but through necessity, to buy my books and paid my school fees etc. etc. When I comes to Monrovia I has been living at Camp Johnson Road to one Bassa man house. Yes there is many huts that I been lived in [*because of*] this difference of rents. At this present I living in one house build by can-coom sticks and it cost $4.50 a ROOM, four dollars and fifty cents a month. Some rooms cost $6.50, to $17.50 a month, therefore I been lived in so many. This circumstance [*that is, because he lives alone and not with a family*] cause me to have someone of doing my shopping when I come home from work to meet something to eat before I go to school. I am nobody eating [*that is, I eat with nobody*] because of uncleanness unless I have found out that you or he, she, her, has been learned. I have saw many of the AFRICA people some of them never washed they face and began to eat nor [*without*] washing hands. I realised not to eat with anyone nor to drink with anyone's cup or spoon. I don't even like anyone to laid by me, except my honey or Darling Girl. I not ever thinking of marriage right now, till I get my education, so if I have anyone, should be called a girl friend, not wife. If I having to graduated from school I hoping to marry an American [*that is, a civilized*] woman. The girl friend here in Liberia I used to give her $10.00 out of the $25.00 to buy her things from the store. I always sending my families in Cap Palmas a few money after three months' period. From the $25.00 I take and buy foods, pay rent, paid for my books also school fees, upon that circumstance I only paying a visiting 2 times for highship.

That is, because of his financial hardships he had made only two visits to his family in Cap Palmas. He explained orally that he did not like to visit his home because his family thought of him as a wealthy and successful person, and he could not meet their expectations by taking gifts.

My biggest problem I always thinking about is to become a aviator in Liberia, if Liberian Government would allowed me to learning. My reason of asking God to [*let me*] do this sort of work, is my Father he very poor and we the children he bore are many and I the older one. In consider of my life, if I don't do anything then my child will become the same way I am today. The treatment here in Liberia is, if your father are not known by the Americo-Liberians you shall never be anybody in this Liberia. Before you will be known by Liberians you should be a member of Civilized Society. For this reason if I go to church I always asking in my daily prayer 'Hear me crying, oh God, give ear unto my prayer, when my heart is in heaviness O set me upon thy Rock which is higher than I, for me to see a sort of work during of time I shall appear before President of Liberia W. V. S. Tubman.

That is, he wanted a job which would bring him to the President's notice. He wanted to become a member of civilized society not so much for his own sake, but because only in that way, he felt, he could become 'somebody'. Like many other young men, he was struggling on with his schooling with considerable sacrifice of leisure time and money, but he had little hope that education alone would get him anywhere, without the social backing of an influential patron.

Category D also includes several other types of person whose status is ambiguous—for example, those who have moved at different rates along the different dimensions of the system of social stratification,[4] and who display some, but not all, of the characteristics of the 'civilized'. One such person is Mr. W, 60 years old, educated to Grade 8, a Methodist, a retired mason by trade. His house is of definitely civilized type and its contents include shelves of books—a very unusual feature in Monrovia. But he has chosen to remain living in a tribal community, and moreover, he is openly polygynous. By his neighbours, he is regarded with some awe as an 'educated' man; by the civilized, however, he is classed among the uncivilized tribespeople. Others may be characterized as downwardly mobile: one such example is Mrs. T, a high school graduate who was formerly married to an Honorable. She divorced him and married a clerk from a tribal community; they first lived in a house, which she built from her savings, on the edge of the community, but now they rent it to a Lebanese while they themselves have moved back into the community. During the same period she lost a post in Government because of a quarrel with her superior officer. Her household interior, her attitudes, and her way of life mark her off sharply from her neighbours, including her mother, who lives next door and teases her about her *kwi* ways—her dress, her way of eating, and so on. On the other hand, her former friends in the Town Centre, shocked at her choosing to live 'among all those tribal people' have largely ostracized her. Such aberrant individuals as Mr. W and Mrs. T are not very numerous, but their fate serves to show more generally accepted behaviour in sharp relief.

The characteristics of the large section of the population represented by category E have been discussed in previous chapters. They are by no means an undifferentiated mass, but are divided vertically according to tribes, the tribal divisions being reflected in, although not entirely coinciding with, religious, occupational and residential ones. Most of the people falling into this category are illiterate or have only a few years of schooling: it will be recalled that 61 per cent. of the adult men in my sample had not passed Grade 6. A large proportion—probably the

4 See Mayer, 1955, p. 25.

majority—are Christians, most usually Methodists, Baptists, or members of the Pentecostal or similar separatist churches. Even where they are Methodists or Baptists, they do not normally attend the same churches as the civilized. Of the total adult population in my sample, 29 per cent. had joined neither church nor mosque, and such people normally belonged to no other voluntary association (except in so far as the Poro and Sande societies can be so identified), but relied on their own families and kin both for their social life and for social security. Those who do join associations, most frequently join those formed within their own tribe. They are aware of their position at the bottom of the social ladder, but—like working-class people elsewhere—are interested more in increasing their income and material standard of living than in improving their social status. As Little writes of Sierra Leone:

... the non-literate individual is alive to and is fully prepared to acknowledge that 'education' has certain advantages—it can be a means to a higher income and a less arduous life—but he is quite unmoved by the spiritual and other non-material benefits it is supposed to confer... It is doubtful if he feels that the educated African is his superior in any intrinsic sense of the term, and he is inclined to scoff at and regard as completely faddy the emulation of some Western customs—such as boiling drinking-water and protecting food from flies.[5]

They encourage their children, or at least their sons, to 'learn book' so that they can get better-paid jobs, while at the same time deploring the rifts in the family which inevitably result from education. Ambivalent attitudes towards civilized status are often apparent in the use of the adjective *kwi*. Originally a Kru term for 'white-man-fashion' it is now used by people of many tribal origins in a joking sense, with underlying disapproval. Thus, one who changes his eating habits, drinks tea or coffee, eats potatoes, complains that the food is over-peppered, or one who sits alone reading and writing or complains about household noise (a very real problem for many young students) may be teased for being *kwi*. The same joking use crops up among the educated themselves: an Honorable of tribal origin, who had sent his niece to school in England, told me that: 'She came back talking so *kwi*, you couldn't understand a word'—and proceeded to give an excellent imitation of public school English. The existence of a

5 Little, op. cit., p. 228.

graded social hierarchy which one may reasonably characterize as an embryonic social class structure, and the fact that there is a high rate of upward social mobility, does not mean (any more than it does in other societies based on social class) that people at *all* grades want to raise their social, as distinct from their economic, status. A great many of the young tribespeople, however, are reacting against the rigid system in which their parents grew up, in which tribespeople in general formed an inferior caste. A class of thirty-eight night school students—clerks, drivers, policemen and so on—wrote, at my request, an essay explaining why they wanted an education. All listed, and elaborated at some length, the material rewards of education. But over half also mentioned that, by getting an education, they hoped to gain in prestige or 'respect':

Before, my people were all slaves. Government made them work, hard work on roads and farms, no pay. Now I go to school, I get respect, I be no longer slave.

In Figure IV I have summarized the characteristics of the various strata in the urban population in terms of position in the power structure, occupational groupings, membership of voluntary associations, and a variety of factors which may be called 'style of life'. I now examine in more detail the extent to which occupation-income categories form the basis of social ranking.

THE SOCIAL RANKING OF OCCUPATIONS

In Western industrial societies, occupation and income are the basic criteria of social ranking, but in Monrovia, as in other developing African towns, other factors, especially education and style of life, are at least as important.[6] Often the groupings ranked on all these criteria coincide: for the 'civilized way of life' demands a certain minimum income level, and income relates to occupation. For the most unambiguously 'civilized' occupations—those in the professional and clerical category—a degree of formal schooling is a prerequisite, and the prestige attached to education, as such, gets transferred to the job. Authority over others is also an important criterion of social status. A senior official has authority arising out of his job; his salary and other emoluments make him a wealthy man in relation to the mass of the population, and the manner in which he invests his wealth spreads his influence. As

[6] See Mitchell and Epstein, 1959, p. 30.

owner of a rubber-farm, for example, he has command over a private labour force, as owner of land or buildings rented out, he has authority as a landlord. Even clerks and messengers on the lowest level of the bureaucratic hierarchy have a great deal of power because they are the persons through whom approaches must be made to higher levels.

TABLE 20. *Occupation and income*

	Wages or Income					
	Under $20 %	$20–49 %	$50–99 %	$100 or more %	Average $	Effective samples
Professional and clerical	1	32	51	17	72	100% = 138
Skilled and semi-skilled, and drivers	3	60	33	3	48	100% = 216
Stevedores, port-workers, domestics, unskilled	29	67	3	1	24	100% = 171
Traders, craftsmen, fishermen	14	52	18	16	60	100% = 121

The correspondence between social ranking based on occupation, education, wealth, and authority is, however, incomplete. There is in the first place the anomalous position of the traders, conspicuously absent as an occupational category in Figure IV. Table 20 shows the distribution of incomes in the four main occupational categories among the men questioned in my sample survey. Nearly as high a proportion of the 'traders, craftsmen and fishermen' as of the white-collar and professional men were making at least $100 a month. Fishermen and craftsmen were here grouped with traders as representing the bulk of the self-employed population: in fact, of the traders alone, nearly half had incomes at this level and one in four was making more than $200 a month. That is, they include men—diamond dealers, for example —who have considerable wealth yet lack both political authority and recognized 'civilized' status. For the majority of the wealthy Liberian traders are Mandingo or Vai who retain their Islamic religion, their tribal dress, and polygynous marriage. The general scale of status-ranking depends not only on wealth but also on the adoption of the Christian religion, Western dress, and at least the formality of monogamous marriage. Some of the Mandingo traders have fine houses and sleek American limousines, and several have had a Western-style education. By a strange anomaly, their magnificent and graceful traditional dress is the style which the civilized Liberians, including the Americo-Liberians, most often adopt when travelling abroad, that is, in situations where they want to be identified as Africans. But in Monrovia the Mandingo traders—and the Muslim population as a whole—are largely isolated from the rest of the population. It is generally said to be impossible for one who publicly remains a Muslim to get a government job, and none of the professional and clerical workers in my sample were in fact Muslims. Goldthorpe writes of the trading class in East Africa:

At first, the business class are quite separate from the educated élite; very many of them are illiterate and quite usually many are not Christians... This separation can last only for a time, however. Members of the élite become farmers and businessmen part-time and in retirement. ... And even more importantly, the children of both classes go to the same schools, while education overseas is an aspiration of both also...[7]

The same outcome is possible in Liberia, although it would, among other things, depend on a weakening of the entrenched position of Christianity. In Monrovia, the pattern was laid in the nineteenth century for an association between the socio-political and commercial élite. I have discussed in Chapter I the reasons for its disappearance. During the first half of the twentieth century, commerce was almost entirely in the hands of foreigners—American, European, or Lebanese. The Mandingo traders—in diamonds, gold, foreign exchange, cattle, curios and so on—are a post-war phenomenon. And recently a number of 'civilized' people, including upper-class Americo-Liberians—have started shops, laundries, beauty parlours, taxi companies, hotels, etc. Some are full-time businessmen, others have government posts and operate businesses as a sideline. They are not yet a large enough group to affect the bureaucratically based social hierarchy. But their existence indicates the possibility of a return to the situation where commerce was an acceptable alternative to 'government, politics and the law' for the civilized Liberian.

For different reasons, the 'skilled and semi-skilled workers'—including electricians, mechanics, building artisans and drivers

[7] Goldthorpe, 1961, p. 153.

—cannot be placed, as an occupational category, on the social hierarchy illustrated in Figure IV. For among them— even among the more highly skilled—there is considerable variation in levels of income, education, and the outward evidences of 'civilization'. Of those in my sample, nearly half had had some formal schooling, although less than one in ten had completed Grade 8, and only 6 per cent had entered high school. Of the professional and clerical workers, on the other hand, nearly three-quarters had had at least some high school education. Nevertheless,

TABLE 21. *Occupation and education*

	Education				
	None %	Elementary* %	High school* %	College* %	Effective sample
Professional and clerical	3	25	52	19	100% = 153
Skilled and semi-skilled	55	38	6	—	100% = 241
Port-workers, stevedores, domestics, unskilled	73	21	6	—	100% = 193
Traders, craftsmen, fishers	70	22	7	1	100% = 155

* The proportions given indicate those with at least *some* education on each of these three levels, i.e. they had not necessarily *completed* schooling at this level.

social distinctions between these two categories of occupation, as such, are not very clearly drawn. Neither is the prestige attached to white-collar, as distinct from manual and technical, work, so marked as it was—at least in colonial days—in other African territories.

This was illustrated in the replies of 362 schoolboys to the question: 'What do you want to do when you leave school?' The boys were drawn from the two top grades of elementary school and the first grade of high school, and were, as I describe later, of mixed ethnic and socio-economic backgrounds. Their replies are summarized in Table 22. I have included, for comparison, the results obtained by Schwab from a similar questionnaire completed by 268 schoolboys in Gwelo, Southern Rhodesia.[8] Identical proportions in the two samples wanted to take up farming or other agricultural work: in Monrovia these included rubber-farmers and

[8] Schwab, 1961, p. 135.

workers in agricultural development. A somewhat lower proportion of the Monrovia than of the Gwelo boys aimed to become professional or white-collar workers, and a higher proportion were interested in skilled manual occupations. The trend in Monrovia

TABLE 22. *Occupational aspirations of schoolboys*

Occupational category	Gwelo %	Monrovia %
Professional and white collar	66	50
Skilled and supervisory (including police)*	12	21
Agricultural	16	16
Commercial	4	1
Miscellaneous	1	2
Unskilled	—	—
Total samples	100% = 268	100% = 362

* My occupational categories are here adjusted to match Schwab's.

is much clearer if we ignore the occupational categories and list the actual occupations most frequently aimed at:

Occupation	Numbers aspiring
Medical doctor	59
Farmer, agriculturalist	59
Electrician or mechanic	48
Engineer	41
Lawyer or judge	27
Minister, priest, missionary	19
Accountant, clerk, secretary, book-keeper	18
Statesman, politician, head of department, diplomat	16
Teacher	13
Scientist, geologist, chemist	13

Aspiring doctors and agriculturalists came well in the lead, but would-be electricians, mechanics and engineers were next; after a considerable gap came the lawyers, the judges, accountants, clerks and so on, with teachers and scientists at the bottom of the list. Schwab does not give the actual distribution of choices within each occupational category, but from studies of other

Rhodesian towns one may guess that there is an emphasis on clerical work and teaching. Xydias found such preferences in replies to a similar questionnaire completed by schoolchildren in Stanleyville in 1953—when it was under Belgian rule: 59 per cent. wanted to be clerks, 24 per cent. teachers, 9 per cent. doctors or medical assistants, 4 per cent. to take Holy Orders, and so on.[9] Interest in technical and mechanical work was much greater among the Monrovia students, despite the prestige long attached to 'government, politics and the law'.

It was also apparent from this inquiry that, despite the established role of the Americo-Liberians, the Monrovia students (most of whom were from the tribes) did not feel that their chances were necessarily circumscribed by their ethnic origins: their choices, that is, were not inhibited, as those of the Gwelo and Stanleyville children were, by the operation of a colour bar. And a further interesting point emerged from the particular occupational preferences of the Monrovia children. Apart from farming, the three types of work most favoured are all new ones for Liberians. Most of the doctors and engineers in the republic are in fact foreigners: a number of young Liberians are now studying abroad for these professions, although they often have difficulty in qualifying because of their lack of basic educational qualifications. Electricians and mechanics, on the other hand, more usually learn their work on the job, and large numbers of Liberians are already in these occupations, although few are as yet fully trained. Most of them are employed by foreign firms and are being trained by foreigners. Air pilots and scientists in Liberia are also almost all foreigners. Is one, then, to conclude that the preference for these occupations reflects prestige attached to foreign, that is, for the most part, to white, occupations as distinct from those of the Americo-Liberian élite? This may be partly true, but it does not explain the actual selection of occupations, for whites in Monrovia are also diplomats, teachers, businessmen and entrepreneurs.

The schoolboys were also asked to state the reasons for their choice of occupations. Like schoolchildren elsewhere, they found this a difficult task, and also like children elsewhere, a large proportion (half of the 141 who attempted to answer the question) 'wanted to be useful' to their country or their 'people' or their families, and some added that Liberia needed doctors, engineers,

[9] Xydias, 1956, p. 357.

P

farmers and so on. But Liberia also needs qualified teachers, for example. One thing that the most favoured occupations have in common is the possibility of having a good income. Another is a certain dramatic quality: the medical profession has a particular and immediate appeal in a country where poor health is widespread. The schoolgirls also were attracted to the medical professions: of the 151 girls who replied to this section of the questionnaire, 75 wanted to be nurses, 14 doctors, 14 clerical workers, and seamstresses, hairdressers and dieticians followed well in the rear. Finally, the favoured occupations all offer the possibility of independent employment, or at least employment outside Government. Only three of the boys explicitly gave this as the reason for their choice of occupation, but in conversation quite a few young students claim that they do not want to work for Government or 'have anything to do with politics'. This by no means implies that they do not take government jobs when it comes to the point, but it does indicate a trend away from the established scale of occupational prestige which follows the government hierarchy.

THE EXTENT AND NATURE OF SOCIAL MOBILITY

Mobility from the tribal into the civilized section of the population depends primarily on education. Now, most young people— or at least most young men, whatever their background, would like an education to high school level at least. But only a few get as far as this, and many do not succeed in getting to school at all. In principle, school attendance is compulsory between the ages of 6 and 16 years,[10] but in practice this does not apply because of the shortage of school places—as in many other African towns with a large number of recent immigrants. In Monrovia in 1956, rather less than half the school-age population (in this case taken to be 5 to 19 years) was enrolled in schools, although the proportion among the boys was higher than among the girls.[11] Which young people, then, succeed in getting an education? The answer may be expected to throw some light on the process of social mobility. For education, though not a guarantee of civilized status, is a prerequisite for upward mobility into the civilized class.

[10] Liberian *Code of Laws*, 11:1.
[11] Census of the Population of Monrovia, 1956, and Census of Schools in Monrovia, 1956.

The simplest way of finding an answer to this question was to examine the backgrounds of those who were attending schools in Monrovia at the time of my study. It was primarily for this reason that I administered a questionnaire (some of whose results I have already quoted) to all students in Grades 7, 8, or 9, who attended class on the days of my visits, in ten schools. These are the top two grades of elementary school and the first grade of high school, and they were selected because Grade 7 is now a minimum qualification for clerks, a high school certificate providing a much better guarantee of such employment. The students in the three final grades of high school were omitted for lack of time, but in any case there is a marked falling off in enrolment after Grade 9, and students in this grade account for nearly half of the total high school population.[12] The inquiry was carried out in ten day-schools, including government, mission and private ones, and covered the great majority of children in these three grades in Monrovia. There is no system of external examinations in Monrovia, and educational standards vary greatly. To some extent, a student's future success depends on which school he has attended. Most of the ten schools selected were, however, those generally regarded as having a relatively high standard, so this did not greatly affect the significance of the results. The final sample included 368 boys and 166 girls. The average age of the boys was 18 years, of the girls 16 years, and of the boys one in four was over 20. The children born in Monrovia had reached these grades at an earlier age than had those brought or sent in from the tribal areas or smaller townships. Some had had interrupted school careers.

Fees vary from school to school: tuition fees are not charged in government elementary schools, although various other charges are made. All students need some sort of financial support to cover their clothing and maintenance. A very small proportion (if we exclude night-school students) are earning on their own account, and a few have scholarships or grants. But the great majority depend at least in part on their families or guardians, or on patrons. Obviously, then, a child's chances of getting educated will relate to some extent to the socio-economic status of his family. Therefore, the basic questions concerned the ethnic origins, educational levels, and religious adherence of the students' parents, and the occupations of their fathers. However, only 45 per

[12] Census of Schools in Monrovia, 1956.

cent. of the boys and 60 per cent. of the girls were living with one or both of their parents, and among these many were illegitimate or from homes broken by divorce or separation. Of the remainder, many were of illiterate parents (sometimes living in Monrovia), but had been sent to live with educated relatives or adoptive parents or guardians, and were being supported by these. On the other hand, a number of children, especially those of upper-class parents, are sent to schools abroad. For these reasons, examination of the parental backgrounds of those actually attending schools in Monrovia gives only a rough indication of the extent to which, among Monrovia children in general, their backgrounds affected their chances of getting an education.

TABLE 23. *Ethnic origin of schoolchildren*

Father's tribe	Boys %	Girls %	Estimated proportion in total urban population
Kru-Grebo	24	25	25
Bassa-De	20	18	20
Vai-Gola-Mende-Mandingo	20	21	15
Kpelle-Loma	13	7	10
Other Liberian tribes	10	2	7
Americo-Liberian or Congo	10	13	16
Foreign origin	7	14	7
Total effective sample	100% = 358	100% = 165	100

To what extent is success in getting an education dependent on one's ethnic origin? This is the first and most obvious question. In Table 23, I compare the ethnic distribution of the students' fathers, with the estimated ethnic distribution of the total population in Monrovia (p. 36). There is a broad correspondence between the two sets of figures, suggesting that no overwhelming advantage attaches to membership of any particular ethnic group. The proportion of Vai students was relatively high, as one might expect, since among all the coastal tribes, it was the Vai who were earliest drawn into government service and 'civilized' society. On the other hand, Americo-Liberian students, especially the boys, were represented in *smaller* numbers than one would expect from their estimated distribution in the total population.

However, this must be set against the fact that while *some* children of tribal parents are sent to schools abroad, it is *customary* for America-Liberian children, especially boys, to be sent overseas. In the higher grades, not covered by my sample, the effect of the absence of the America-Liberian boys is more obvious. From a survey of students at the University of Liberia in 1957, carried out by Professor Robert T. Roberts, it emerged that 69 per cent. of the girls but only 20 per cent. of the boys had had English as their first language.[13]

TABLE 24. *Education of fathers of schoolchildren*

Fathers' education	Boys %	Girls %
Nil	47	14
Elementary*	17	11
High school*	24	49
University*	11	26
Total effective sample	100% = 336	100% = 150

* That is, at least some education at this level.

In the selective process there was a very clear weighting in favour of children of parents who were themselves educated. One would expect this, both because educated peope are more likely than uneducated to see that their children get to school, and because they are more likely to be able to afford it. Over half the boys and 86 per cent. of the girls had fathers with at least some schooling, while a third of the boys and no less than three-quarters of the girls had fathers who had attended high school or university (Table 24). These high proportions are particularly striking since in the parental generation education to this level was much more rare than it is today. But as an indication of the present pace of social change, it was made significant that nearly half of the boys were the sons of illiterate men. Many of these fathers had occupations arising out of tribal economies—fishers, farmers, hunters, and chiefs—although 'farmer' in Table 25 also included several full-time rubber-planters. (In addition, of course, a number of the 'professional' fathers also owned rubber-farms.)

[13] I am grateful to Professor Roberts for this information.

In many ways, the most interesting feature of the results of this inquiry was the contrast between the backgrounds of the girls and the boys. A relatively small number of girls are sent to school at all, and of those who are, many drop out before they reach the seventh grade—because they get married, or have babies, or are expected to help with household chores, or simply for lack of incentive to continue. In the case of the girls, selectivity in favour of those with educated parents, and in favour of those whose fathers' occupations fell into the 'professional and clerical' category, was very marked indeed (Tables 24 and 25). Seventy-five per cent. of the girls, but only 35 per cent. of the boys, had fathers with at least some high school education, and half the girls, but only a quarter of the boys, had fathers in the accepted 'civilized' occupations.

TABLE 25. *Occupations of fathers of schoolchildren*

Father's occupation	Boys %	Girls %
Professional and clerical	27	49
Skilled manual, driver	6	7
Trader, craftsman	10	14
Seaman, port-worker, domestic, labourer	3	2
Police, army, etc.	4	3
Fisher, farmer, hunter, chief	50	25
Effective sample	100% = 336	100% = 155

Americo-Liberians were also much more numerous among the girls: 13 per cent. had Americo-Liberian fathers (Table 23), but many were of mixed parentage and in fact one out of three had at least one Americo-Liberian parent. This means that there is often a big social gap between boys and girls in the classroom. This, and the overall scarcity of educated girls, affects the boys' chances of upward social mobility, since it is difficult to establish a civilized household unless one can find an educated wife.

Roughly half of the school students, then, had illiterate parents. But this does not mean that the next generation of 'civilized' will be twice the size of the present one, because education alone does not guarantee upward social mobility. In the course of the social survey, we came across several instances of labourers and domestics who had high school certificates. The students' chances of completing their schooling, and, having completed it, of finding suitable jobs, depend in large part on their contacts or on their finding influential patrons. Things are much easier for a young man who, although his parents are illiterate, has at least one relative, or, failing that, a person from his home town (with whom fictitious kinship ties may be established), already in 'civilized society'. It has often been pointed out that kinship obligations in Africa hinder the development of social classes, since a heavy burden falls on the wealthy members of a kin group, and this slows down differentiation in standards of living.[14] This is also true in Monrovia, especially with the decline of the old practice of 'passing for America-Liberian' and cutting oneself off from kinsfolk and tribespeople. But there is another aspect to this: family obligations can also promote social mobility. One of the most usual obligations pinned on the civilized is that of educating the children of illiterate kinsfolk and/or of finding them jobs. We have seen in Chapter IV that most civilized households contain children of uneducated relatives who have been sent to learn civilized ways and to attend school. Over the years, a great many children may pass through one household in this way, and become incorporated into the civilized population. That is, the upward mobility of one individual can be followed by the upward mobility of a wide group of relatives—real or fictitious—and over several generations this has a cumulative effect.

SOCIAL CLASS AND ETHNIC ORIGINS

From a comparative point of view, the most interesting feature of Monrovia's social structure is the fact that for well over a century rulers and ruled have been of the same race. In other African urban areas, including Freetown, whose history is most nearly parallel to that of Monrovia, the presence and role of the European has, in the past, determined the manner in which stratification has taken place, and the speed with which social classes have emerged.[15] The Europeans provided the model for the 'civilized way of life'. Because of their dominant political

[14] See, for example, Goldthorpe 1956, p. 151, and references quoted in Forde (ed.), 1956, p. 215.
[15] Banton, 1957, chap. vi. See also Mitchell, 1957 and essays by Schwab and Goldthorpe in Southall (ed.), 1961.

positions, their monopoly of important economic ones, and their social exclusiveness, socio-economic differentiation was slow to develop among Africans. Moreover, opposition to the Europeans served, in varying degrees, to unite the ethnically disparate people they ruled and minimize the political effects of tribal loyalties. Balandier wrote in 1955:

> The groups to which [the term social classes] would normally apply are not as yet clearly differentiated, and they are being formed by a process very different from that which resulted in their emergence in Europe, for instance, after the industrial revolution. Their formation is bound up with an economic development conditioned by intervention from without (that of a colonizing power), and the resultant social categories, whatever their relationship to one another, are all in a position of inferiority *vis à vis* the dominant European community. The stronger the antagonism felt towards the colonial (European) community, the less will be the friction between the socially unequal elements in the African population. Moreover, there is a limit to the expansion of new social categories . . . the colonizing power's authority goes far to prevent the ascent of individuals who might prove capable of forming an upper class of sufficient size to play a leading role.[16]

The pace of political change has been such that in many African countries the situation which Balandier described is now a matter of history. However, for many decades to come, students of social stratification in the independent territories will have to take into account the formative influence of the white colonial powers.

Now, in Liberia, economic development has been 'conditioned from without', but *not* by the colonizing power. The crucial question is, to what extent the Americans and Europeans, on the one hand, and the Americo-Liberians on the other, have filled the role which Europeans have filled in other countries.

(a) *The white foreigners*

I use the invidious adjective 'white', for lack of a better one, to cover Europeans and white Americans. The social position of American Negroes, West Indians, and Africans from other territories, is a more complex one, depending largely on whether they come as settlers, or on short-term contracts with Government, foreign companies, or international organizations. For they,

---

[16] Balandier, in Forde (ed.), 1956, p. 501.

unlike the whites, can become naturalized Liberians. The relevant clause in the Constitution (Article V, Section 13) reads:

The great object in forming these Colonies, being to provide a home for the dispersed and oppressed children of Africa, and to regenerate and enlighten this benighted continent, none but Negroes or persons of Negro descent shall be eligible to citizenship in this Republic.

Before the Second World War, white foreigners were only a handful in Monrovia. With the post-war commercial boom, they have come in large numbers, and now number about a thousand persons (p. 36). From time to time individual whites have had considerable economic powers in the republic,[17] but since 1848 they have had no political authority. The republic depends for its economic development on foreign capital, but the question of the possible effects of this fact on government policy is a quite separate one from the question of the social role of the white personnel of foreign organizations in Monrovia. Or to put it in other words, whatever influence the American Government and the Directors of the Firestone Company may or may not have on the Liberian Government, such influence is not apparent to the general public, and whites in Monrovia in no sense form a political élite. They cannot become citizens. Only citizens can own land, and only citizens may be employed in the civil service—although a few individual foreigners work on contract with Government, as technicians, doctors, teachers, or advisers, under Liberian Heads of Department. Government is still the largest single employer— giving work to about one in four of the adult men in the Monrovia population and, significantly, to over half of the professional and clerical workers who form the bulk of the civilized population. Social ranking, as we have seen, follows the pattern provided by the government hierarchy: whites fall outside this hierarchy and the question of their social position is peripheral and not central to the topic of social stratification. (We are here concerned specifically with Monrovia: the situation is somewhat different in the unitary, paternalist community at Firestone plantation.) Senior foreign administrative and managerial staff in commercial firms and technical missions, heads of Christian missions, and of course diplomats, are regularly invited to formal functions at the Executive Mansion and elsewhere, but even at such functions they

---

[17] Brown, 1941, discusses the role of foreign financial and economic advisers who were appointed from time to time.

tend to form separate cliques. Potentially they are of significance in that their way of life sets a model for 'civilization' which provides an alternative to the Americo-Liberian one. Their influence is limited, however, by the fact that most white foreigners have little informal social contact with Liberians. Their private social life takes place within the foreign community, which is itself split along lines of nationality. The Lebanese, many of whom have lived for most of their lives in Monrovia, have a social club, while the social activities of other foreigners centre around their respective embassies. Most of the men meet Liberians in the course of their work, but their wives seldom get a chance to chat informally with Liberians other than domestic servants, taxi-drivers, shop assistants, and so on, and their attitudes, like those of colonial wives in other territories, are conditioned by this situation.

Finally, the foreigners do not form a model for the indigenous élite, as they did, in the past at least, for the Creoles in Freetown.[18] The Americo-Liberians regard their culture as 'Western', but consider their version of the 'Western way of life' to be as valid as any other. The different roles of the Europeans in Free-town on the one hand and Monrovia on the other may be illustrated by considering who sets styles of dress. Porter, in his recent study of Creole society in Freetown, describes how in the nineteenth century Creoles wore the heavy, formal, Victorian style of dress which, as we have seen, was also worn by the Americo-Liberians. During the 1920's, the European population (which during the same period increased considerably in size), began to dress more lightly.

The open-neck shirt now rivals the semi-stiff collar except on more formal occasions, and a pair of shorts is as popular as trousers for day to day work. . . . The younger elements among the Creoles soon came to similar conclusions; so while their fathers dressed and sweated in woollen suits, their sons dressed in lighter textures or were unencumbered by tie or jacket. Thus when the tribal individual in the 1920's began to challenge Creole ascendancy in the economic order, he tried also to justify and validate his material or economic success by enjoying that 'style of life' which had traditionally characterized the Creole class. They entered the race, however, at a stage when the Creole had abandoned the top hat and coat for khaki shorts and shirt.[19]

[18] See Porter, 1963, many references.   [19] Ibid., p. 103.

In Monrovia, on the other hand, the style—for foreigners and for tribespeople—is set by the indigenous, largely Americo-Liberian, élite. Suit and tie are *de rigueur* for the civilized population. No one, Liberian or foreign, enters a government office in shorts, and even foreigners very seldom adopt this wear in the street—much as they would like to, for Monrovia has one of the most oppressive climates in the world. Such dress reforms as have been suggested —usually by persons of tribal origin—are towards the adoption, not of less formal Western style, but of the loose-fitting gowns worn by local tribespeople.

Attitudes of Liberians to whites differ greatly, with both degree of sophistication and frequency of contact, the more positive attitudes being expressed by those lower in the social scale. Whites may be admired for their technical skills, for their financial reliability (especially their punctual payment of wages), and for their even-temperedness—they 'respect one another', 'do not show anger or get excited' and so on. On the negative side, they may be considered cold, formal and insincere, 'out to make money'. Particularly by educated Liberians (tribal as well as Americo-Liberian) who work with whites, the latter are suspected, often with justification, of being hypercritical and hypocritical, and unsympathetic in spite of apparent friendliness. Official ideology, as expressed in newspaper editorials and history text-books, makes foreigners the scapegoats for all kinds of anti-social and anti-governmental activities: thus, in a recent history book in general use in schools:

Unification has steadily progressed in spite of rebellions instigated by treacherous foreigners.[20]

This interpretation of events is not necessarily accepted by the general population: nevertheless, it underlies a situation in which many Liberians actively avoid contact with whites, seldom inviting them to their homes, and seldom accepting invitations. And this perpetuates the social isolation of the white foreigners. However important the governments or commercial firms they represent, they fall outside the Liberian social hierarchy.

(b) *The Americo-Liberians*
In Figure IV I have indicated by vertical shading the approximate proportions of Americo-Liberians in the civilized population.

[20] Henries, 1950, p. 26.

This is only an estimate based on personal impressions, and refers to people who identify themselves as America-Liberians, since the descendants of the nineteenth-century immigrants can no longer be clearly demarcated as an ethnic group. America-Liberians in the former sense still provide the basis of the socio-political élite, despite the entry of tribespeople into upper-class society. They also form an élite in terms of wealth, for although foreign interests play a vital part in the republic's economy, certain America-Liberians are manifestly richer than the local representatives of such interests. They probably have higher incomes, but—what is more important—they have finer houses, motor cars, and clothes, and entertain on a grander scale. Of course, this does not mean that *all* America-Liberians are either powerful or wealthy, although it is unusual for those in Monrovia to have occupations other than those which I have grouped under the heading 'professional and clerical', and I have never heard of one who was a manual labourer. In the popular image, however, the two upper strata of the social hierarchy, and sometimes the entire civilized population, are often classed as 'America-Liberian' on the basis of their way of life and their association with the source of political authority. Uneducated tribespeople are usually able to identify members of their own tribes among the civilized; civilized from other tribes are lumped together as 'America-Liberians', 'Liberians' or 'The Government'. Underlying this is the sentiment that 'he who is not with us is against us'.

This image seems to be a survival from the period which lasted until the 1940's, when Monrovia's social structure was based on a caste-like system, in which the America-Liberians were the upper caste, the tribespeople the lower. Tribespeople were being incorporated into the America-Liberian community, usually by intermarriage and adoption, but such people normally changed their names and removed themselves from the orbit of tribal life. The 'passing' was usually secretive, in so far as it could be in so small a community, and was possible because of the similarity in appearance between the two castes.[21] By the end of the 1930's, however, it seems that class divisions were beginning to appear within the tribal section of the population, in that a number of tribespeople were coming to be regarded as 'civilized' or 'educated' without necessarily attempting to 'pass'. The vital period of

[21] Cf. Rose, 1958, p. 225.

transition seems to have been the years following the evacuation of Krutown in 1945, the division of its population along class lines, and the movement of the educated teachers, lawyers, and so on, to residential areas outside the new tribal communities. Answers to a question on previous places of residence in Monrovia, asked in the course of my social survey, suggested that similar movements were taking place from other tribal communities at about this time.

During the intervening fifteen years, the class structure has become more and more an open one, and differentiation within the urban tribal population has rapidly increased with the greater number and variety of jobs available both within Government and outside it. Few young people today attempt to 'pass' for Americo-Liberian. One symbol of this is the retention of tribal names by the civilized, and the official resumption of tribal names by those who had previously discarded them. The correspondence between ethnic origin and the two main tiers of the social hierarchy has broken down, but the *image* of all Americo-Liberians as powerful and wealthy, and, conversely, of all those in high positions in Government as Americo-Liberians, has outlived it. It is accompanied by a deep-seated hostility of the have-nots towards the haves, which has been intensified by the exodus of white colonial powers from other West African territories. Said one illiterate Kru stevedore:

Independence? We got no independence. The people on France side, the Gold Coast people, they got it. The Americo-Liberians, they got it. We can't say anything, if we do, they put us in the B.T.C. [gaol]. Some of our people now get jobs in Government. But we poor people, we never get anywhere . . . ten years ago, stevedores 40 cents, now 55 cents. In Gold Coast, they have new ships, men being sent overseas to learn captain, engineer, pilot. We no sent overseas, we don't get anywhere. [Then he added illogically]: So I tell my son, you learn book. . . .

And a Kpelle university student:

We students had to elect a class president. Some of the Americo-Liberians got together and said they didn't want anyone from the tribes. So we interior students got together, and we agreed to elect a Gio boy. We felt we had a majority. These people are too hard in their hearts, they cannot change. . . . There will be a civil war. They think so much of themselves, and who are they. You know, they think they are better than us, but they are all sons of slaves—they were slaves here in Africa before they went to America, that is how they were sent.

To my disputing this, however, he replied, with rare objectivity: 'Yes, I know, but when someone hits you, you look for weapons to hit back.' Among the students, tensions between the two main ethnic groups are particularly strong because this is one of the few situations where long-ingrained prejudices come into the open in a face-to-face situation. It is apparent, however, that neither the stevedore nor the student saw his life-chances as entirely circumscribed by his tribal origin: the first, concluding that his son must 'learn book', implied that he did see a way of 'getting somewhere', while the second was in fact himself one of the privileged, since he was about to leave for overseas on a scholarship provided by a foreign government and subsidized by the Liberian Government; immediately before, he had been discussing the problem of what to do with so much money. Should he travel and see the world, during university holidays, or should he save money to start a rubber-farm when he returned? The roots of resentment were expressed more clearly by a third man, a Vai who held a fairly senior position in Government:

The Unification program. What is it? Look, the President goes around the country and talks nicely, and the poor people are taken in. He brings them into the House of Representatives—what use are they there, these tribal people—they understand nothing, they don't even speak English. He doesn't put people like us there to speak for our people, we might say something! Anyway, the House of Representatives is nothing, it does what the President wants, it is all for the Americo-Liberians. Those poor ignorant tribal people, they think they are big men, because they sit there! Look, it's like this: before, the Americo-Liberians had all the bread. There were ten loaves, and they had them all. Then this Tubman comes along, and says 'here are three loaves', and the people say, 'what a wonderful President we have'. But the other seven he keeps for himself, for his own people. With them three loaves he bought our manhood.

My research in Monrovia was primarily concerned with social change in the tribal population. I would hesitate to assess the extent to which privilege does, in fact, attach to ethnic origins, as such, as distinct from membership of the socio-economic strata characterized in Figure IV as the 'Honorables' and the 'élite'. That persons in official positions, and their families, have certain privileges is quite evident. One important context in which this issue often arises is in the allocation of funds for overseas scholarships. Until recently, such funds were available, not only for university students, but also for students in elementary and high school grades. In 1958, an executive (i.e. a presidential) order discontinued grants for students in elementary grades: there had been a great deal of public resentment over the practice of using government funds for grants on this level. Commented one of the local newspapers with unusual bluntness:

This means . . . that the parents of 76 Liberian students of elementary standard now studying abroad will have to reach down into their pockets or vaults or wherever they stack their kudos and finance their children's education. Of course, there is the alternative of bringing them home. This, however will hardly create many problems. A check of the list of students abroad by our reporters at the Department of Public Instruction reveals that most of the elementary school children studying abroad on government money have parents who possess the ways and means to take care of their children themselves. In other words the great majority of the children . . . come from families in the top bracket of our society.[22]

The 'top bracket', however, is not exclusively Americo-Liberian, and these seventy-six students included, to my knowledge, at least half a dozen children of tribal origin—that is, of parents who identified themselves as tribespeople. Probably they were much more numerous than this; certainly many more of the seventy-six were drawn from families where intermarriage with tribespeople had taken place.

To the extent that privilege attaches to those in official position, it attaches primarily to the Americo-Liberians who have the monopoly of the most senior positions, but it also attaches to membership of specific tribes. For it is the coastal tribes who had mission schools in the nineteenth century, and have long been in contact with 'civilization', whose members have attained senior positions in Government. Since advancement depends very largely on family connexions and patronage, this situation is self-perpetuating, since there is an unwritten obligation for a 'big man' to help his kinsfolk and tribespeople. We have seen that a young educated man seeking a job is likely to approach an official who is a relative, or at least one from his own tribe, and the result of this situation is obvious enough in the homogeneous tribal clusters within several government departments—the Vai and related peoples in the Interior Department, the Kru in the

[22] *The Listener*, Monrovia, 19.7.58.

Department of Public Health, and so on. This is leading to the emergence of a new alignment of the immigrants from the interior tribes, especially the young students, *vis à vis* the coastal people as a whole.

A further trend of change in the relationship between ethnic grouping and the social hierarchy is already apparent. Persons of the established upper class are becoming less dependent on Government for a living. Foreign commercial enterprises provide opportunities for legal advisers, personnel officers, and so on, although most of their managerial and technical staff, as yet, is foreign. A few Liberians have started their own commercial enterprises. But the development of private rubber farms has now become a very common spare-time occupation for the upper class, and as the farms mature they provide their owners with an economic alternative to government service. A number of people have already moved out of Government (and out of Monrovia) to their rubber-farms, and others privately consider doing so. They include not only Americo-Liberians, but also tribespeople, especially Vai, who were earliest drawn into government service and have, until recently at least, predominated among educated tribespeople in Monrovia. And on the other hand the Kru, who have in the past showed less interest in entering Government, are now coming into it in greater numbers than any other tribe—as is obvious from examination of the lists of successful Civil Service candidates. The present period is one of transition. The correlation between ethnic origin and social class remains a significant one, but the pattern of alignment of particular ethnic elements with particular social positions is changing.

In conclusion, the relationship between the Americo-Liberians and the tribespeople in Liberia has differed basically from that between white colonists and Africans elsewhere. Despite initial differences of culture and attitudes, social intermingling and, in particular, intermarriage, has been comparatively easy, because a person's ethnic origin is not apparent from his appearance. One seemingly paradoxical result of this is the comparative strength of tribal cohesiveness, since the inter-tribal unity which might have been engendered by opposition to the ruling class has been continually diluted by the assimilation into that class of the more educated and articulate of the tribespeople. *Comparative* ease of intermingling does not mean that all Americo-Liberians have been more 'open' than white colonists in their attitudes towards African tribespeople. Some have 'superior' attitudes as deep-seated as the settler population in southern Africa, and indoctrinate their children with such attitudes. Others have moved a long way towards feeling inferior to those whom they were taught to look down on. Women appear to be more 'die-hard' in their attitudes than men, and the older generation is, as one would expect, more conservative than the younger one. It is only since the Second World War that young people, especially men, have been sent abroad for their education, and during that period they have come into contact with a changing climate of world opinion. The situation has been affected also by the emergence of other independent African states, and by Liberia's taking the position of an *African* state rather than that of an outpost of Western civilization. Whether the Americo-Liberians will be prepared, as more and more educated and experienced tribespeople appear on the scene, to continue to surrender their entrenched position in Government, remains to be seen. The present development of private rubber- and other cash-crop plantations suggests that one direction of social change may be towards the formation of a landed aristocracy.

Q

APPENDIX A

THE SOCIAL SURVEY OF
EIGHT RESIDENTIAL AREAS: METHODS

THE unit of the survey for the purpose of sampling was the household, which was taken to include all persons who lived in the houses selected, including lodgers and tenants. Fifty houses in each of the eight residential areas were chosen, that is, 400 houses in all. The absence of any type of register or system of street numbers in most areas, and of arrangement in streets in some, would have made the construction of a random sample a long and complex process. In seven of the eight areas we therefore selected on the following basis: the interviewer started with any one house (sometimes his own), interviewed all his neighbours, and then all their neighbours, and so on, until he had covered the required number of houses. Where we knew in advance that an area contained sub-sections with special socio-economic characteristics, the sample was split accordingly into two or more widening circles of houses. In the Town Centre, however, sampling by this method would have frustrated the purpose of the inquiry in the area, which was to determine the characteristics of a predominantly 'civilized' population. Sampling in circles by the method I have described would have taken us away from the more prosperous street front and the houses of the plot-owners into the poorer houses and huts in the back-yards, whose inhabitants are not socially a part of the street-front neighbourhood. In this case, therefore, we simply interviewed fifty contiguous houses facing on to one street— which took us practically the whole length of the street. Because of this method of sampling, there is a faint possibility that individual households might be recognized, and I have therefore given the street a fictitious name—Kwi Street.

All persons living in each house were interviewed, including persons renting rooms. Details on household members temporarily absent—for example, stevedores at sea or women visiting relatives—were obtained from the household head or from other members of the household. One schedule listed all occupants and their relationship to the household head, and separate schedules were completed in addition for each man or woman aged 15 years or more, details being collected, as far as possible, from the individuals concerned. This, of course, frequently meant that interviewers had to return several times to the same house.

Most interviewees co-operated willingly. Some required assurance that the survey was not being made for the Government, others that it was being made with the permission of Government. Only three house-holders finally refused to be interviewed. In the tribal communities, the assistance of tribal chiefs, governors, and other local leaders was most helpful in explaining the purpose of the survey to the householders.

The bulk of the interviewing was carried out by eight men and one woman assistant. All had at least some high school education. Two were university students, one a high school student, one a teacher, two were trainees in government departments, one was a stevedore, and one a housewife. All were either residents in the areas where they interviewed, or had friends in those areas who could vouch for them. An attempt was made to exclude possible errors on the part of individual interviewers by having two or three work in each area, but this was not always possible because of the travelling distances involved.

The published report of the 1956 Census of Monrovia covered the age-sex structure of the population, educational levels, and size of households. A more detailed sample survey, covering birthplace, length of residence, and occupations, was carried out simultaneously with the census, the sample including 10 per cent. of the households in each of the eighteen residential areas, selected on a random basis. The survey was intended primarily as a scheme for training interviewers, the sample was incomplete for some areas, and the results were not published. However, with the kind permission of President Tubman and the officials concerned, I was permitted to tabulate the results of the survey for my own information. This was of great assistance when I came to select areas for detailed survey, and also as a check on the results of my own 1959 survey. There was a very clear general correspon-dence between the two sets of figures on the four topics which could be tabulated from both surveys: occupations, educational levels, birth-place, and length of residence in Monrovia. Where discrepancies seemed to arise from bias in my own sample, I have indicated this in the text.

APPENDIX B

STEVEDORES' WAGES

DEDUCTIONS BEFORE CASH REACHED HOUSEHOLD

In compiling the household budgets for Chapter IV, we found that the amounts which the stevedores, in particular, brought into the household were considerably less than the total amounts they had earned on their trips. To get a more complete picture of the wage-earners' financial obligations to kin, friends, and corporate bodies outside the household, we therefore made a separate analysis of the disposal of the *total* wages from one trip each, of twenty-four stevedores, the sample including three headmen, two second headmen, one checker and eighteen labourers. The men were chosen from different gangs, and the trips were made during the first quarter of 1959. The trips varied in length between thirty-three and fifty days, and the amount of overtime available on different trips also varied. Further, during this period, as a result of a dispute between the stevedores and the shipping companies, wage-rates were increased. The total figures for wages and overtime below are therefore not strictly comparable from one case to another, and are shown rather to set them off against deductions. In Table 26 I give details in full for three individual stevedores.

The men's income from the trip was made up of wages plus overtime, except in the case of the three headmen in the sample, who also received fees from members of their gang. Most of the men also bring home goods in the form of food and clothing, but these we did not take into account. By arrangement between the shipping companies and the Government, the stevedores are paid at the (government) Bureau of Labour, the company handing over to the bureau the total wage-packet for the gang concerned at the conclusion of each trip. The whole gang, or sometimes several gangs, receive payment on the same day, which is usually the day after their return, but this is sometimes delayed. The cash is handed to the individual men by the paymaster, a (Kru) man appointed by the President under bond of $15,000. He receives no salary, but is entitled to collect 25 cents from each stevedore on each trip.

Payments which had been made by the men from their total incomes, before they actually returned from the bureau to their households, are summarized in Table 26 under seven heads:

1. *Government taxes.* The so-called 'head tax' or 'head money tax on seamen' at the rate of \$1 per voyage must be paid 'for each Liberian seaman and sea-going labourer who ships on a vessel engaged in foreign

TABLE 26. *Stevedores' income and amounts deducted before cash reaches household*

	Case 1 Labourer	Case 2 Labourer	Case 3 Headman
Length of trip	48 days	42 days	33 days
Rate per day	60 cents	75 cents	\$ 1.00
Wages and overtime	\$47.88	\$71.10	\$61.00
Headmen's fees	—	—	\$15.50
Total income	\$47.88	\$71.10	\$76.50
Less			
1. *To Government*			
Head tax	\$ 1.00	\$ 1.00	\$ 1.00
'Per capita' tax	\$ 5.00	\$ 5.00	\$ 5.00
2. *To Kru Corporation or officials*			
Corporation fee	75 cents	75 cents	75 cents
Paymaster's fees	25 cents	25 cents	25 cents
Lawyer's fee	25 cents	25 cents	—
3. *To tribal heads*			
Section chairman	25 cents	25 cents	\$ 1.00
Dako chairman	\$ 1.00	\$ 1.00	50 cents
Panton chairman	—	—	\$ 2.50
4. *To ticket-owner*	\$ 7.75	\$ 8.00	—
5. *Personal gifts*			
To relatives outside household	\$ 2.00	\$ 6.00	—
To friends and church people	\$ 1.88	—	\$ 2.25
To headman's club	—	—	\$ 1.00
6. *Interest on advances*	—	\$ 1.00	\$ 1.00
7. *Headman's fee*	—	50 cents	—
Total deductions	\$20.13	\$24.00	\$15.25
Amounts brought home	\$27.75	\$47.10	\$61.25

trade'.[1] The companies are required by law to pay this amount themselves and not to deduct it from the wage-packets. Company officials informed me that the amount is *added* by them in the total assessment of

[1] *Code of Laws*, 35: 992.

wages and subtracted by the Government from the total wage-packet when wages are paid out at the Bureau of Labour; the labourers, however, think of the head money as having been advanced by the company and returnable to it, and in their calculations of their total income the extra dollar does not appear.

The 'per capita' tax is the annual tax to cover water, health, street lighting, etc., payable by all adults and mentioned in Chapter II. It was paid by all twenty-four men because the trips concerned were the first they had made during the year.

2. *Kru Corporation*. The composition and role of the Corporation have been discussed in Chapter III. Each stevedore pays a fee of 75 cents a trip to the Corporation, the amounts being collected at the Bureau of Labour on pay-day by the Corporation Treasurer, who at the time of my study, at least, was also the Paymaster mentioned above. Because of his dual capacity I have listed him as a corporation rather than as a government official.

The lawyer's fee collected on this trip was a special levy to cover the costs of hiring a well-known Kru lawyer to present the stevedores' case in the wage-dispute I have mentioned above.

3. *Tribal heads*. The Corporation, as described in Chapter III, has seven sections. In the more organized sections, the chairmen collect either regular subscriptions or special levies from members. Jloh and Gbeta sections provided the majority of the stevedores. Of the twenty-four stevedores in the sample, eighteen were Jloh and fifteen of them paid dues, usually of 25 cents, to the Jloh headman or his representative. In addition, nearly all the men paid amounts varying from 50 cents to $2 to the Monrovia chairman for their home town or group of towns: thus in the three cases given in detail, the men paid the amounts to the chairmen for Betu, Wissepo and Kabor respectively. Finally eighteen of the men made payments to their *panton* chairman in Monrovia, whose role has been discussed. All these chairmen, or their representatives, are normally present on pay-day to collect their dues. One man who was in financial trouble was let off his payments under all three heads, and promised to pay on his next trip.

4. *The ticket-owner*. The shipping company gives the headman concerned a number of 'tickets' corresponding to the number of men required for the trip. The headman hands over a quarter of these tickets to the Corporation, and the men who work on such tickets are regarded as corporation employees. In some cases, the headman himself retains tickets and employs several young men to work them by a similar arrangement. Usually, such men are lads on their first trip, undergoing a kind of apprenticeship. Of the twenty-four stevedores in the sample nine were working for 'ticket-owners'—either the headman

or the Corporation. From their total wages they paid amounts varying from $3 to $14.50 to the ticket-owner.

5. *Personal gifts.* Many of the men made personal gifts to relatives and/or friends who were present on pay-day or whom they met before they reached home. One of the three headmen paid a dollar to his 'headmen's association' to cover the costs of entertainment. These associations are groups of three or four headmen, each of whom by private arrangement gives the others in the group a ticket for 'his' ship, the idea being to tide the headman, and also the man whom he chooses to work on the ticket, over the time of financial stringency which arises between trips.

6. *Interest.* The companies normally make advances of $4 to $8 to the men before they go on the ship, to cover personal expenses aboard and to assist the men in providing for their households while they are away. No interest is paid on such advances. Many of the men also receive advances from their headman, and in all such cases in the sample, the men paid the money back with 25 per cent. interest (for 33 to 42 days' loan) after their return. The headman who paid interest had borrowed from his shore-headman.

7. *The headman's fee.* The three headmen received, in addition to their wages and overtime pay, a fee of 50 cents from each of the men in their gang. This custom is sanctioned by law—actually the headmen appear to be entitled to collect $1.

Nor shall any headman deduct . . . any other contribution, except the one dollar which by immemorial usage each labourer pays his headman (*Code of Laws*, 22:370).

However, only eight of the gang members on the sample actually paid a fee to the headman of their respective gangs. I was told that some of the headmen waive such payment altogether, and few ask it of gang members who are relatives or who have long worked with them.

In summary, the stevedores had then paid out amounts which in some cases totalled over a third of their income, to cover extra-household obligations, before they returned home with their pay-packets. Some of these obligations also fall on other members of the household: time did not permit us to get comparable details from men in other occupations, but it did appear that the financial burden fell most heavily upon the stevedores. In part, this is because of the way they are paid: since they are paid through Government, taxes and fees can be easily collected, and since they are paid in gangs of thirty to fifty men at the same time and in the same place, it is relatively easy for tribal and other officials to attend and collect dues before the cash is spent.

APPENDIX C

A NOTE ON INTERIOR ADMINISTRATION

THE hinterland and 'areas within the counties wholly inhabited by uncivilized natives' (to quote the Interior Regulations), are administered by a type of indirect rule modelled on that of British colonial practice. The hinterland is divided into three provinces, containing in all ten districts, under the supervision of provincial and district commissioners who are officers of the Interior Department. The districts and the tribal areas within the (coastal) counties are subdivided into chiefdoms, under the immediate authority of Paramount Chiefs. These chiefdoms differ very greatly in size one from another, some containing only three or four towns or villages, some fifty or sixty. Few tribes are grouped in only one chiefdom: for the Kpelle there are six or seven, the Vai about twelve, the Kru-Grebo about forty, many of them very small. The chiefdoms are listed in *Republic of Liberia: Geographical Place Names*, printed by the Liberian Cartographic Service, RL, 1956.

Each chiefdom—there are about a hundred altogether—is subdivided into clans, under the authority of Clan Chiefs, and under each Clan Chief are the Town Chiefs, i.e. the headmen of the towns and villages of which the clan is composed. The term 'clan' is used in a purely geographical sense and has no necessary reference to a kin relationship between residents within it. The Kru do have *dispersed* clans, in the anthropological sense, but no clan heads; the Vai appear to have localized clans, with clan heads, but these are, as far as I could make out, not the same officers who form part of the official system of administration. In practice, considerable flexibility is allowed for in the internal subdivision of chiefdoms, and the hierarchy Town Chief—Clan Chief—Paramount Chief is not always as straightforward as the regulations suggest. Chiefs at all levels are elected—although the actual process of election differs from one tribe to another—by their respective subjects, but the appointment of the Paramount is subject to the President's approval. They receive no salaries, but are compensated by a commission on taxes collected within their jurisdictions, and in the case of a Paramount or Clan Chief by fees for settling litigation and by an annual tribute of rice from their people.

Judicial authority is exercised by Provincial and District Commissioners and also by Paramount and Clan Chiefs. The Clan Chief's jurisdiction covers:

(*a*) Civil cases arising within the clan involving a maximum amount of $25.

(*b*) Cases arising within the clan relating to personal status, marriage and divorce under native law.

(*c*) Misdemeanours subject to a maximum fine of $5 or one month's imprisonment.

And the Paramount has authority over:

(*a*) Civil cases arising within the chiefdom involving $25 and less than $100.

(*b*) Criminal cases involving a fine of $10 or imprisonment for three months.

(*c*) All cases arising between strangers and members of the tribe, except they be civilized people.

I am here quoting from the Interior Regulations, not the *Code of Laws* (see page 95 above). That is, the Chiefs have authority to hear minor cases arising out of the general civil and criminal law of the republic, in addition to those arising out of tribal customary law. They are, however, precluded from hearing cases involving 'civilized' people, cases between the latter being heard on the court of the District Commissioner, those between a 'civilized person' and a 'native' in the Joint Court of the District Commissioner and the Paramount Chief.

REFERENCES

AZIKWE, NNAMDI, *Liberia in World Politics*, Stockwell, London, 1934.

BAËTA, C. G. *Prophetism in Ghana*, Student Christian Movement Press, 1961.

BALANDIER, G. 'Urbanism in West and Central Africa', in Forde (ed.), *Social Implications*, 1956.

BANTON, M. *West African City: A Study of Tribal Life in Freetown*, Oxford University Press for International African Institute, 1957.

BANTON, M. 'The Restructuring of Social Relationships', in Southall (ed.), *Social Change in Modern Africa*, 1961.

BROWN, GEORGE W. *The Economic History of Liberia*, Associated Publishers Inc., Washington, 1941.

BUELL, RAYMOND LESLIE. *The Native Problem in Africa*, Macmillan, New York, 1928.

BUELL, RAYMOND LESLIE. *Liberia, A Century of Survival, 1847–1947*, University of Pennsylvania, African Handbooks, no. 7, 1947.

BÜTTIKOFER, J. *Reisebilder aus Liberia*, E. J. Brill, Leiden, 1890.

CRONON, EDMUND DAVID. *Black Moses: The Story of Marcus Garvey and the Universal Negro Improvement Association*, University of Wisconsin, 1955.

CHATFIELD TAYLOR, WAYNE. *The Firestone Operations in Liberia*, Fifth Case Study in an NPA Series on U.S. Business Performance Abroad, National Planning Association, Washington, 1956.

COLE, HENRY B. (ed.). *The Liberian Yearbook*, 1956. Diplomatic Press and Publishing Co., London.

EPSTEIN, A. L. *Politics in an Urban African Community*, Manchester University Press for Rhodes Livingstone Institute, 1958.

EPSTEIN, A. L. *Juridical Techniques and the Judicial Process*, Rhodes Livingstone Paper no. 23, Manchester University Press, 1954.

EPSTEIN, A. L. 'The Network and Urban Social Organization', *Human Problems in British Central Africa*, vol. xxix, June 1961.

FAUSET, A. H. *Black Gods of the Metropolis*, University of Pennsylvania Press, 1944.

FORDE, DARYLL (ed.). *Social Implications of Industrialization and Urbanization in Africa South of the Sahara*, UNESCO, 1956.

FRAZIER, E. FRANKLIN, *The Negro Family in the United States*, University of Chicago, 1939.

FYFE, CHRISTOPHER. *A History of Sierra Leone*, Oxford University Press, London, 1962.

GENEVRAY, J. *Eléments d'une Monographie d'une Division Administrative Libérienne* (Grand Bassa County), Mémoires de l'Institut Français d'Afrique Noire, no. 21, IFAN-Dakar, 1952.

GIBBS, J. L., Jnr. 'Some Judicial Implications of Marital Instability among the Kpelle', Ph.D. thesis, Harvard University, 1960 (unpublished).

GOLDTHORPE, J. E. 'Educated Africans: Some Conceptual and Terminological Problems', in Southall (ed.), *Social Change*, 1961.

GREENE, GRAHAM. *Journey without Maps*, Pan Books, London, 1957.

HARLEY, G. W. *Notes on the Poro in Liberia*, Peabody Museum Papers, vol. xix, 2, 1941.

HARLEY, G. W. *Masks as Agents of Social Control in North-East Liberia*, Peabody Museum Papers, vol. xxxii, no. 2, 1950.

HENRIES, A. and DORIS BANKS. *The Liberian Nation: A Short History*, Herman Jaffe, New York, 1954.

HENRIES, RICHARD and DORIS BANKS. *Liberia, the West African Republic*, Bruns, New York, 1950.

HUBERICH, Charles Henry. *The Political and Legislative History of Liberia*, Central Books, New York, 1947.

IZZETT, A. 'Family Life among the Yoruba in Lagos', in Southall (ed.), *Social Change*, 1961.

JOHNSTON, HARRY. *Liberia*, Hutchinson, London, 1961 edition. 2 vols.

KARNGA, ABAYOMI, *History of Liberia*, D. H. Tyte & Co., Liverpool, 1926.

LELONG, M-H. *Monrovia, Capitale pour Rire*, Baconnier Frères, Alger, 1946.

LITTLE, K. L. *The Mende of Sierra Leone: A West African People in Transition*, Routledge & Kegan Paul, London, 1951.

LITTLE, K. L. 'Structural Change in the Sierra Leone Protectorate', *Africa*, vol. xxv, no. 3, July 1955.

MCCALL, DANIEL F. 'Liberia: An Appraisal', *Annals of the American Academy of Political and Social Science*, vol. 306, July 1956.

MCCULLOCH, M. *A Social Survey of the African Population of Livingstone*, Rhodes-Livingstone Paper no. 26, Manchester University Press, 1956.

MCRAE, John D. 'Import and Export Commercial Organization in Liberia', *Liberia*, vol. i, no. 2, October 1958. (Published by Liberian Embassy in Rome.)

MAYER, KURT B. *Class and Society*, Doubleday, New York, 1955.

MITCHELL, J. C. *The Kalela Dance*, Rhodes-Livingstone Paper no. 27, Manchester University Press, 1957.

MITCHELL, J. C. and EPSTEIN, A. L. 'Occupational Prestige and Social Status among Urban Africans in Northern Rhodesia', *Africa*, vol. xxix, no. 1, 1959.

MYRDAL, GUNNAR. *An American Dilemma*, Harper & Brothers, New York, 1944.

NORMAN, OSCAR S. Oration delivered at the Barclay Training Centre, July 26, 1951. Government Printing Office, Monrovia.

NOTTINGHAM, ELIZABETH. *Religion and Society*, Random House, New York, 1954.

PARRINDER, GEOFFREY. *Religion in an African City*, Oxford University Press, 1953.

PORTER, ARTHUR T. *Creoledom: A Study of the Development of Freetown Society*, Oxford University Press, London, 1963.

ROSE, ARNOLD, *The Negro in America*, Harper, New York, 1958.

SCHWAB, GEORGE. *Tribes of the Liberian Hinterland*, Report of the Peabody Mission to Liberia, Peabody Museum Papers, vol. xxxi, 1947.

SCHWAB, W. B. 'Social Stratification in Gwelo', in Southall (ed.), *Social Change*, 1961.

SIMPSON, C. L. *Memoirs*, Diplomatic Press, London, 1963.

SOUTHALL, AIDAN (ed.). *Social Change in Modern Africa*, Oxford University Press for International African Institute, London, 1961.

STAUDENRAUS, P. J. *The African Colonization Movement, 1816–1865*, Columbia University Press, New York, 1961.

STRONG (ed.). *The African Republic of Liberia*, Harvard University Press, 1939.

YANCY, ERNEST JEROME. *Historical Lights of Liberia's Yesterday and Today*, Herman Jaffe, New York, 1954.

XYDIAS, NELLY. 'Labour: Conditions, Aptitudes, Training' (Stanleyville), in Forde (ed.), *Social Implications*, UNESCO, 1956.

The local press:

The Liberian Age, Monrovia.
The Listener, Monrovia.

Liberian Government publications and documents:

Bureau of Information. (1) *This is Liberia: A Bird's Eye View of the Nation*, 1959. (2) *Liberia, Trade, Industry and Travel* (periodical). (3) *Invest, Trade and Prosper with Liberia*, c. 1957. (4) *The National Unification Program of Liberia*, Echoes from the First National Executive Council, Harper, 1954.

Bureau of Statistics, Department of Agriculture and Commerce. (1) *Census of Population of Monrovia*, December 1956. (2) *Census of Schools in Monrovia*, 1956. (3) *Census of the Population of Greenville*, 1958.

Department of the Interior. (1) *Revised Laws and Administrative Regulations for governing the Hinterland*, 1957. (2) *Annual reports*.

Annual Budgets of Republic of Liberia for 1957 and 1958.

Acts passed by the Legislature of the Republic of Liberia, 1956–7.

Liberian Code of Laws of 1956, adopted by the Legislature of the Republic 22 March, 1956. Published under authority of the Legislature and President by Cornell University Press, Ithaca, NY, 1958. (Ed. Konvitz). 4 vols.

Liberian Law Reports, Cases decided in the Supreme Court of the Republic of Liberia from January 1908 to November 1926. Published *c.* 1947. 2 vols.

INDEX

Ahmadiyya Muslim Mission, 154
American Colonization Society, 4, 9, 14, 15, 16, 17
Americo-Liberians, defined, 1, 23; attitudes to and relations with tribes, 13–14, 24 f., 30–32, 228–9; intermarriage with tribes, 7, 12, 27, 35–36; present numbers, 35–36; present social position, 197–8, 216–19, 223 f.
Assembly of God, 157

Bassa tribe, 1, 27, 34, 36; Bassa Brotherhood and Benefit Society, 87; Bassa Community, 47, 52 f., 55–56, 87–89; urban administration, 88–89; Youth Association, 185
Belle tribe, 93
Bishop Brooks, 55
Buzi tribe, 89 (*and see* Loma)

Children, adoption of tribal, 12, 25, 115–20
Christian churches, 14, 151–71; church and state, 152–4; denominations listed, 156–8; separatist churches, 157–70; denomination and tribe, 90, 159; denomination and social status, 158
Church of the Lord, 157, 158
City Council, 65–66
Civilized status, defined, 67–68; 94–95, 196–7, 201–6
Claratown, 47, 52, 73–76
Committee of Industrial Organizations, 190
Congoes, 7, 11–12
Crowds, 192

De tribe, 3, 10, 36, 93
Department of the Interior, role in urban affairs, 92 f.; rural administration, 236–7
Didhwo Twe, 77
Dowry, 104, 105

Élite, general characteristics, 197–200; churches of, 159–60, 168–70; associations, 191–4
Employment, 37–45

Family (*see under* Households)
Fanti tribe, 3, 93
Firestone, 23–24; 27, 29, 35, 221
Fishermen and fish-sellers, 130, 145, 189
'Five tribes', Kru *dako*, defined, 76, 80
Foreigners, white, 36, 213, 220–3; American Negroes, 37, 220–1
Freemasons, Ancient and Accepted Order of, 60, 192–4
Freeport of Monrovia, 28, 40–1
Freetown, 4, 7, 11, 83, 185, 219, 222

Garvey, Marcus, 21–23
Gbande tribe, 93
Geponyano society, 178 f.
Gio-Mano tribe, 93
Gissi tribe, 93
Gola tribe, 1, 10, 36, 84
Grebo tribe, 1, 34, 36

Honorables, defined and general characteristics of, 200–1
Household of Ruth, 193
Households, definitions, 122–7; size, 123; composition, 125–7; functions of extended families in town, 127–50; budgets, 131–50
Housing, 50–52

Immigration from America, 5–9, 16–17, 21–23
Infantile mortality and infertility, 37, 120–2
Intermarriage, between tribes, 126, 201 (*and see under* Americo-Liberians)
International Order of Good Templars, 193
Iron mining, 29

Knights of St. John, 202
Kpelle tribe, 1, 35, 36, 89, 93, 173, 175; Kpelle United Association, 93, 185, 188
Krahn tribe, 93

243